SAINT SIMON DE MONTFORT

Boydell Medieval Texts

Boydell Medieval Texts is a series of parallel text volumes (Latin/English) presenting major medieval works, which aims to meet both the requirement of scholarly editions to the highest standard and the need for readily available translations at an affordable price for libraries and students who require access to the content of the works.

The series volumes will be issued initially in hardback, followed by distribution in electronic form to a variety of platforms such as JSTOR. A year after publication, a paperback version of the translation only will be produced, with appropriately revised introduction and footnotes.

The editors of the series are Rodney Thomson and Michael Bennett, both Emeritus Professors of Medieval History at the University of Tasmania.

Previously Published

William of Malmesbury: Miracles of the Blessed Virgin Mary
edited and translated by R. M. Thomson and M. Winterbottom

For and Against Abelard: The Invective of Bernard of Clairvaux and Berengar of Poitiers edited and translated by R. M. Thomson and M. Winterbottom

The History of Alfred of Beverley
edited by J. P. T. Slevin and translated by L. Lockyer

SAINT SIMON DE MONTFORT

THE MIRACLES, LAMENTS, PRAYERS AND HYMNS

Edited and translated by David Cox

THE BOYDELL PRESS

© David Cox 2024

All Rights Reserved. Except as permitted under current legislation
no part of this work may be photocopied, stored in a retrieval system,
published, performed in public, adapted, broadcast,
transmitted, recorded or reproduced in any form or by any means,
without the prior permission of the copyright owner

The right of David Charles Cox to be identified as
the author of this work has been asserted in accordance with
sections 77 and 78 of the Copyright, Designs and Patents Act 1988

First published 2024
The Boydell Press, Woodbridge

ISBN 978-1-83765-084-2

The Boydell Press is an imprint of Boydell & Brewer Ltd
PO Box 9, Woodbridge, Suffolk IP12 3DF, UK
and of Boydell & Brewer Inc.
668 Mt Hope Avenue, Rochester, NY 14620–2731, USA
website: www.boydellandbrewer.com

A CIP catalogue record for this book is available from the British Library

The publisher has no responsibility for the continued existence or accuracy of URLs for
external or third-party internet websites referred to in this book, and does not guarantee
that any content on such websites is, or will remain, accurate or appropriate

This publication is printed on acid-free paper

In memory of
Iris Mary Pinkstone
1932–2020

Contents

ix	*List of Figures*
x	*Preface and Acknowledgements*
xii	*List of Abbreviations*

INTRODUCTION

xvii	The miracle book
xxi	The miracles
xxvii	The laments, prayers and hymns
xxix	Saint Simon
xxxvii	Preservation and rediscovery

CATALOGUE OF THE TEXTS AND MANUSCRIPTS

xl	The miracles
xli	The laments, prayers and hymns
1	EDITORIAL PROCEDURE

TEXTS AND TRANSLATIONS

2	The Evesham abbey miracle book (**1–197**)
49	Miracles from the Melrose chronicle (**198–201**)
52	A miracle from the Lanercost chronicle (**202**)
53	Anno milleno (**203**)
56	Chaunter mestoit (**204**)
58	Chaunter mestut (**205**)
60	Illos saluauit (**206**)
67	Vbi fuit mons (**207**)
73	Vulneratur karitas (**208**)

CONTENTS

76	Calendar entries (**209–14**)	
77	Salue Symon: antiphon, versicle and response (**215**)	
78	Salue Symon: motet (**216**)	
79	Rumpe celos (**217**)	
80	Mater Syon (**218**)	
81	Nequit stare (**219**)	
83	O decus militie (Cambridge MS) (**220**)	
84	O decus militie (Cologne MS) (**221**)	
85	Miles Christi (**222**)	
87	*Select Bibliography*	
89	*Index of Persons and Places*	

Figures

1. Distribution map of Montfortian estates   xxv
2. Distribution map of miracle stories   xxvi
3. Plan of the abbey church, Evesham   xxxii
4. The Evesham cult sites   xxxv

Preface and Acknowledgements

The forbidden miracle cult of Simon de Montfort earl of Leicester, who died in 1265, produced a remarkable body of literature before expiring from natural causes after some fifteen years. The writings included laments, prayers and hymns, and a book of some two hundred miracles. The products of that creative surge reveal how some people tried to cope with political events that they could feel and describe but could not influence.

In 1840 James Orchard Halliwell published an edition of the miracle book and, whatever the shortcomings of the sole manuscript and however slight his contribution to our understanding of it, Halliwell's edition has been consulted with profit by generations of historians. A century and a half later Iris Pinkstone, founder of the Simon de Montfort Society, was aware that an English translation would be needed if the full potential of the miracle book were to be appreciated, especially as proficiency in Latin ought no longer to be assumed. A further consideration was that many of the names mentioned in the manuscript were unrecognizable after medieval recopying; Halliwell could not overcome that obstacle, but in the present century it can be breached with tools that he never had. Iris therefore tried to find a competent translator. I understood her aspiration at the time and might have offered to help, but I was busy with other publications and sadly, just as I found myself able to make a start, we received the news of Iris's death.

Nevertheless, my belated readiness to carry out her project coincided happily with the re-emergence of another scheme, which I had imagined some decades earlier but had not been qualified to begin at the time: a collected edition and translation of the Montfortian verses and prayers. It became obvious that such an edition would complement that of the miracle book, and the present volume therefore assembles all the known texts that Simon de Montfort's cult produced. Most of them have been printed at least once since 1800, but in scattered places and in various editorial styles. It will be a modest step forward to have them brought together, freshly edited and translated.

♦ ♦ ♦

PREFACE AND ACKNOWLEDGEMENTS

The Simon de Montfort Society has of course encouraged the project from the beginning. I record my thanks to all the repositories that have provided images of manuscripts in their possession. 'Anno milleno' (203), not previously published, is included here by permission of the Master and Fellows of Gonville and Caius College, Cambridge. In matters of detail several individuals have also come to my assistance, among whom I should like to mention Anne Bailey, Paul Cullen, Paul Duffy and Abigail Hartman. Michael Bennett gave wise advice on the organization of the material, and my wife Janice has kindly commented on the Introduction, while Richard Barber and Christy Beale, together with their professional colleagues, have guided the book through the press with meticulous skill and consideration. But the begetter and rightful dedicatee of the project remains, of course, the late Iris Pinkstone.

Abbreviations

Ann. Monastici	*Annales Monastici*, ed. H. R. Luard, 5 vols (Rolls Series, 1864–69)
AN Political Songs	*Anglo-Norman Political Songs*, ed. I. S. T. Aspin (Anglo-Norman Text Soc. 11, 1953)
Barking Ordinale	*The Ordinale and Customary of the Benedictine Nuns of Barking Abbey*, ed. J. B. L. Tolhurst, 2 vols (Henry Bradshaw Soc. 65–6, 1927–28 for 1926–27)
Beauchamp Cart.	*The Beauchamp Cartulary Charters 1100–1268*, ed. E. Mason (Pipe Roll Soc. new ser. 43, 1980 for 1971–73)
Bk of Fees	*Liber Feodorum. The Book of Fees Commonly called Testa de Nevill, Reformed from the Earliest MSS. by the Deputy Keeper of the Records*, 2 vols in 3 (HMSO, 1920–31)
BRUO to 1500	A. B. Emden, *A Biographical Register of the University of Oxford to A.D. 1500*, 3 vols (Oxford, 1957–59)
Cal. Chart. R.	*Calendar of the Charter Rolls Preserved in the Public Record Office*, 6 vols (HMSO, 1903–27)
Cal. Close	*Calendar of the Close Rolls Preserved in the Public Record Office*, 46 vols (HMSO, 1892–1963)
Cal. Fine R.	*Calendar of the Fine Rolls Preserved in the Public Record Office* (HMSO, 1911–in progress)
Cal. Inq. Misc.	*Calendar of Inquisitions Miscellaneous (Chancery) Preserved in the Public Record Office*, 7 vols (HMSO, 1916–68)

Cal. Inq. p.m.	*Calendar of Inquisitions post mortem and Other Analogous Documents Preserved in the Public Record Office* (HMSO, 1904–in progress)
Cal. Pat.	*Calendar of the Patent Rolls Preserved in the Public Record Office* (HMSO, 1891–in progress)
Chron. Canterbury–Dover	*The Historical Works of Gervase of Canterbury*, ed. W. Stubbs (Rolls Series, 1879–80) 2, pp. 106–324
Chron. et Annales	'Willelmi Rishanger, monachi S. Albani, chronica', *Chronica S. Albani [I]* 2, pp. 1–230
Chron. Evesham	*Chronicon Abbatiae de Evesham, ad annum 1418*, ed. W. D. Macray (Rolls Series, 1863)
Chron. Furness	'Continuatio chronici Willelmi de Novoburgo ad annum 1298', *Chronicles of the Reigns of Stephen, Henry II, and Richard I*, ed. R. Howlett (Rolls Series, 1884–89) 2, pp. 503–83
Chron. Lanercost (1839)	*Chronicon de Lanercost. M.CC.I–M.CCC.LXIV*, ed. J. Stevenson (Bannatyne Club, 1839; Maitland Club, 1839)
Chron. Melrose (1835)	*Chronica de Mailros*, ed. J. Stevenson (Bannatyne Club, 1835)
Chronica S. Albani	*Chronica Monasterii S. Albani*, ed. H. T. Riley, 12 vols (Rolls Series, 1863–76)
Close R.	*Close Rolls of the Reign of Henry III Preserved in the Public Record Office*, 14 vols (HMSO, 1902–38)
Close R. (Suppl.)	*Close Rolls (Supplementary) of the Reign of Henry III Preserved in the Public Record Office, 1244–1266* (HMSO, 1975)
Complete Harley 2253	*The Complete Harley 2253 Manuscript*, ed. S. Fein, 3 vols (Kalamazoo, 2014–15)
Complete Peerage	G. E. C[ockayne], *The Complete Peerage*, ed. V. Gibbs and others, 13 vols (London, 1910–59)
Cron. Maiorum	*De Antiquis Legibus Liber. Cronica Maiorum et Vicecomitum Londoniarum*, ed. T. Stapleton (Camden Soc. 34, 1846)

ABBREVIATIONS

EHR	*English Historical Review*
English Baronies	I. J. Sanders, *English Baronies: A Study of their Origin and Descent 1066–1327* (Oxford, 1960)
Feudal Aids	*Inquisitions and Assessments relating to Feudal Aids; with Other Analogous Documents Preserved in the Public Record Office, A.D. 1284–1431*, 6 vols (HMSO, 1899–1920)
Flores Historiarum	*Flores Historiarum*, ed. H. R. Luard, 3 vols (Rolls Series, 1890)
Heads	*The Heads of Religious Houses: England and Wales*, ed. D. Knowles, C. N. L. Brooke, V. C. M. London and D. M. Smith, 3 vols (Cambridge, 2001–8)
Liturgische Reimofficien	*Historiae Rhythmicae: Liturgische Reimofficien des Mittelalters*, ed. G. M. Dreves and C. Blume, 8 vols (Leipzig, Analecta Hymnica, 1889–1904)
London Wills	*Calendar of Wills Proved and Enrolled in the Court of Husting, London, A.D. 1258–A.D. 1688*, ed. R. R. Sharpe, 2 vols (London, 1889–90)
Marlborough, *Hist.*	Thomas of Marlborough, *History of the Abbey of Evesham*, ed. and transl. J. Sayers and L. Watkiss (Oxford, OMT, 2003)
Miracles, ed. Halliwell	'Miracula Simonis de Montfort', *The Chronicle of William de Rishanger, of the Barons' Wars. The Miracles of Simon de Montfort*, ed. J. O. Halliwell (Camden Soc. [15], 1840), pp. 67–110
Mon. Angl.	W. Dugdale, *Monasticon Anglicanum*, ed. J. Caley, H. Ellis and B. Bandinel, 6 vols in 8 (London, 1817–30)
Northumb. Pleas	*Northumberland Pleas from the Curia Regis and Assize Rolls 1198–1272* [ed. A. Hamilton Thompson] (Publications of the Newcastle upon Tyne Records Committee 2, 1922 for 1921)
ODNB	*Oxford Dictionary of National Biography*, ed. H. C. G. Matthew and B. Harrison (Oxford, 2004, and online)

ABBREVIATIONS

OMT	Oxford Medieval Texts
Oxnead	*Chronica Johannis de Oxenedes*, ed. H. Ellis (Rolls Series, 1859)
Peterborough Abbey (CBMLC)	*Peterborough Abbey*, ed. K. Friis-Jensen and J. M. W. Willoughby (Corpus of British Medieval Library Catalogues 8, 2001)
PN	*The Survey of English Place-Names* (English Place-Name Soc.) [cited by county volume]
Political Songs	*The Political Songs of England, from the Reign of John to that of Edward II*, ed. T. Wright (Camden Soc. [6], 1839)
Reg. Giffard	*Episcopal Registers, Diocese of Worcester: Register of Bishop Godfrey Giffard, September 23rd, 1268, to August 15th, 1301*, ed. J. W. Willis Bund, 2 vols (WHS, 1902)
Rishanger, *De Bellis*	'Chronicon Willelmi de Rishanger. De duobus bellis apud Lewes et Evesham commissis', *Chronica S. Albani [IV]* 3, pp. 491–565
Rob. Gloucester	*The Metrical Chronicle of Robert of Gloucester*, ed. W. A. Wright, 2 vols (Rolls Series, 1887)
Rolls and Reg. Sutton	*The Rolls and Register of Bishop Oliver Sutton 1280–1299*, ed. R. T. Hill, 8 vols (Lincoln Record Soc. 1948–86)
Rolls Series	*Rerum Britannicarum Medii Aevi Scriptores, or Chronicles and Memorials of Great Britain and Ireland during the Middle Ages* (London, 1858–99)
Rot. Hund.	*Rotuli Hundredorum Temp. Hen. III et Edw. I in Turr' Lond' et in Curia Receptae Scaccarii West. Asservati* [ed. W. Illingworth], 2 vols (Record Commissioners, 1812–18)
Rot. Selecti	*Rotuli Selecti ad Res Anglicas et Hibernicas Spectantes, ex Archivis in Domo Capitulari Westmonasteriensi Deprompti*, ed. J. Hunter (Record Commissioners, 1834)

ABBREVIATIONS

Song of Lewes	*The Song of Lewes*, ed. C. L. Kingsford (Oxford, 1890)
TNA	London, The National Archives
VCH	*The Victoria History of the Counties of England* [cited by county volume]
WHS	Worcestershire Historical Society
Worcs. Subsidy	*Lay Subsidy Roll for the County of Worcester, circ. 1280*, ed. J. W. Willis Bund and J. Amphlett (WHS, 1893)

Secondary works frequently cited are given in an abbreviated form in the footnotes; full details may be found in the Select Bibliography.

Introduction

The texts in this edition are all related to the sudden death of Simon de Montfort earl of Leicester, which occurred on 4 August 1265 at the battle of Evesham in Worcestershire. As a revolutionary politician and soldier he had been so popular and successful in England that during his lifetime some had begun to portray him as a Christ-like saviour. The shock of his death, magnified by horror at the royalist mutilation of his corpse, launched a miracle cult so vigorous that it soon spread to parts of the British Isles that were well beyond his burial place at Evesham abbey.[1] In defiance of royalist threats the cult lasted some fifteen years, during which Earl Simon's devotees compiled a miracle book and composed laments, prayers and hymns.

The miracle book

The monks of Evesham welcomed pilgrims at Simon de Montfort's grave and recorded every miracle story that came to them. Some miracles had been generated locally but reports of many more were received from other parts of the country. It seems that they usually came by word of mouth; in only two instances is there some indication that a report was delivered in writing (**127, 190**).[2] When a story was given orally, the monks' first task was to write a summary, not necessarily in complete sentences, of what may have been a long-winded or unstructured tale.[3] At Evesham the note needed to record the identity (not necessarily the name) of the miracle's recipient and that of the informant (if it was someone else); where the recipient lived (unless they were a prominent person whose residence was well known); the nature of the miracle; and who else could vouch for the story. When the informant referred to a minor place outside Worcestershire and beyond the adjoining counties nearest to Evesham (Gloucestershire and Warwickshire) they

---

[1] R. C. Finucane, *Miracles and Pilgrims: Popular Beliefs in Medieval England* (London, 1977), p. 169.
[2] Bold numbers refer to items edited below.
[3] Evidence for such notes elsewhere is given by L. E. Wilson, 'Writing miracle collections', in S. Katajala-Peltomaa, J. Kuuliala and J. McCleery (eds), *A Companion to Medieval Miracle Collections* (Leiden, 2021), pp. 15–35 (at pp. 20–3).

were asked for its county or its nearest well-known town.[4] Those details were enough to make the story credible and verifiable.[5] There are only two references to testimony on oath (**127–8**) and none was needed, for there was no prospect of the formal canonization proceedings that would have called for sworn statements.[6] The recording monk could choose to include more details than those described, but he often settled for the minimum. In particular, the date of a miracle was not of the essence and was not routinely taken down. The monks' preliminary notes would thereafter have remained a collection of loose sheets until a miracle book was started. Meanwhile they did not have to be kept in the exact order in which the stories had arrived; that may be why reports that reached Evesham simultaneously are sometimes found separated in the book (e.g. **29** and **31**; **41–5** and **47**). In any case, the monks were more interested in the substance of the stories than in their precise chronology.[7]

To find the earliest date at which the notes could have been entered in a miracle book one need look no further than its first item (**3**), which happens to record an incident that can be closely dated and provides the *terminus a quo*. The following extract from it contains the pertinent clues:

> One Richard, surnamed Badger, from Evesham, was on his way towards Stratford upon Avon with his merchandise when a large army came into view, approaching from Kenilworth. In fear he turned back along the road and there he met Sir William Beauchamp with all his retinue … Richard said, 'Take care! Look, here come your enemies.' … And this was a year later [than the battle of Evesham]; that is, in the second year and during the war.

Since William Beauchamp died in the earlier part of 1269,[8] the incident must have occurred before then. Closer dating comes from the reference to an armed force of Beauchamp's enemies from Kenilworth approaching Evesham from the direction of Stratford upon Avon. Kenilworth castle, thirty miles north-east of Evesham, was the chief stronghold of the Montfortian rebels immediately after the battle of Evesham. The king laid siege to it in late June 1266[9] but until then the occupants were able to range over Warwickshire and prey upon the population.[10] The first

---

[4] This practice sometimes helps the translator to distinguish between major and minor places that have the same name, and to identify places of which the names are garbled in the MS.
[5] R. Bartlett, *Why can the Dead do Such Great Things?* (Princeton and Oxford, 2013), pp. 564–5.
[6] See Wilson, 'Writing miracle collections', pp. 23–5.
[7] See also Bartlett, *Why can the Dead do Such Great Things?*, pp. 562–3.
[8] *Reg. Giffard* 1, pp. 7–9; *Cal. Inq. p.m.* 1236–72, p. 220.
[9] *Cron. Maiorum*, p. 87.
[10] D. C. Cox, 'The battle of Evesham in the Evesham chronicle', *Historical Research* 62 (1989), pp. 337–45 (at p. 344).

miracle in the Evesham book had evidently occurred before the siege, while the Kenilworth rebels were still at large.

The item's final clause, though difficult to construe, holds even more dating evidence. In the unique and late manuscript it reads thus (with capitalization and abbreviation exactly as here):

& h° a° reuoluto. In E s'c'do A & T G[11]

Correct interpretation of this is not straightforward[12] but a simple reading is possible if one assumes that abbreviations have led to scribal errors during recopying. In some earlier copy of the miracle book it is possible that 'In E' had read 'I E', thus:

& h° a° reuoluto. I E s'c'do A & T G

which can be extended as:

Et hoc anno reuoluto. Id est secundo anno et tempore guerre.

which translates as:

And this was a year later; that is, in the second year and during the war.

By that reading, it seems that the first miracle to be entered in the Evesham book had occurred in the 'second year' (which presumably began on 25 March 1266) and before late June that year, when the Kenilworth rebels were finally contained. The phrase 'during the war', if that is the correct translation of 'T G', would suggest further that the entry was not copied into the book until after the rebellion had come to an end; 'during the war' would have been redundant while the war was in progress, but afterwards it would have given a context for the story.[13] All in all, it seems to me that the Evesham miracle book was probably started some time after 1 July 1267.[14]

---

[11] London, British Library, Cotton MS Vespasian A VI, fol. 163v.
[12] Cf. C. Valente, 'Simon de Montfort, earl of Leicester, and the utility of sanctity in thirteenth-century England', *Journal of Medieval History* 21 (1995), pp. 27–49 (at pp. 45–6 n. 90); J. E. St Lawrence: 'The *Liber miraculorum* of Simon de Montfort: Contested sanctity and contesting authority in late thirteenth-century England' (Univ. of Texas Ph.D. thesis, 2005), pp. 17, 143.
[13] In the 1950s and 1960s my father and his contemporaries often used the phrase 'during the war' when referring to the years 1939–45.
[14] The end of the rebellion: A. Jobson, *The First English Revolution: Simon de Montfort, Henry III and the Barons' War* (London, 2012), p. 160.

INTRODUCTION

Some decades earlier, the abbey had had good experience of setting out a miracle book after St Wulfsige, an eleventh-century recluse, was buried in the abbey church. His book had been compiled c.1200[15] and two leaves have survived from an early-thirteenth-century fair copy of it, a handsome production written in double columns with red rubrics and red and blue pen-flourished initials.[16] The organizer of Simon de Montfort's miracle book is likely to have known it and may therefore have visualized something similar as a fair copy of his own collection. He may be cautiously identified as the sacrist of the abbey, who was by custom a senior monk charged with custody of the abbey church and its contents and with keeping all the offerings made there;[17] by 1271 that man was Reynold of Inkberrow,[18] who had been a monk of Evesham since 1259 or earlier.[19] As sacrist, Reynold may have been the person who started Earl Simon's miracle collection and who at some point had the items copied into a book.

Such a book was desirable as a convenient file of stories from which to tell visitors to Evesham about past miracles and to suggest the wonders that their own offerings might bring about; Earl Simon's miracle book eventually offered so wide a variety of tales that the monks could cite whichever seemed relevant to the concerns of any particular visitor. Pilgrims, thus instructed, could go away and tell others about what they had learnt, just as the book's epigraph (2) recommends. The epigraph reads simply 'Nichil opertum quod non reueletur, etc.' (Nothing is covered that should not be revealed, etc.) It alludes to the Sermon on the Mount and was an appropriate saying at a time when everyone needed to treat the miracles with secrecy. The 'etc.', however, conceals an exhortation that was considerably more defiant of authority:

> Therefore fear them not. For nothing is covered that shall not be revealed: nor hid, that shall not be known. That which I tell you in the dark, speak ye in the light: and that which you hear in the ear, preach ye upon the housetops. And fear ye not them that kill the body, and are not able to kill the soul: but rather fear him that can destroy both soul and body in hell.[20]

---

[15] D. Cox, *The Church and Vale of Evesham, 700–1215: Lordship, Landscape and Prayer* (Woodbridge, 2015), p. 175.
[16] London, British Library, Harley MS 4242, fols 65–6. Described in C. Drieshen, 'The lost miracles of Wulfsige of Evesham' <https://blogs.bl.uk/digitisedmanuscripts/2021/07/the-lost-miracles-of-wulfsige-of-evesham.html>.
[17] Marlborough, *Hist.* p. 544.
[18] *Mon. Angl.* 2, p. 31; *Chron. Evesham*, p. 282.
[19] *Cal. Pat.* 1258–66, p. 58.
[20] Matt. 10: 26–8 (cf. Luke 12: 2–5).

Christ's injunction would have been closely applicable in the early years of Simon de Montfort's cult if the abbey wanted visitors to reject the threat of secular punishment and to tell everyone about the miracles. Exposition of the epigraph and of stories from the rest of the book would have stimulated them to spread the word, and for a time there was certainly publicity enough to generate a spectacular influx of funds to the abbey. The Lanercost chronicle refers to the 'daily' offerings of Earl Simon's devotees at Evesham and to the impressive building works that were made possible with their money.[21] A description of the new Lady chapel, begun ten years after the battle, tells of 'windows, a beautiful vault, and gilded bosses' and 'the story of the Saviour and the stories of various virgins splendidly painted'.[22] The miracle book helped with the cost of such works; indeed, nothing suggests that it had any other public purpose.[23]

The miracles

The progress of Simon de Montfort's miracle cult can be traced in broad outline by reference to the few datable stories that appear in the Evesham book.[24] Since the datable miracles are mostly entered in date order, each undatable miracle probably occurred at some time between the nearest datable ones before and after it. One may therefore suggest that the events between **3** and **103** can mostly be assigned to 1265–66 and that most of the miracles between **103** and **175** would have happened between c.1266 and 1272.[25] The latest datable miracle was reported to Evesham in 1279 (**195**) and two further stories were entered before the book was closed; it thus appears that the abbey received some twenty reports between c.1272 and c.1280 but none after that. The miracle cult had evidently been widely supported until the early 1270s, but outside Evesham abbey it had declined thereafter and had reached virtual extinction c.1280.

◆ ◆ ◆

The nature of Simon de Montfort's miracles is well attested by the Evesham book. John Theilmann compared Earl Simon's reported cures with those of seven other English cult figures, from Earl Waltheof to King Henry VI, and found that cases of

---

[21] *Chron. Lanercost* (1839), p. 77.
[22] *Chron. Evesham*, p. 286. For the date see London, British Library, Cotton MS Nero D III, fol. 222r.
[23] A point also made by St Lawrence, 'The *Liber miraculorum*', pp. 24–5, 338–41; J. [E.] St Lawrence, 'A crusader in a "communion of saints": Political sanctity and sanctified politics in the cult of St Simon de Montfort', *Comitatus: A Journal of Medieval and Renaissance Studies* 38 (2007), pp. 43–67 (at p. 44).
[24] **3, 14** (see **198**), **94, 103, 108, 115, 160, 175, 187, 189–90, 194–5, 197**. Those MS dates that depend solely on roman numerals are disregarded here because of the possibility, and in some cases the certainty, of scribal error.
[25] Some miracles are known to have occurred well before they were entered in the book (e.g. **115, 160**) but they are too few to invalidate these rough calculations.

INTRODUCTION

blindness and of mental illness formed a smaller proportion of Montfort's cures while his proportion of chronic and crippling conditions was greater.[26] The miracle book usually describes a patient's symptoms but rarely has a diagnosis, and it uses the blanket term *gutta* (gout) over a broad range of painful ailments. Meanwhile, of the accidental injuries presented to the earl, about half were to children.[27]

One in ten of the cures in the book resulted from a visit to Evesham abbey or to the nearby 'Earl's well' but most of the rest were obtained at home, usually by 'measuring' and penny-bending. John Brown had been suffering from a form of paralysis:

> after being measured to the earl he made up his candle to the measurement, and when he came to Evesham he recovered from the disability to which he had been subject. (**16**)

The story refers to a custom whereby the patient or an affected part was measured with a piece of string in the name of a saint.[28] Seven in ten of the cures in the Evesham miracle book were achieved in that way. After the cure, the string was sometimes used to make the wick of a candle,[29] to be taken to the saint's resting-place as a token or offering. But people who could not afford beeswax were not obliged to make a candle, because tallow, a cheaper alternative, was not acceptable in a church.[30] The few candles mentioned in the Evesham book were therefore made for patients of superior means, and they usually charged a subordinate or friend with taking their candle to Evesham. Likewise only better-off patients sent waxen thank-offerings in the form of images of themselves or of their cured limbs. As an alternative to measuring, one could just bend a penny in Earl Simon's name, but that was relatively rare. A bent penny alone would sometimes produce a cure, but if a penny was bent it was usually done to accompany a measuring, the two actions together resulting in a miracle. The penny might be gilded as well as bent (**86**); it could also be sent to Evesham in token of a cure obtained by other means (**6**); and it could even be sent in memory of someone who had prayed to Earl Simon and failed to be cured (**186**).

---

[26] J. M. Theilmann, 'English peasants and medieval miracle lists', *The Historian* 52 (1990), pp. 286–303 (at p. 292).
[27] E. C. Gordon, 'Accidents among medieval children as seen from the miracles of six English saints and martyrs', *Medical History* 35 (1991), pp. 145–63 (at p. 151).
[28] Finucane, *Miracles and Pilgrims*, pp. 95–6. See **96, 160, 193**.
[29] See **72, 95**.
[30] C. Dyer, *Standards of Living in the Later Middle Ages: Social Change in England c.1200–1520*, 2nd edn (Cambridge, 1998), pp. 73–4.

INTRODUCTION

Most of the miracles in the book had been granted in response to prayers and measurings, but some had occurred unexpectedly after dreams or visions involving Earl Simon. A miracle of that kind might be bestowed on one of his supporters, but it was more likely to be experienced by a sceptic or critic. In one vision Simon de Montfort told a former enemy that, 'Some are penitent, some will be penitent and some without penitence will die a bad death.' (**169**) By appearing in person Montfort would bring about repentance or else contrive a drastic punishment.

◆ ◆ ◆

In 1844 W. H. Blaauw suggested that 'persons of all ranks' had attested Earl Simon's miracles,[31] and as late as 2019 I carelessly echoed that opinion;[32] but within the pages of the miracle book it cannot properly be said that all ranks are represented. There I have counted 182 recipients of miracles, including children;[33] the proportion of children is markedly smaller than in comparable collections.[34] Of all recipients at least a third had noble, knightly, gentry, mercantile or ecclesiastical status; the secular and religious clergy made up a fifth of all recipients, and thus a much higher proportion than they did in the general population.[35] Altogether Simon de Montfort's miracle cult attracted greater than usual proportions of men and upper-class people, including senior churchmen.[36] Meanwhile as many as two-thirds of recipients mentioned in the book may have belonged to the households of manual workers;[37] about half of all miracle recipients who appear in it are actually of unstated occupation or rank, but they probably belonged to manual households because their names rarely if ever occur in contemporary public records. Those supposed manual workers might have included anyone from substantial farmers and master craftsmen downwards, but in practice a lack of money or leisure probably prevented many at the lower end of the manual scale – not to mention paupers, vagrants and criminals – from making their stories known at Evesham, if indeed they had any. Servants and the poor do occur in the book but only as the observers of miracles, not as the recipients.

◆ ◆ ◆

---

[31] W. H. Blaauw, *The Barons' War including the Battles of Lewes and Evesham* (London and Lewes, 1844), p. 258.
[32] D. Cox, *The Battle of Evesham: A New Account*, 2nd edn (Evesham, 2019), p. 35.
[33] This is fewer than the number of entries in the miracle book because some people appear in more than one entry.
[34] Gordon, 'Accidents among medieval children', p. 151; C. Valente, 'Children of revolt: Children's lives in the age of Simon de Montfort', in J. T. Rosenthal (ed.), *Essays on Medieval Childhood: Reponses to Recent Debates* (Donington, 2007), pp. 91–107 (at p. 99n).
[35] J. C. Russell, 'The clerical population of medieval England', *Traditio* 2 (1944), pp. 177–212 (at p. 179).
[36] Finucane, *Miracles and Pilgrims*, p. 135.
[37] For the criteria defining social rank I have followed Dyer, *Standards of Living*, pp. 17–25.

INTRODUCTION

The miracle book's careful recording of place-names enables one to estimate the geographical extent of Earl Simon's cult. Ronald Finucane[38] noted some concordance between the distribution of Montfortian estates (Fig. 1)[39] and that of the reported miracles (Fig. 2);[40] and Clive Knowles demonstrated that the distribution of Montfortian estates corresponded to the most economically advanced, most densely populated areas of England, that is to say the Midlands and the east.[41] Thus Finucane and Knowles between them showed that miracles and population density coincided. And their observations hold good, because I have been able positively to identify and map eighty-two English and Welsh sources of miracle stories (Fig. 2), some of which generated more than one report;[42] another ten such places, though not identified, are known to have been in Berkshire, Cheshire, Derbyshire, Devon (two places), Gloucestershire, Kent (two), Northamptonshire, Northumberland and Oxfordshire. Fig. 2 therefore confirms that most reports of miracles did come from eastern England and the Midlands; within the Midlands there was naturally a loose concentration around Evesham. The map shows a separate concentration in Kent and Sussex, which were less populous but had a disproportionate number of Montfortian supporters.[43]

The miracle clusters in some of the more populous towns were not necessarily a reflection of their size; after all, there are no identifiable reports from Leicester or Worcester. They were both under royalist control after the battle of Evesham[44] and it therefore seems that lordship, as well as size, may have influenced miracle numbers. Where there is evidence, it often shows that a miracle comes from an estate that is or has been held at some level by an active contrariant. And the tenants of a detested royalist might also lean towards the cult of Earl Simon, as at the royal manor of Brill in Buckinghamshire (**109–10**) and at Filby in Norfolk (**76**) and Gainsborough in Lincolnshire (**162**), which were held by the king's 'alien' half-brother William de Valence. Nothing was predetermined, however, and at that period any direct influence of a particular individual on the personal

---

[38] Finucane, *Miracles and Pilgrims*, p. 170.
[39] For the estates see W. H. Blaauw, *The Barons' War including the Battles of Lewes and Evesham* [ed. C. H. Pearson] (London and Lewes, 1871), pp. 365–80; C. H. Knowles, 'The disinherited, 1265–1280: A political and social study of the supporters of Simon de Montfort and the resettlement after the Barons' War' (Univ. of Wales Ph.D. thesis, 1959), pt 2, pp. 108–9 (with map 3); D. Williams, 'Simon de Montfort and his adherents', in W. M. Ormrod (ed.), *England in the Thirteenth Century: Proceedings of the 1984 Harlaxton Symposium* (Harlaxton, 1985), pp. 166–77 (at pp. 172–3).
[40] On the distribution of the miracles see also Valente, 'Simon de Montfort and the utility of sanctity', pp. 32, 34.
[41] Knowles, 'The disinherited, 1265–1280', pt 2, pp. 110–11 (with maps 4–5).
[42] The map does not include the story from Kinclaven, Perthshire, found only in the Lanercost and Melrose chronicles (**201–2**).
[43] C. Valente, *The Theory and Practice of Revolt in Medieval England* (Aldershot and Burlington, VT, 2003), pp. 92–3.
[44] *VCH Leics.* 4, p. 4; *VCH Worcs.* 4, pp. 381, 391.

INTRODUCTION

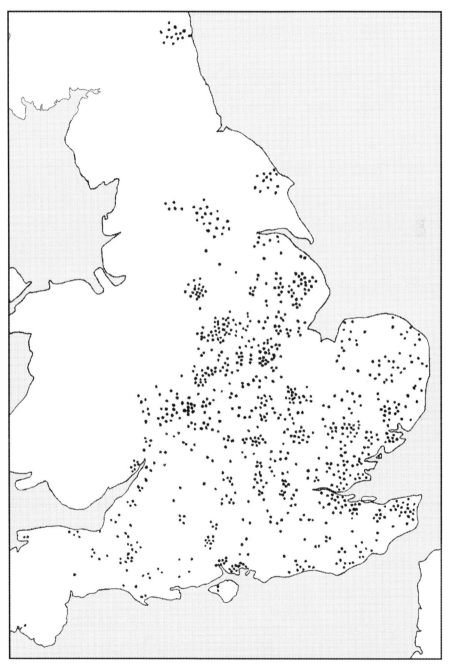

Figure 1 Montfortian estates forfeited after the battle of Evesham.
After Knowles, 'The disinherited, 1265–1280', map 3.

INTRODUCTION

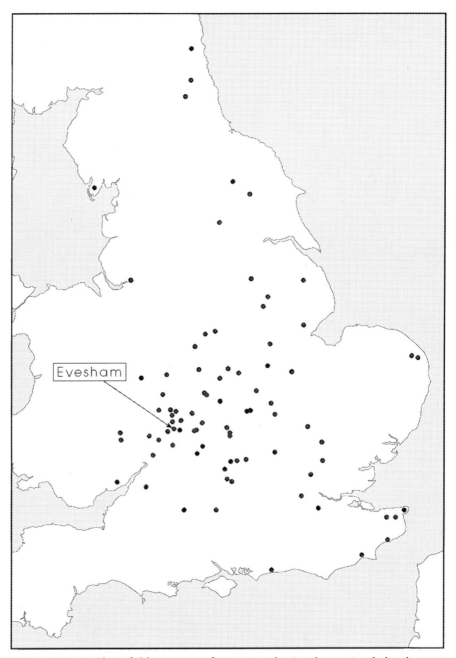

Figure 2   Identifiable sources of stories in the Evesham miracle book.

inclinations of another was, of its nature, rarely if ever documented.[45] It seems likely, indeed, that in densely occupied regions any miracle story might spread instantly of its own accord and be widely believed without reference to anyone in authority. Stories shared in common in that way appear to underlie the miracle book's many instances of whole households or neighbourhoods bearing witness to a particular event.

The laments, prayers and hymns

While miracle stories were accumulating at Evesham abbey, Simon de Montfort's death and the continuing brutalities of the rebellion inspired verse laments and a longing for peace. Three surviving laments can be dated to the period between the battle of Evesham and the peace agreement of 1 July 1267, and the rest probably should be. Since the authors had access to writing materials, had a fluent command of Latin or French, and had the still rarer ability to use them in verse, they were probably professional people, secular churchmen, or members of religious orders, writing on their own behalf or at the request of a colleague or patron (e.g. **206**). While it is hardly likely that all literary people were devoted to Earl Simon, none of the extant verses made in the years of controversy 1258–67 is directed against him, and the writers of chronicles applauded him almost without exception.[46] Some of the laments, however, were as much about the disorder and suffering caused by both sides in the rebellion, and one of them does not mention Simon at all (**208**).

None of the laments is modelled directly upon another and no two are alike in formal structure, but the authors share several assumptions as if each is drawing independently upon an unwritten consensus. The verses agree, for instance, that after the death of Simon de Montfort the country was bereft of justice, peace, truth and the rule of law; they agree, too, that his death amounted to a martyrdom freely suffered for great ideals, like the murder of Thomas Becket; and that Earl Simon's martyrdom qualified him for sainthood – one of the laments does call him a saint (**203** lines 58, 70). The laments deal in ideas that were common currency at the time. But they also express personal anguish, and confused or bitter feelings could be alleviated by turning them into verse, making the ugly and threatening into the elegant and controlled. In the words of John Donne,

---

[45] See M. Fernandes, 'The Northamptonshire assize jurors: The role of the family as a motivating force during the Barons' War', in R. Eales and S. Tyas (eds), *Family and Dynasty in Late Medieval England: Proceedings of the 1997 Harlaxton Symposium* (Donington, 2003), pp. 38–55; Valente, *Theory and Practice of Revolt*, pp. 93, 100–4.

[46] A. Gransden, *Historical Writing in England c.550 to c.1307* (London, 1974), pp. 461–2, 468–9, 478–9.

INTRODUCTION

> Griefe brought to numbers cannot be so fierce,
> For, he tames it, that fetters it in verse.[47]

That seems to have been the essential purpose of each lament. None of them favours a continuance of the rebellion; far from it, they call on all parties to return to peace and harmony and they beg for divine, not human, retribution upon those who will not do so.[48]

The verses probably circulated privately on loose sheets or rolls, and only one copy of each is now known.[49] The former existence of other copies can be assumed, and is attested by the variant readings or alternative versions that have survived (e.g. **203** lines 9, 11, 76; **204–5**); even so, the texts need never have passed beyond the acquaintance of a cultured few. Had the laments been intended for wider consumption they would have been in English, and if they had been consumed more widely there would probably be more extant copies. No-one without advanced Latin or French could understand them, and their sentiments could not be relayed to a wider audience through the official structures of shire and diocese or by the preaching orders; those had been the most effective channels of Montfortian ideas before the battle of Evesham, but now they were blocked.

◆ ◆ ◆

In the seclusion of their precincts religious houses in several parts of England began to remember the death of Earl Simon and his companions every year on 4 August; so much is evident from entries in their calendars. The texts of prayers and hymns for Earl Simon have also survived and some of them were clearly designed to be heard in church; two are motets and were included in large service books (**216, 222**), and we have elements of at least three different offices or *memoriae* (commemorations), presumably from three separate churches (**215, 220–1**). The annual commemorations were apparently intended for use at the evening office of Vespers and the night-time offices of Matins and Lauds.[50] Like the laments, the prayers and hymns draw upon feelings that were current in the disordered period 1265–67. They are addressed to God, to Christ, to the Blessed Virgin or to the earl himself and evidently assume that he is a saint or that he should be. In so doing, however, they offended against the Dictum of Kenilworth, which in 1266

---

[47] 'The triple Foole', lines 10–11.
[48] See H. Shields, 'The *Lament for Simon de Montfort*: an unnoticed text of the French poem', *Medium Aevum* 41 (1972), pp. 202–7 (at pp. 205–6); A. J. Hartman, 'Poetry and the cause of Simon de Montfort after the battle of Evesham', *The Mediaeval Journal* 9 (2019), pp. 41–61 (at pp. 55–8).
[49] See D. B. Tyson, 'Medieval French occasional verse: Another fair field needing folk', *Nottingham Medieval Studies* 61 (2017), pp. 115–45 (at p. 134); J. Jahner, *Literature and Law in the Era of Magna Carta* (Oxford, 2019), p. 201.
[50] See **215, 217, 220**.

recommended corporal punishment for treating Earl Simon as a saint. Indeed, certain Franciscans

> out of his excellent deeds composed an admirable office about him, that is to say readings, responses, versicles, a hymn, and other things that belong to the glory and honour of a martyr, which will not obtain a solemn performance in God's church, as is hoped, while Edward is alive.[51]

That was apparently written before November 1272, because it refers to 'Edward', not 'King Edward' or 'the king'. It is therefore uncertain whether the extant prayers and hymns could have been used in church at the time they were composed. But it is hard to believe that the attempt was never made.

Saint Simon

The writers of Montfortian literature were not trying to stimulate public opinion after the battle of Evesham but to express it in a satisfying way. In order to construct such noble abstractions as 'the English people', 'justice', 'betrayal', 'martyrdom' and 'revenge' they alluded repeatedly to the then familiar details of Simon de Montfort's person, career, death and miracles.

In 1258 as earl of Leicester Simon had been one of the barons who forced Henry III to accept a programme of reforms in central and local government. Each of the reformers then swore an oath to support the rest, and in the eyes of Earl Simon their mutual oath transformed a campaign for secular reform into a sacred mission. For years he had tried to absorb the advice of pastors like Robert Grosseteste but had progressed far less in piety than the chief object of his contempt, King Henry. After 1258, however, Montfort was to be found urgently seeking appropriate godliness through severe private penance. By taking up self-sanctifying exercises that included nightly vigils, the continuous wearing of a hair shirt and an abstinence from marital intercourse, he hoped to become a knight of Christ.

The cause to which he then dedicated himself went by the broad name of 'justice', which to its adherents meant honesty, fairness, or righteous conduct. It promised to remedy the abuses then practised by local officials; it would stop the king's indulgence of his foreign relatives in England, which had amplified the public's aversion to all 'aliens'; and it would rectify royal and papal interference in the English church. The intended result would be a harmonious 'community of the realm'. In the pursuit of those ideals Simon de Montfort's oath and privations

---

[51] *Chron. Melrose* (1835), p. 212.

would give him the strength to withstand all doubters and opponents, to become a popular hero and to lead the reform movement not only to victory at the battle of Lewes in 1264 but also to its annihilation a year later on the field of Evesham.[52]

There was a setback in 1261 when King Henry regained control of government; Montfort, alone among the leading reformers, would not abandon his oath but chose instead to leave the country. Nevertheless, the cause of reform still had many supporters in the English localities and in 1263 they enabled him to return to England, his oath intact, and with a dominant position in the movement. After becoming God's pre-eminent champion of 'justice' in England, 'the hope of the oppressed, the voice of the common people' (**203** line 30), Earl Simon was able to attract many followers, especially idealistic young men. Turmoil and civil war ensued, and at Lewes in May 1264 Montfort's army unexpectedly defeated and captured the king and his son and heir, Edward.[53] There followed a fragile truce in which Earl Simon began to introduce further reforms. His career had by then reached a precarious summit and the *Song of Lewes*, a long poem written between the battles of Lewes and Evesham, argues learnedly that Earl Simon's new regime could claim both political legitimacy and divine support. At one point the *Song* likens Simon to Christ because he was ready to die at Lewes for the good of the many, and it attributes his victory there to God's favour.[54] The *Song* portrays him as the people's only salvation, the long-rejected 'cornerstone' that could unite a divided nation;[55] it was a metaphor that Jesus had applied to himself.[56]

In March 1265, in the presence of lords, knights and burgesses summoned by Earl Simon from all parts of England, a dramatic ceremony in Westminster Hall memorably reasserted the holiness of his movement. The proceedings were ordered to be announced in every shire court for onward transmission to the manors, and each bishop had a diocesan structure through which to pass down the notion of Montfortian sanctity to the parishes.[57] At the same time the Franciscan friars were using their special status in towns and rich households to preach in Earl Simon's

---

[52] The standard biographies of Simon de Montfort are currently those of John Maddicott and Sophie Ambler: J. R. Maddicott, *Simon de Montfort* (Cambridge, 1994); S. T. Ambler, *The Song of Simon de Montfort: England's First Revolutionary and the Death of Chivalry* (London, 2019). On the period of reform and rebellion (1258–67) see also Jobson, *First English Revolution* and David Carpenter, *Henry III: Reform, Rebellion, Civil War, Settlement 1258–1272* (New Haven and London, 2023), in both of which Simon de Montfort is a central figure.

[53] Edward's Latin title as heir to the throne, 'dominus Edwardus', is usually rendered as 'Lord Edward' or 'the Lord Edward' but contemporaries called him 'Sir Edward' in English: e.g. *Political Songs*, p. 71; Rob. Gloucester 2, pp. 727, 731, 735. To avoid argument I refer to him simply as 'Edward'.

[54] *Song of Lewes*, p. 12, lines 345–6, 358–9.

[55] Ibid. p. 9, lines 261–8.

[56] Matt. 21: 42; Mark 12: 10; Luke 20: 17. Cf. Ps. 117 (AV 118): 22; Isa. 28: 16.

[57] S. T. Ambler, *Bishops in the Political Community of England, 1213–1272* (Oxford, 2017), pp. 176–82. On use of the shire courts for Montfortian announcements see also Carpenter, *Henry III 1258–72*, p. 404.

INTRODUCTION

favour.[58] As one of King Henry's councillors had observed in 1261, 'If the lord king had preachers on his behalf such as the opposite side has, it would be better for him.'[59]

Edward escaped from custody in May 1265 and in coalition with barons from the marches of Wales gathered an army recruited from Earl Simon's enemies. They included men who had known and once admired Earl Simon and had sworn to uphold the plan of reform but were now ready to put aside their oaths; Gilbert of Clare earl of Gloucester was only the most prominent of the defectors. War broke out again and on 4 August 1265 at the battle of Evesham Earl Simon died with many of those who had remained loyal to him, including his eldest son Henry and the chief justiciar Hugh le Despenser.[60] On the battlefield Simon had been singled out by a squad of twelve fighters, selected by Edward to find and kill him. When the twelve surrounded him[61] they called upon him to surrender,[62] with good reason to believe that he would not; 'I will never surrender to dogs and perjurers, but only to God,' he cried,[63] and was then brought down. There followed the notorious mistreatment of Earl Simon's corpse where it lay: the head, hands, feet and genitals were cut off and all dispersed as trophies. Meanwhile such was the disparity of forces that the Montfortian army was soon overwhelmed and slaughtered. As Robert of Gloucester wrote, 'Such was the murder of Evesham, for battle was it none.'[64]

Later that day the monks of Evesham abbey retrieved what remained of Earl Simon's body and buried it in the most prestigious position they had, near the tomb of St Wulfsige in the choir of the abbey church, immediately in front of the steps to the presbytery (Fig. 3). Henry de Montfort and Hugh le Despenser had died with the Earl and were laid to rest beside him.[65] Simon's remaining adherents interpreted his battlefield assassination as a martyrdom, especially as it was accompanied by immediate evidence of his extraordinary piety: the hair shirt was revealed when his armour was stripped off. Montfort's cause had indeed been sacred to him personally but it was also intrinsically popular, and that would

---

[58] *Flores Historiarum* 3, p. 266.
[59] *Royal and Other Historical Letters Illustrative of the Reign of Henry III* 2, ed. W. W. Shirley (Rolls Series, 1866), p. 158. For the context see Carpenter, *Henry III 1258–72*, p. 220.
[60] On the course of the battle see O. de Laborderie, J. R. Maddicott and D. A. Carpenter, 'The last hours of Simon de Montfort: a new account', *EHR* 115 (2000), pp. 378–412; Cox, *Battle of Evesham*.
[61] *Chron. Lanercost* (1839), p. 76.
[62] 'Fragment d'une chronique rédigée à l'abbaye de Battle, sur la guerre des barons', C. Bémont, *Simon de Montfort comte de Leicester* (Paris, 1884), pp. 373–80 (at p. 380); 'Annales prioratus de Dunstaplia', *Ann. Monastici* 3, p. 239; Oxnead, p. 229.
[63] *Miracles*, ed. Halliwell, p. xxx n, quoting London, British Library, Cotton MS Faustina B VI (annals of Croxden abbey).
[64] Rob. Gloucester 2, p. 765.
[65] D. Cox, 'The tomb of Simon de Montfort: an enquiry', *Transactions of the Worcestershire Archaeological Soc.* 3rd ser. 36 (2018), pp. 159–71 (at pp. 159–62).

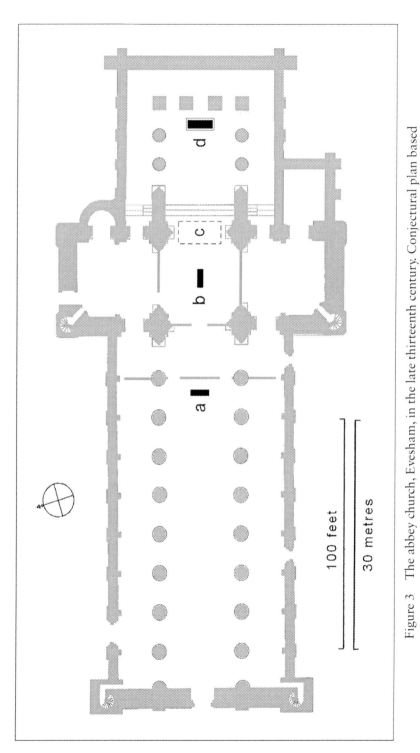

Figure 3 The abbey church, Evesham, in the late thirteenth century. Conjectural plan based on archaeological and historical records. **a** Altar of the Holy Cross. **b** Tomb of St Wulfsige. **c** Graves of Simon de Montfort, Henry de Montfort and Hugh le Despenser. **d** High altar.

be the vital force in shaping and sustaining his reputation as a saint. Meanwhile, however, martyrdom alone did not prove that Simon de Montfort was in fact a saint; confirmation of his ultimate glorification would depend on God sending miracles,[66] and it was not inevitable that he would do so. For not everyone was dismayed to hear that Earl Simon was dead: the constable of Bridgnorth castle in Shropshire maintained a posthumous aversion to him, 'because he deprived me of many valuable things' (**79**), and others continued to disparage him for political reasons, even within religious houses that had been enthusiastically Montfortian (**74, 200**). Nevertheless, everybody who had remained attached to Simon's fight for reform felt bereavement and anger, and while they had to give up hope of social change they clung to the possibility that in their personal difficulties God would allow Earl Simon to intercede for them in heaven. Predictably, when news of his miracles broke, 'Sighs were changed into shouts of praise, and the former level of gladness was revived.'[67]

The first stories had emerged quickly, and by 1266 reports of Earl Simon's miracles were common knowledge: according to one royalist, 'Nearly everybody is saying that Sir Simon, the earl of Leicester, is a saint.' (**3**) Moreover, the popular mood was enough to elevate his dead companions Henry de Montfort and Hugh le Despenser to a similar level:

> With the father, the son Henry was taken, died and was buried, a martyr and a virtuous knight. A thousand signs show that both of them were saints, with a thousand sick people telling their praises. (**203** lines 56–9)

> God made several signs of sanctity through Hugh, for the blind received sight on coming to his tomb, and cripples their proper means of walking.[68]

Any impression that a wave of confidence in Simon de Montfort's miraculous powers had flooded the country soon after the battle ought, however, to be examined. For some of the miracle cures, the patient did not turn to him spontaneously but did so only after being prompted in a dream or by a friend. Meanwhile the earl's cult faced not only occasional indifference but also severe royalist opposition. Immediately after the battle of Evesham there was an uncontrolled 'orgy of vengeance' against the Montfortians, and then in September 1265 the king began the formal seizure of contrariants' estates.[69] Well into 1266, therefore, royalists were

---

[66] See **203** lines 58–9, **217** line 2.
[67] Rishanger, *De Bellis*, p. 546.
[68] *Chron. Melrose* (1835), p. 201.
[69] C. H. Knowles, 'The resettlement of England after the barons' war, 1264–67', *Transactions of the Royal Historical Soc.* 5th ser. 32 (1982), pp. 25–41 (at pp. 25–30).

finding opportunities to intimidate not only Montfortian rebels but also personal enemies whom they alleged to be contrariants. It is hardly surprising, therefore, that the miracles 'were not revealed in public because of royalist intimidation',[70] and that 'No-one has dared to make known anything like this for fear of the king and his followers.'[71] Nevertheless, Montfortian rebels were still holding out in defensible places like Kenilworth castle and the Isle of Ely and pillaging the surrounding areas. Amid the discord and violence the signatories of the Dictum of Kenilworth in October 1266 asked the papal legate to forbid anyone to call Earl Simon a saint or a just man or to speak of his 'vain and fatuous miracles'; and they asked the king to inflict corporal punishment on everyone who disobeyed.[72] At the abbey of Bury St Edmunds, which was heavily fined for its abbot's support of the contrariants, someone decided to erase from John de Taxter's chronicle an assertion that there were miracles;[73] other chroniclers would refer only to rumours of miracles and cited none in particular.[74]

Official efforts to suppress Simon de Montfort's cult were aimed especially at its focal point, Evesham abbey:

> the monks of Evesham, among whom Simon is buried, dare neither to show the tomb nor to publish the miracles, because of royalist intimidation.[75]

> concealment is sought by the power of his enemies, which is directed towards covering up the fame of him and his own; through their minions they cause the ways and paths of those who come [to Evesham] to be blocked by day, although many of them try to go there on pilgrimage by night.[76]

The probable organizer of the Evesham roadblocks was the sheriff of Worcestershire, Sir William Beauchamp of Elmley,[77] a royalist who had sent two sons to fight in the battle.[78] His castle at Elmley stood five miles south-west of the town and his

---

[70] *Chron. et Annales*, pp. 36–7 (for *regum* read *regium*).
[71] *Chron. Furness*, p. 548.
[72] *Documents of the Baronial Movement of Reform and Rebellion 1258–1267*, ed. R. F. Treharne and I. J. Sanders (Oxford, OMT, 1973), pp. 322–3.
[73] Gransden, *Historical Writing c.550 to c.1307*, pp. 396, 401 and plate XI (a).
[74] e.g. *Chron. et Annales*, pp. 36–7; *Chron. Furness*, p. 548; *Chronica Buriensis: The Chronicle of Bury St Edmunds, 1212–1301*, ed. A. Gransden (London, Nelson's Medieval Texts, 1964), p. 33; *Chron. Canterbury–Dover*, p. 243; 'Gesta sanctae memoriae Ludovici regis Franciae; auctore Guillelmo de Nangiaco', *Recueil des historiens des Gaules et de la France* 20, ed. P.-C.-F. Daunou and J. Naudet (Paris, 1840), pp. 309–462 (at p. 418).
[75] *Polychronicon Ranulphi Higden Monachi Cestrensis* 8, ed. J. R. Lumby (Rolls Series, 1883), p. 250n.
[76] *Chron. Lanercost* (1839), p. 77.
[77] *List of Sheriffs for England and Wales from the Earliest Times to A.D. 1831* (Public Record Office, Lists and Indexes 9, 1898), p. 157.
[78] *ODNB*, s.n. 'Beauchamp, William de, ninth earl of Warwick'.

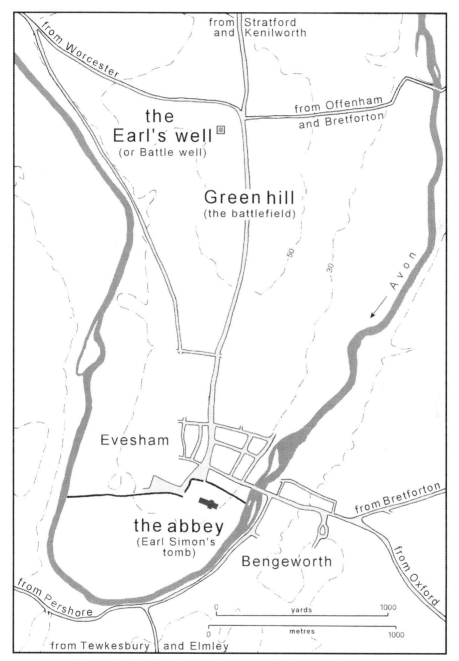

Figure 4 The Evesham cult sites in the thirteenth century, and the roads to them. Contour heights in feet.

Worcestershire estates almost surrounded the abbey's.[79] There is certainly one recorded case of interception by his men, in which staff of Elmley castle stopped a girl on her way from Evesham to Elmley on suspicion that she was bringing back healing water from the battlefield (9).

Once inside the abbey church, however, pilgrims could make their way in peace to the east end of the nave and pray there before the rood and the altar of the Holy Cross (195). Able-bodied visitors could do that without intruding on the monks' regular services, and if sick or disabled persons arrived they and their companions, including women, might be allowed to pass into the choir to visit the Montfortian graves, even while a service was in progress (196); some patients even ascended to the presbytery to sleep in front of the high altar (194). But notice was being taken that the monks had hosted the Montfortians before the battle, had given Christian burial to the remains of Earl Simon and had admitted pilgrims to his tomb, and William of Marlborough, the abbot-elect, was held to account for those offences. Since William had not yet received papal confirmation the legate was able to bar him from the abbacy in 1266 and replace him with someone from another house.[80] Inevitably the Evesham monks 'feared to incur the indignation of the great' and under external pressure they removed Earl Simon's remains from the choir and hid them.[81] In spite of everything, however, Earl Simon's empty grave remained a cult site,[82] and next to it were the undisturbed bodies of Henry de Montfort and Hugh le Despenser. Also very near was the miracle-working tomb of St Wulfsige (29). A pilgrimage to St Wulfsige could therefore be a visitor's pretext for illicit veneration of the dead Montfortians. It was fortunate too, or perhaps contrived, that in 1266 an alternative cult site became available outside the town when a pond of healing water was identified on the battlefield (3).[83] It was then called the Earl's well or Earl Simon's well and became a permanent place of pilgrimage.[84] Known as the Battle well by the 1450s and ever afterwards, the pond can still be seen,[85] and in the nineteenth century local people would use its water to bathe 'weak' eyes.[86]

[79] C. J. Bond, 'The estates of Evesham abbey: a preliminary survey of their medieval topography', *Vale of Evesham Historical Soc. Research Papers* 4 (1973), p. 4 (map); *Beauchamp Cart*. p. lvi (map).
[80] Cox, *Battle of Evesham*, pp. 33–4.
[81] 'Opus chronicorum', *Chronica S. Albani [II]*, pp. 3–59 (at p. 20); 'Annales monasterii de Oseneia', *Ann. Monastici* 2, pp. 3–352 (at pp. 176–7). They may have been consigned to a quiet corner of the crypt: Cox, 'Tomb of Simon de Montfort', pp. 166–8.
[82] On public access to saints' shrines and tombs see A. E. Bailey, 'Reconsidering the medieval experience at the shrine in high medieval England', *Journal of Medieval History* 47 (2021), pp. 203–29. I am grateful to Dr Bailey for a copy of this article.
[83] See *Chron. Furness*, p. 548.
[84] J. R. Maddicott, 'Follower, leader, pilgrim, saint: Robert de Vere, earl of Oxford, at the shrine of Simon de Montfort, 1273', *EHR* 109 (1994), pp. 641–53 (at p. 649).
[85] Cox, *Battle of Evesham*, pp. 36–8.
[86] 'F.P.', 'The Battlewell, Evesham', in E. A. B. Barnard (ed.), *Notes & Queries concerning Evesham and the Four Shires* 2 (Evesham, 1911), p. 152.

INTRODUCTION

Preservation and rediscovery

Social conflict gradually subsided in the 1270s after an enlightened royal policy allowed disinherited rebels to resume their estates and made institutional changes that satisfied reformist aspirations.[87] The last entry in the Evesham miracle book was made c.1280 and, as far as one can tell, no more laments, prayers, or hymns were composed after that. The existing texts continued to be read but they were no longer topical. Instead, they acquired an appeal as historical documents, literary relics and moral tales. After all, to thoughtful people Simon de Montfort remained a figure of great moral and historical interest, a name to be mentioned when discussion turned to such perennial topics as the changefulness of Fortune or the need for constitutional change.[88] Like Charles XII of Sweden,

> He left the name, at which the world grew pale,
> To point a moral, or adorn a tale.[89]

A lesson from Montfort's career is cited, for instance, in the *Vita Edwardi Secundi*, written in the early fourteenth century: 'It is not safe to rise up against the king, because the outcome is likely to be unfortunate. For even Simon earl of Leicester was at last laid low in battle at Evesham.'[90] The ancient Wheel of Fortune continued to turn and had been invoked soon after the battle in one of the Montfortian hymns (**219**), and later in that century one of the laments (**205**) was copied into a book next after a diagram of the Wheel of Life, another representation of a man's rise and fall. Elsewhere a version of that lament (**204**) was copied poignantly next to verses that had celebrated Simon's victory at Lewes. Edward II himself, son of the victor of Evesham, was willing to pay two women for 'singing of Sir Simon de Montfort and other songs' in 1323[91] and probably relished a reminder of the mighty rebel's downfall.

Montfortian texts seem to have been valued in the later Middle Ages as specimens of poetry, and perhaps as records of religious and constitutional history. Laments are found copied in books on theology (**203**) and canon law (**207**), and

---

[87] Knowles, 'Resettlement of England'; J. R. Maddicott, 'Edward I and the lessons of baronial reform: local government, 1258–80', in P. R. Coss and S. D. Lloyd (eds), *Thirteenth Century England I: Proceedings of the Newcastle upon Tyne Conference 1985* (Woodbridge, 1986), pp. 1–30.
[88] C. Knowles, *Simon de Montfort 1265–1965* (Historical Association General Ser. 60, 1965), pp. 7–10; D Waley, 'Simon de Montfort and the historians', *Sussex Archaeological Collections* 140 (2002), pp. 65–70; S. Walker, *Political Culture in Later Medieval England*, ed. M. J. Braddick (Manchester and New York, 2006), pp. 213, 221–2 n. 117.
[89] Samuel Johnson, *The Vanity of Human Wishes* (1749), lines 221–2.
[90] *Vita Edwardi Secundi: The Life of Edward the Second*, ed. and transl. W. R. Childs (Oxford, OMT, 2005), pp. 76–7.
[91] *The Honor and Forest of Pickering* 3, ed. R. B. Turton (North Riding Record Soc. new ser. 3, 1896), pp. 225–6.

INTRODUCTION

another (**208**) formed part of a handsome compilation of law texts, where there was an intention to set the verses to music. At St Augustine's abbey, Canterbury, the monk Ralph of Gatwick (fl.1297–1325) gave the house a volume (now lost) that included not only political tracts but also 'Planctus Anglie de morte Simonis de Montis Fortis' (England's Lament on the Death of Simon de Montfort).[92] And local history in particular was served by a copy of 'Illos saluauit' (**206**) embedded in a chronicle kept at Peterborough abbey, where the verses preserved references to local strife in the post-Evesham rebellion.

Montfortian writings, enjoyable simply as literature, were also a useful bank of *exempla* for religious teachers. One of the laments (**205**) was evidently copied by Franciscans in Ireland as sermon material, and the surviving copy of the miracle book was made for a collection of texts that illustrated contacts between living people and the other-world. Churches, too, may have valued Montfortian prayers and hymns as literature, and also as records of a liturgical tradition; church calendars made a hundred years after Simon de Montfort's death still included his anniversary, and prayers and hymns were being copied even later (**221**). But such materials did not imply continued devotion to Earl Simon. Only at Evesham did his cult show signs of life after c.1280; at least, the Earl's well seems to have maintained a reputation for sanctity, for by c.1448 it was marked by a stone Crucifixion under a canopy, and by 1457 Abbot John Wykewone seems to have built a chapel there.[93] The Battle well chapel was short-lived, however. A printed missal that was given to it before 1502[94] migrated to the abbey church before the Dissolution, and the chapel was no more than a vague local memory by the mid-eighteenth century.[95]

Secular interest in Simon de Montfort outlived the Reformation but his reappearance in imaginative literature came later, in response to the romantic medievalism and liberal politics of the late eighteenth and early nineteenth centuries. It was then that the original Montfortian texts began to appear in print and in some cases to be translated. The first lament published in full was an English verse translation of 'Chaunter mestoit' (**204**) by the young Walter Scott; in 1840 the miracle book was printed; and the first full biography, by Reinhold Pauli, appeared in German in 1867.[96] In that process of rediscovery Simon de Montfort acquired the popular image of a fearless champion of democracy and

---

[92] MLGB3 ('Medieval Libraries of Great Britain' website), BA1.871; A. B. Emden, *Donors of Books to S. Augustine's Abbey Canterbury* (Oxford Bibliographical Soc. Occasional Publication 4, 1968), p. 10.
[93] *Evesham Abbey and Local Society in the Late Middle Ages: The Abbot's Household Account 1456–7 and the Priors' Registers 1520–40*, ed. D. Cox (WHS, new ser. 30, 2021), pp. 26–7.
[94] Oxford, Bodleian Library, Gough Missals 33: Bodleian Libraries 'Bod-Inc Online' website.
[95] Cox, *Battle of Evesham*, pp. 41–2.
[96] *Simon de Montfort, Graf von Leicester, Schöpfer des Hauses der Gemeinen* (Tübingen, London and Edinburgh, 1867). Published in English as *Simon de Montfort, Earl of Leicester, the Creator of the House of Commons*, transl. U. M. Goodwin (London, 1876).

INTRODUCTION

civil rights; and although Pauli and all subsequent historians refer to his faults and misdeeds, no academic or humanitarian assessment has yet erased that image. Places associated with Earl Simon, especially Evesham, Leicester and Lewes, have named streets and public buildings after him and set up monuments in various forms. And since the 1880s he has had a leading role in several works of fiction, including poems and plays; until the 1950s most of them chose to use an archaic diction that is now little appreciated, but a succession of exciting novels about his life and times has emerged since then, more or less in current English. Nevertheless, the monuments, poems, plays and novels of the last two centuries are essentially commemorations of a secular hero; they cannot draw upon the sincere distress and devotion that once powered the laments, prayers, hymns and miracle stories meant for a martyr and a saint.

Catalogue of the Texts and Manuscripts

The miracles

The Evesham abbey miracle book (**1–197**). London, British Library, Cotton MS Vespasian A VI, fols 162r–183r. The present copy of the miracle book survives within a booklet of six texts (fols 134–83). The booklet was copied by a single scribe in the last quarter of the fourteenth century or the first quarter of the fifteenth. It is not luxurious but neither is it careless, and it is of a size suitable for private reading. All six of its items concern conversations between living people and inhabitants of the other-world: *Spiritus Guidonis* (The Ghost of Gui) by Jean Gobi the younger; H[enry] of Sawtry's *Purgatorium sancti Patricii* (St Patrick's Purgatory); *Pene inferni* (The Pains of Hell); *Passio sancte Iuliane* (The Passion of St Julian); *Vita sancti Alexii* (The Life of St Alexius); and finally the Evesham abbey miracle book. It was evidently included because it was relevant to the theme of the collection, not from a special regard for Earl Simon. Each entry in the miracle book has a red display initial. After the last miracle entry the scribe has copied two short liturgical items from Evesham abbey (**214–15**). They may have descended to his exemplar from additions made in the original book. There are sixteenth-century pen-trials on the last page of the booklet (fol. 183v), which is also the last page of the parent volume; they mention a John Kempt of 'Cliffton', a Roger Causefeylde esquire and a Robert Smyth.

A prologue (**1**) was added to the miracle book at some time before the present copy was made. It is an account of events immediately before and after the battle of Evesham, and seems to descend from a separate narrative composed at Evesham (and used again in a chronicle compiled there in or after 1392);[1] that narrative in turn was derived from one composed at Evesham in French within months of the battle.[2] The prologue was probably not part of the original miracle book; it lacks effusions of praise for Simon de Montfort or of horror at his death,

---

[1] Oxford, Bodleian Library, MS Laud Misc. 529, fols 70r–71v. Some extracts by John Stow from another 'prologue' text are in London, British Library, Harley MS 542, fol. 49r.
[2] London, College of Arms, MS 3/23B: Laborderie, Maddicott and Carpenter, 'Last hours of Simon de Montfort'.

and it makes no mention of miracles. In the present manuscript the beginning and greater part of the prologue fills an unattached leaf inserted between two gatherings. The unattached leaf (fol. 162) was evidently inserted by the scribe of the miracle book copy, because he has written the catchword *Henricus* at the foot of fol. 162v. Oddly the leaf had suffered extensive clumsy erasures beforehand. Multispectral photography by the British Library has succeeded in enhancing some of the erased material, and other versions of the same narrative supply some deficiencies; nevertheless, it remains impossible to produce a completely uninterrupted edition.

Previous edition: *Miracles*, ed. Halliwell, pp. 67–109 (without transcription of the prologue's damaged first leaf).

Miracles from the Melrose chronicle (**198–201**).   London, British Library, Cotton MS Faustina B IX, fols 67v–68v, 71v–72r. The chronicle of Melrose abbey in Roxburghshire, a house of Premonstratensian canons, has Montfortian miracle stories in the *Opusculum de nobili Simone de Monte Forti editum* (A Short Work written about the Noble Simon de Montfort), which was added to the chronicle (at fols 64r–73v) in or after 1289[3] and probably by c.1291.[4] Previous editions: 'Chronica de Mailros', *Rerum Anglicarum Scriptorum Veterum* [ed. W. Fulman] 1 (Oxford, 1684), pp. 135–244 (at pp. 232–4, 238–9); *Chron. Melrose* (1835), pp. 202–4, 212–13. Previous translation: 'Chronicle of Melrose', *The Church Historians of England* 4, transl. J. Stevenson, pt 1 (London, 1856), pp. 79–241 (at pp. 224–7, 233–4).

A miracle from the Lanercost chronicle (**202**).   London, British Library, Cotton MS Claudius D VII, fol. 192v. This story comes from a lost chronicle by Richard of Durham, a Franciscan, which ended in 1297 and was later incorporated in the chronicle of Lanercost priory, a house of Augustinian canons in Cumberland.[5] Previous edition: *Chron. Lanercost* (1839), p. 95. Previous translation: *The Chronicle of Lanercost 1272–1346*, transl. H. Maxwell (Glasgow, 1913), pp. 7–8.

The laments, prayers and hymns

Anno milleno (**203**).   Cambridge, Gonville and Caius College, MS 349/542, fol. 10v. This copy of the lament, hitherto unpublished, is an addendum to one of the booklets that make up the host volume. The booklet consists mainly of

---

[3] It mentions John de Vescy as deceased: see *ODNB*, s.n.
[4] *The Chronicle of Melrose Abbey: A Stratigraphic Edition* 1, ed. D. Broun and J. Harrison (Scottish History Soc. 6th ser. 1, 2007), pp. 168–9.
[5] A. G. Little, 'The authorship of the Lanercost chronicle', *Franciscan Papers, Lists, and Documents* (Manchester, 1943), pp. 42–54 (at pp. 42–6).

Book IV of the *Sententiarum libri quatuor* (Four Books of Sentences) by Peter Lombard, which is prefaced by a bifolium (fols 9–10) containing a list of the chapters. The booklet has been dated to the thirteenth century.[6] The lament was neatly copied a little later in ruled columns on the unwritten verso of the second leaf of the chapters list, a page that had become available after the erasure of some domestic jottings, e.g. 'ijd. ad uinum'. The lament's assumption that Earl Simon's son Richard is still alive (line 75) suggests a date of composition no later than c.1266.

Chaunter mestoit (**204**). London, British Library, Harley MS 2253, fols 59r–59v. This copy of the lament is integral to a well-known medieval collection, the 'Harley Lyrics'. The manuscript is a large volume, handsome but not luxurious. The verses were copied between 1331 and 1341 by the manuscript's 'Scribe B', who worked in the area of Ludlow, Shropshire. The text begins with a red display initial. The lines of each stanza except the first are bracketed together as are the two lines of the refrain, which is marked to be repeated between the stanzas. Each line is divided into three sections by light oblique pen-strokes. The lament appears next after a triumphant Montfortian poem ('Sitteth alle stille') written some time before the battle of Evesham, and is juxtaposed to it as if to illustrate the mutability of human affairs; and the lament is followed by epitaphs on vanity.[7] A date of composition c.1266 is suggested by the references to peace being 'far off' in 1265 (line 3 and **205** line 3) and to Montfortians in prison (line 46 and **205** line 28); imprisoned Montfortians are also mentioned in **203** (line 81), apparently written no later than c.1266. The author of the lament had a special regard for Earl Simon's third surviving son, Amaury (lines 34–5), but does not name him or his elder brother Simon, and it ignores the other brothers Guy and Richard. It is not impossible that Amaury, a learned cleric, was the author; if so, he may have thought it prudent to withhold the brothers' names.

Previous editions: The first printed edition was that of Francis Cohen (later Palgrave) on pp. xli–xliiii of a rare and untitled private publication (London, 1818) of which the incipit is *Cy ensuyt une chanson moult pitoyable*. Subsequent editions (to 1953) are listed in *AN Political Songs*, p. 25, where another edition is provided on pp. 28–32 (with prose translation at pp. 32–3). The lament has since been edited in *Complete Harley 2253* 2, pp. 88–97 (with parallel prose translation). There are also verse translations by Walter Scott, in *A Select Collection of English Songs* 2,

---

[6] Further details of the MS are in M. R. James, *A Descriptive Catalogue of the Manuscripts in the Library of Gonville and Caius College* (Cambridge, 1907), pp. 393–4 (which cites an earlier foliation).
[7] *Complete Harley 2253* 2, pp. 8–9, 383–6.

ed. J. Ritson, 2nd edn (London, 1813), pp. 380–3,[8] and by George Ellis, in *Ancient Songs and Ballads* 1, ed. J. Ritson (London, 1829), pp. 18–21.[9]

Chaunter mestut (**205**). Dublin, Trinity College, MS 347, fols 2v–3r. The late-thirteenth-century host manuscript is a small thick portable volume, evidently of Irish Franciscan origin, and consists mainly of sermon topics together with some minor tracts and, at the end, a set of annals completed in the late thirteenth century. The lament was inserted by two thirteenth-century scribes. The first leaf is perhaps a replacement and the whole lament may formerly have been in the hand of fol. 3r.[10] The scribe of that page brackets the lines in pairs. The two formerly blank pages (fols 1v–2r) that precede the lament come after a thirteenth-century diagram of the Wheel of Life on fol. 1r.[11] Previous edition: H. Shields, 'The *Lament for Simon de Montfort*: an unnoticed text of the French poem', *Medium Aevum* 41 (1972), pp. 202–7 (at p. 203).

Illos saluauit (**206**). London, British Library, Cotton MS Otho D VIII, fols 261r–262r. These verses conclude an account, otherwise mainly in prose, of the dispute between Henry III and his barons (fols 256r–262r); the verses begin in the aftermath of the battle of Lewes and end with the lawless period after Simon de Montfort's death at Evesham. The author of the verses, called Michael (line 57), gives special attention (at lines 137, 140) to the abbey of Ramsey in Huntingdonshire. The abbey likewise receives special attention in the prose part of the account (at fols 256v–257r). The author calls the whole a *memoriale* and dedicates it to 'pater H.' (fol. 256v), probably Hugh of Sulgrave abbot of Ramsey (d.14 February 1268). Michael's verses bemoan the lot of those whom the king has disinherited since the battle of Evesham (lines 202–5, 224–5), and thus seem to antedate the settlement of October 1266.[12] A reference in the present tense to Lent (line 215) and another to 'the coming Easter' (line 226) suggest that the lament was completed in Lent 1266 (10 February–27 March). The *memoriale* (including the lament) is the first item in a booklet within the present composite volume. The booklet (fols 256–69) is well produced though plain, and was probably made in the late fourteenth century; its last item is a chronicle of British history to 1388. The lament is set out in double columns; guide letters at the beginnings

---

[8] Scott produced this translation at the request of Joseph Ritson (d.1803), who supplied a copy of the French text. A note (on p. 380) states that 'It was the object of the translator to imitate, as literally as possible, the style of the original, even in its rudeness, abrupt transitions, and obscurity; such being the particular request of Mr Ritson.'
[9] A note (on p. 18) states that Ellis wrote this translation at Ritson's request, i.e. in or before 1803.
[10] D. Tyson, 'Lament for a dead king', *Journal of Medieval History* 30 (2004), pp. 359–75 (at p. 371).
[11] Further details are in *The 'Annals of Multyfarnham': Roscommon and Connacht Provenance*, ed. B. Williams (Dublin, 2012), pp. 20–2; Trinity College Dublin 'Manuscripts and Archives Online Catalogue' website.
[12] Jobson, *First English Revolution*, p. 157.

of lines 1 and 125 indicate the positions of display initials, but none is provided. The verses break off abruptly on fol. 262r, leaving the rest of the second column blank; the whole verso of that leaf, however, was originally ruled in two columns as if ready for more lines of verse. This unfinished copy of the lament (and thus of the *memoriale*) may have been made at Peterborough abbey; on the verso of its last leaf (fol. 262v) a similar hand begins the record of a dispute between the abbey and the inhabitants of Dogsthorpe. Incidentally, the abbey owned a work described in the late fourteenth century as *Vita Simonis de Monteforti rithmice* (The Life of Simon de Montfort in Verse).[13]

Previous edition: *Miracles*, ed. Halliwell, pp. 139–46. The manuscript had been badly burnt in 1731 and Halliwell worked from the remains of the damaged leaves, by then detached. Some words and characters had already been lost and after his edition was published the fragments remained susceptible to further losses. When the leaves were eventually inlaid in paper frames, some remaining characters at the edges were unavoidably covered up.[14] Halliwell's edition therefore enables textual losses incurred after his involvement to be restored.

Vbi fuit mons (**207**).   Cambridge, Gonville and Caius College, MS 85/167, fol. ii r. These verses were copied, apparently in the owner's hand, on a flyleaf of the host volume, a later-thirteenth-century collection of treatises on canon law. The manuscript seems to have belonged c.1270 to a Walter 'de Hyda', clerk, who became or aspired to be rector of Broadwater in Sussex.[15] He may have been related to Walter de la Hyde, a layman whose father-in-law John de Neville and mother-in-law Hawis of Gaddesden were patrons of Broadwater rectory.[16] The scribe has bracketed the lines in threes. The reference to a hoped-for Montfortian invasion by sea (lines 158–9) and to the landing of a ship bringing discord (lines 161–2) would be consistent with composition in 1267. Previous edition: F. W. Maitland, 'A song on the death of Simon de Montfort', *EHR* 9 (1896), pp. 314–18 (at pp. 316–18).

Vulneratur karitas (**208**).   London, British Library, Harley MS 746, fols 103v–104r. The lament is integral to a handsome collection of material on the laws of England that was probably compiled between c.1279 and 1285.[17] The verses are added in some blank ruled columns left over at the end of the volume, and in a similar book-hand to the rest. They are divided into stanzas, each beginning with a

---

[13] *Peterborough Abbey* (CBMLC), p. 158, no. BP21.285f.
[14] *Miracles*, ed. Halliwell, p. xx n; A. Prescott, '"Their present miserable state of cremation": The restoration of the Cotton library', in C. J. Wright (ed.), *Sir Robert Cotton as Collector: Essays on an Early Stuart Courtier and his Legacy* (London, 1997), pp. 391–454.
[15] James, *MSS of Gonville and Caius* 1, pp. 82–4; H. G. Richardson, 'Studies in Bracton', *Traditio* 6 (1948), pp. 61–104 (at pp. 61–2); Tyson, 'Lament for a dead king', p. 373.
[16] *VCH Suss.* 6, pt 1, pp. 69, 77; below, **117**.
[17] *AN Political Songs*, p. 149.

paragraph mark, red for the Latin stanzas and blue for the French. Each stanza is copied without line-breaks, the columns being too narrow for whole lines of verse. The lines of the first stanza are spaced for the insertion of musical notation; in performance the music would have been repeated for every stanza. No such notation was inserted, but a sketch of music for the first seven words (the first two lines of that column) is discernible as a single stave on fol. 107r (formerly blank). The stave antedates the pen-trials above and below it. The manuscript probably resided in Lincolnshire in the mid fourteenth century; Hugh of Obthorpe (fl.1355–69) from Baston[18] is mentioned on fol. 104v and again in the pen-trials. References to robbers roaming the country (lines 49, 53, 59, 63) suggest that the verses were composed between 1265 and 1267, when other laments made similar references (**206** line 209; **207** lines 155–6). Previous editions: *Political Songs*, pp. 133–6 (with prose translation beneath); *AN Political Songs*, pp. 152–5 (with prose translation of the French at pp. 155–6).

Calendar from Barking abbey (**209**). London, British Library, Cotton MS Otho A V, fol. 2v. The calendar fragment (not seen) in which this entry appears was copied in the later fourteenth century.[19]

Calendar from Barking abbey (**210**). Oxford, University College, MS 169, fol. 4v. The calendar in which this entry appears is part of a manuscript (not seen) copied in 1404.[20] Previous edition: *Barking Ordinale* 1, p. 8.

Calendar from Beaulieu abbey? (**211**). London, British Library, Harley MS 2951, fol. 129v. The calendar (not seen) was apparently begun c.1250. It is bound into a Cistercian hymnal believed to have been made for Beaulieu abbey, Hampshire.[21] The entry seems to have been added in the later thirteenth century,[22] possibly in the time of Abbot Dennis (d.1280), who is commemorated on fol. 130v. He had been summoned to Simon de Montfort's parliament of 1265.[23] After Evesham he was accused of involvement in the destruction of royalist property.[24] Previous edition: P. M. Lefferts, 'Two English motets on Simon de Montfort', *Early Music History* 1 (1981), pp. 203–25 (at p. 210n).

Calendar from Tavistock abbey (**212**). Cambridge, Corpus Christi College, MS 210, p. 30b. The manuscript of c.1480 in which this note appears is William

[18] Royal Commission on Historical MSS 77, *De L'Isle I* (1925), p. 16.
[19] *Barking Ordinale* 1, p. ix; British Library 'Exploring archives and manuscripts' website.
[20] *Barking Ordinale* 1, p. v.
[21] R. W. Pfaff, *The Liturgy in Medieval England: A History* (Cambridge, 2009), p. 258.
[22] P. M. Lefferts, 'Two English motets on Simon de Montfort', *Early Music History* 1 (1981), pp. 203–25 (at p. 210n).
[23] *Close R.* 1264–68, p. 86.
[24] E. F. Jacob, *Studies in the Period of Baronial Reform and Rebellion, 1258–1267* (Oxford, Oxford Studies in Social and Legal History 8, 1925), p. 296.

Worcester's autograph record of his journeys through England.[25] The calendar that he saw at Tavistock in Devon is not known to survive. The calendar entry may have been added in the time of John Chubb, abbot 1262–69, who had been summoned to Simon de Montfort's parliament of 1265.[26] Previous editions: *Itineraria Symonis Simeonis et Willelmi de Worcester*, ed. J. Nasmyth (Cambridge, 1778), p. 115; William Worcestre, *Itineraries*, ed. J. H. Harvey (Oxford, OMT, 1969), p. 112.

Calendar from Evesham abbey (**213**).   London, British Library, Lansdowne MS 427, fol. 13r. The present manuscript is an early-eighteenth-century copy of a medieval calendar that was badly burnt in 1731 (British Library, Cotton MS Vitellius E XVII, fols 241–6). The remains of that manuscript do not include Simon de Montfort's entry, which was added at some time before c.1425 (the latest probable date for **214**).

Calendar from Evesham abbey (**214**).   London, British Library, Cotton MS Vespasian A VI, fol. 183r. The scribe of the Evesham miracle book copied this note, which quotes from **213**, on his last page, where it is followed without a break by **215**. The note does not relate to the scribe's theme of human encounters with the other-world, and so was probably already present in his exemplar. Previous edition: T. Warton, *The History of English Poetry*, ed. R. Taylor (London, 1840) 1, p. 45n; *Miracles*, ed. Halliwell, p. 109.

Salue Symon: antiphon, versicle and response (**215**).   London, British Library, Cotton MS Vespasian A VI, fol. 183r. The scribe of the miracle book copied these lines immediately after **214** and presented them without line-breaks. Like **214** they were probably in his exemplar. They appear to be elements of an office or *memoria* in honour of Simon de Montfort, lacking a collect. The versicle and response follow 'a common formula, used in *memoriae* and as the bridge between Matins and Lauds in the office of many saints'. The antiphon text occurs again elsewhere as a motet (**216**).[27] Previous editions: *Political Songs*, p. 124 (with prose translation beneath); Warton, *History of English Poetry* 1, p. 45n; *Miracles*, ed. Halliwell, pp. 109–10; *Receuil de chants historiques français*, ed. A. Le Roux de Lincy, 1st ser. (Paris, 1841), pp. 195n–6n; Lefferts, 'Two English motets', p. 223 (with parallel prose translation). A verse translation by Gilbert Murray is in *Simon de Montfort & his Cause 1251–1266*, ed. W. H. Hutton (New York and London, 1888), p. 169. Another, by Oswald Greenwaye Knapp (1859–1947), is in *The Evesham Journal & Four Shires Advertiser*, 16 January 1892, p. 3.

---

[25] Corpus Christi College, Cambridge 'Parker Library on the web' website.
[26] *Close R*. 1264–68, p. 86.
[27] Lefferts, 'Two English motets', pp. 212–13.

Salue Symon: motet (**216**). Cambridge, Jesus College, Old Library Manuscripts, Old Library, QB5, fol. 139r. This fragment of a motet for three voices survives on what remains of a bifolium from a large volume, perhaps of the fourteenth or fifteenth century but possibly older. The verses are presented with no linebreaks. The bifolium was later removed from its parent volume, cut down and bound sideways as a flyleaf (fol. 139) at the end of a gradual (or *cantatorium*) of c.1300 from Durham cathedral.[28] The motet seems to have been part of an office or *memoria* in honour of Simon de Montfort.[29] The surviving text is also that of the antiphon in **215**. Robert of Stichill bishop of Durham (1261–74) had been moderately sympathetic to the Montfortian regime and was accused of offences against the peace after the battle of Evesham.[30] Previous edition: B. Cooper, 'A thirteenth-century canon reconstructed', *The Music Review* 42 (1981), pp. 85–90 (at p. 86, with musical reconstruction); Lefferts, 'Two English motets', p. 223 (with parallel prose translation), with musical reconstruction at p. 224. A reconstruction by Danil Ryabchikov is sung by Ensemble Labyrinthus on their digital album *Carmina Anglica*, released in 2019.

Rumpe celos (**217**). Cambridge, Cambridge University Library, MS Kk.4.20, fol. 77v. The hymns **217–20** appear to be addenda to the manuscript, which is a collection of homiletic works and was acquired by Norwich cathedral priory between 1272 and c.1325, having formerly belonged to the monk Ralph of Frettenham (fl.1273).[31] The scribe inserted the four items in the later thirteenth century, using two blank ruled columns left over at the end of the volume. The hymns **217–19** were inserted first in a careful book-hand. After a blank line, **220** was added, apparently by the same scribe. The lines of **217** are bracketed in threes. Hymns **218** and **220** are copied without line-breaks, the ruled columns being too narrow for whole lines of verse. George Prothero suggested that **217–20** belonged together as 'portions of an office in memory of Simon de Montfort', and it was Henry Bradshaw's opinion that the hymns **217–19** 'are probably those used at First Vespers, at Matins, and at Lauds'.[32] It seems probable that **217–18** were composed before March 1266 like **219**, with which they are associated in the manuscript. Previous editions: G. W. Prothero, *The Life of Simon de Montfort Earl of Leicester*

---

[28] Ibid. pp. 212–13, 216, 221; P. M. Lefferts, 'Sources of thirteenth-century English polyphony: Catalogue with descriptions', Univ. of Nebraska-Lincoln Faculty Publications: School of Music 45 (online).
[29] Lefferts, 'Two English motets', p. 211.
[30] Ambler, *Bishops in the Political Community*, pp. 137, 180.
[31] *A Catalogue of the Manuscripts preserved in the Library of the University of Cambridge* (Cambridge, 1856–67) 3, pp. 666–8; N. R. Ker, 'Manuscripts from Norwich cathedral priory', *Transactions of the Cambridge Bibliographical Soc.* 1 (1949), pp. 1–28 (at pp. 7, 13).
[32] G. W. Prothero, *The Life of Simon de Montfort Earl of Leicester with Special Reference to the Parliamentary History of his Time* (London, 1877), p. 388.

with Special Reference to the Parliamentary History of his Time (London, 1877), pp. 388–9 (**217**), 389 (**218**), 390–1 (**219**), 391 (**220**).

Mater Syon (**218**).   Cambridge, Cambridge University Library, MS Kk.4.20, fol. 77v. The manuscript presents the hymn in separate stanzas, with a rubricated title. See also **217**.

Nequit stare (**219**).   Cambridge, Cambridge University Library, MS Kk.4.20, fol. 77v. The manuscript brackets the lines in pairs. References to piracy at sea (lines 25–8) suggest composition before March 1266. See also **217**.

O decus militie: antiphon, versicle and collect (**220**).   Cambridge, Cambridge University Library, MS Kk.4.20, fol. 77v. The collect appears to be in the same hand as the rest of **220** but in a slightly larger script. Item **220** comprises elements of an office or *memoria* in honour of Simon de Montfort, to be said at the close of First Vespers or Lauds.[33] In Bradshaw's opinion, 'the *Suffragium* [**220**] was probably the Commemoration at Lauds'.[34] Another version of the antiphon (with different versicle and collect) is in **221**. See also **217**.

O decus militie: antiphon, versicle and collect (**221**).   Cologne, Historisches Archiv der Stadt Köln, Best. 7010 (Wallraf) 28, fol. 84v. These are elements of an office or *memoria* in honour of Simon de Montfort (cf. **220**). The copy is integral to the manuscript, a portable paper volume written in a single cursive hand. It is a later-fifteenth-century collection of prayers that belonged to the Cologne charterhouse or to one of its monks.[35] The antiphon is presented without line-breaks. and the whole is followed immediately by an antiphon and collect for Thomas of Lancaster. Another version of the Montfort antiphon (with different versicle and collect) is in **220**. Previous edition: *Liturgische Reimofficien* 2, p. 7.

Miles Christi (**222**).   Cambridge, St John's College, MS F.1 (formerly MS 138), detached leaf (formerly fols 127v–128r). A fragment of this motet for three voices survives, on a leaf from a large service book that was perhaps compiled in the third quarter of the thirteenth century. The fragment shows the beginnings of two voices, with musical notation, which were copied separately in parallel columns and with no line-breaks, starting at the foot of a verso page and continuing on the facing recto. The fate of that second leaf and of any others is unknown, but the first became detached from the parent volume; it was turned sideways, folded and inserted as a pastedown and flyleaf at the back of a thirteenth-century volume from the abbey of Bury St Edmunds. The leaf is now kept separately

---

[33] Lefferts, 'Two English motets', pp. 210–12.
[34] Prothero, *Life of Simon de Montfort*, p. 388.
[35] *Liturgische Reimofficien* 7, pp. 5–8; Historisches Archiv der Stadt Köln 'Das digitale Historische Archiv Köln' website.

and unfolded.[36] Previous edition: Lefferts, 'Two English motets', pp. 222–3 (with parallel prose translation), with musical reconstruction at pp. 219–20. A line-by-line prose translation is in A. Gransden, 'Some manuscripts in Cambridge from Bury St Edmunds abbey: Exhibition catalogue', in A. Gransden (ed.), *Bury St Edmunds: Medieval Art, Architecture, Archaeology and Economy* (British Archaeological Association Conference Transactions 20, 1998), pp. 228–85 (at p. 268).

---

[36] Gransden, 'Some manuscripts in Cambridge from Bury St Edmunds', pp. 236, 267–8.

Editorial Procedure

Nearly every text has been edited from its manuscript or from a digital copy of it. The only exceptions are three of the calendar entries, which are taken from reliable published editions. Items are numbered and titled editorially. The translations are my own, and references to others are provided. In the editorial matter quotations from the Vulgate are given in Latin from the Stuttgart edition and in English from the Douay–Rheims translation. Scribal contractions and abbreviations are extended silently unless ambiguous, when they are represented by an apostrophe. Punctuation and capitalization are my own. Medieval spellings have been retained, except that in Latin words *J/j* and *U/v* have been standardized to *I/i* and *V/u* (only in roman numerals are *j* and *v* preserved); in vernacular words *J/j* and *V/v* are used as consonants; and medial *c* and *t* in Latin are transcribed according to English derivatives of the same word, e.g. *iusticia* from 'justice' and *militia* from 'military'. Diacritical marks have not been added to medieval French words; they are not present in the manuscripts and any ambiguities are resolved in the translation. The following editorial signs are used:

    < >   damaged, corrupt or incomplete matter reconstructed
    † †   words of unclear meaning, possibly corrupt
    ***   lost or damaged matter deemed irrecoverable
    \ /   matter originally inserted above the line
    [ ]   matter inserted by the editor

TEXTS AND TRANSLATIONS

The Evesham abbey miracle book
London, British Library, Cotton MS Vespasian A VI

1 [fol. 162r] [Prologus.] Anno Domini M°CC° <sextodecimo quinto primo die>[a] augusti dominus Edwardus <primogenitus regis et Gilbertus>[b] de Clare ***[c] Quo peruento dominum Symonem de Monteforti iuniorem et exercitum suum in prioratu et papilionibus suis extra castrum inuenerunt inermes et dormientes. Dominus autem Symon de Monteforti in castrum cum difficultate non modica susceptus euasit. Et paucis interemptis ibidem captiuati sunt Gilbertus de Graunt, comes Oxonie, Willelmus de Mouncheinysy, Ricardus de Gray, Adam de Newmarche, Baldewinus Wake, Walterus de Colevile, Iohannes de Gray filius Ricardi de Gray, Hugo Nevill ***[d] quod uia pacis inueniri non potuit. Dominus rex et dominus Symon comes Leycestrie cum exercitu suo de Kemesey ante horam diei primam apud Evesham uenientes ***[e] circa horam diei tertiam audito de aduentu dictorum dominorum Edwardi et Gilberti de Clare et eorum exercitus qui de ciuitate Wigorniensis profecti fuerant ***[f] Caligauit enim terra sub nubilo et celum tenebris inhorrens inconsuetam et procellosam set breuem imbrium emisit tempestatem. [fol. 162v] <Demum declinata>[g] terribili tempestate predicta factus est aer serenior et aura clementior. Exeuntibus igitur domino rege et domino Symone comite Leycestrie et eorum exercitu extra uillam Eueshamie Vnfredus de Boun cum omnibus peditibus quoniam ductor eorum [erat][h] constitutus in acie posteriori extra uoluntatem dicti Symonis comitis Leycestrie moratus est. Prenominati domini Edwardus et Gilbertus de Clare cum exercitu suo ut alios

---
[a] M°CC° sexto decimo quinto primo die] 1265 primo die *C. These sigla are used in the Prologue: B (Oxford, Bodleian Library, MS Laud Misc. 529, fols 70r–71v); C (London, British Library, Harley MS 542, fol. 49r).*
[b] primogenitus regis et Gilbertus] *B.*
[c] *About four lines.*
[d] *About four lines.*
[e] *About eight words.*
[f] *About four lines.*
[g] Demum declinata] *B;* Deinde *MS.*
[h] erat] *B.*

The Evesham abbey miracle book

London, British Library, Cotton MS Vespasian A VI, fols 162r–183r

1 [Prologue.] In the year of our Lord 1265 on the first day of August Sir Edward, the king's first-born, and Gilbert of Clare *** On reaching there,[1] they found Sir Simon de Montfort the younger and his army in the priory and in their tents outside the castle, unarmed and asleep. But Sir Simon de Montfort, with considerable difficulty, escaped into the castle. Few were killed, but Gilbert de Gaunt, the earl of Oxford,[2] William de Munchensi, Richard de Grey, Adam of Newmarket, Baldwin Wake, Walter de Coleville, John de Grey son of Richard de Grey and Hugh de Neville were taken prisoner there *** that the 'way of peace'[3] could not be found. The king and Sir Simon earl of Leicester with his army, coming from Kempsey,[4] reached Evesham before the first hour of the day *** and having heard, about the third hour of the day, of the arrival of the said lords Edward and Gilbert of Clare and their army, who had travelled from the city of Worcester *** Now, the land grew dark beneath clouds. The heavens, menacing with gloom, sent an extraordinary and stormy downpour, though it was short. When the terrible storm abated at last, the air turned calmer and the weather more kind. While the lord king and Sir Simon earl of Leicester and their army were therefore leaving the town of Evesham, Humphrey de Bohun had been appointed commander of all the foot solders, but remained with them in the rear against the wishes of Simon earl of Leicester. Those lords, Edward and Gilbert of Clare, with their army

---

[1] Kenilworth (Warwickshire).
[2] Robert de Vere.
[3] Luke 1: 79.
[4] The residence of Walter Cantilupe bishop of Worcester.

circumcluderent tripartito montem ascenderunt partibus igitur iuxta locum qui dicitur Siveldeston hostiliter congredientibus. <Vmfredus>[a] de Boun et omnes Walenses et ceteri pedites plusquam sex <milia>[b] cum pluribus armatis quorum animos timor arripuit in fugam conuersi sunt. Videntes igitur dominus Symon comes Leycestrie et ceteri proceritatis uiri quod ipsos moneret ineuitata necessitas aut cedere turpiter aut certare uiriliter pauci in multos impetum fecerunt militarem. Vtrumque autem uiriles <animos>[c] erigentes in acerbitate facinoris dimicarunt preliatores et quisque sanguinem alterius requirebat cui sanguine fuerat copulatus. Demum laborantibus in certaminis ***[d] uiris cecidit strages super Symonem de Monteforti et eius exercitum. Extunc dictus comes sicut ex parte fortitudinis et audacie uir annosus set animosus pondus belli diu sustinuit. Demum pluribus armatorum in ipsum impetum facientibus et <dextrario>[e] suo quem mors inuaserat deficiente solo prostratus abscisis manibus et pedibus decapitatus est. Equestres autem ex parte illa et pedestres si qui remanserant aliis persequentibus disgregatim fugerunt. Et erat tanta fuge celeritas quod multi ruinam fluminis Auene credebant fore terre tutiorem et plures ibi incurrebant periculum ubi speratur effugium ***[f] periculorum. Interempti fuerunt illo die ex parte domini comitis preter comitem [fol. 163r] Henricus filius eius, Hugo Dispensator, Willelmus de <Mandevill>,[g] Radulphus Basset de <Drayton>,[h] Petrus de Monteforti, Hugo de <Hoyvile>,[i] Iohannes de Bellocampo de Bedford, Thomas de Hesteleie, Willelmus Devereus, Guydo <Baylole>,[j] Ricardus Trussell, Willelmus de Burmingham, Robertus de <Creppyng'>.[k] <Et captiuati sunt Guydo de Mounteforti, Iohannes de Vesci, Vnfredus de Boun comes Herfordie, a fuga reuersus apud Wygorniam, Iohannes filius Iohannis, Nicholaus de Segrave, Henricus de Hastinges>.[l] Ex parte domini Edwardi cecidit Hugo de Troia miles et Adam de Ridmark et pauci alii. In uilla, in cenobii curia, in monasterio, et capellis earumque atriis populi more pecudum obtruncati iacuerunt. Et quod uisu fuit horribile et auditu tam mirabile quam miserabile chorus et alia quecumque monasterii loca fuerunt interemptorum et

---

[a] Vmfredus] *B*; Vmfredo *MS*.
[b] milia] *B*.
[c] animos] *B*.
[d] *One or two words*.
[e] dextrario] dextrareo *B*; de dextrario *MS*.
[f] *One or two words*.
[g] Mandevill] Moundewylle *B*; Arundevil *MS*.
[h] Drayton] *B*; Draycote *MS*.
[i] Hoyvile] *C*; Hopvile *MS*.
[j] Baylole] *B*; Baysell *MS*.
[k] Creppyng'] *B*; Sepinges *MS*.
[l] Et captiuati sunt … Hastinges] *B*; Guydo de Mounteforti, Iohannes de Vesci, Vnfredus de Boun a fuga reuersus apud Wygorniam et captiuati sunt Iohannes filius Iohannis, Roche de Segrave, Henricus de Hastinges comes Herfordie *MS*.

ascended the hill,[5] in three divisions in order to encircle the others, thus gathering in warlike fashion in an area near the place called 'Siveldeston'.[6] Humphrey de Bohun and all the Welshmen and other foot soldiers, more than six thousand of them, together with many of the armoured men, turned and fled after fear had gripped their minds. Thus when Sir Simon earl of Leicester and the other leading men realized that inexorable necessity would force them either to surrender shamefully or die bravely, the few launched a knightly attack upon the many. Now all the combatants, raising up their manly spirits, fought as with the ferocity of sin and each sought the blood of another to whom he was linked by blood. Eventually, as *** men struggled in combat, carnage descended upon Simon de Montfort and his army. Thereafter the said earl, a man aged but vigorous, bore the weight of the battle for a long time as if he was the embodiment of strength and courage. Finally, with many armed men attacking him and without his warhorse, which death had overcome, while prostrate on the ground his hands and feet were cut off and he was beheaded. Then the mounted men of his side and the foot soldiers, if any remained, scattered and fled, with the others in pursuit. And such was the haste of their flight that many thought that a fall into the river Avon[7] would be safer than one on land, and many ran into danger where an escape from *** danger was to be hoped for. That day there were killed on the side of the lord earl, apart from the earl, his son Henry, Hugh le Despenser, William de Mandeville, Ralph Basset of Drayton, Piers de Montfort, Hugh de Hoyvill, John Beauchamp of Bedford, Thomas of Astley, William Deverois, Guy de Balliol, Richard Trussel, William of Birmingham and Robert of Crepping. And there were taken prisoner Guy de Montfort, John de Vescy, Humphrey de Bohun earl of Hereford[8] at Worcester after coming back from his flight, John fitz John, Nicholas of Seagrave and Henry Hastings. On Sir Edward's side fell Hugh de Troye, knight, and Adam of Ridware and a few others. In the town, in the abbey precinct, in the abbey church and the chapels and in their churchyards, people lay slaughtered like beasts. And, which was horrible to see and astonishing and pitiful to hear of, the choir and other places in the abbey

---

[5] Green hill, overlooking Evesham from the north.
[6] An ancient standing stone on the east flank of Green hill: Cox, *Battle of Evesham*, pp. 17–19.
[7] The river encloses Evesham and the battlefield on three sides (Fig. 4).
[8] Humphrey is here confused with his father of the same name, the earl of Hereford.

uulneratorum sanguine purpurata. <Cum autem uenirent>[a] in unum temeritatis filii <rapacitatisque>[b] eorum ministri quicquid substancie concupiscibilis inueniri potuit in uilla et cenobio prede patuit et direptioni.

2   [fol. 163r] Nichil opertum quod non reueletur, etc.[c]

3   Quidam Ricardus nomine Bagard de Evesham cum transiret cum mercatu suo uersus Stretford super Auenam apparuit ei ma[g]nus exercitus ueniens de Kenelworth. Iste metu reuersus est in uia. Habuitque obuiam dominum Willelmum de Bello Campo cum tota sequela sua. Et inter eos fuit dominus Petrus de Saultmareis. Dictus Ricardus ait, 'Cauete! Ecce inimici uestri super uos.' Ait dominus Willelmus de Bello Campo, 'Reuertentur sarcine' et fecerunt moram in loco ubi sancti martires occubuerunt. Tunc ait dominus Petrus, 'Fere omnes dicunt dominum Simonem comitem Leycestrie esse sanctum. Ideo deprecemur Iesum Christum eiusque sanctam Dei genitricem [fol. 163v] geniculando forte deridendo. Si sanctus est demonstret uirtutem suam et det nobis in loco isto aquam uiuam.' Et arripuit os scapule caballi et cepit fodere. Mira Dei uirtus! De terra arida et petrosa aque dulcissime in uertice montis persiliunt. Et hoc anno reuoluto. <Id est secundo anno et tempore guerre>.[d]

4   Henricus Chaunteler laicus guttam habens in renibus ita quod uix per tres dies incedere non potuit nisi cum sustamento baculi. Hic autem obuians casu cuidam homini de Mucleton deferenti aquam in quodam uase de fonte qui dicebatur comitis Simonis petiit ut eidem daret de aqua predicta ad qantitatem quam tenere posset in manu. Qui eidem concessit et dedit, et cum locum guttatum linisset conualuit. Huius rei testes sunt Iohannes de Bretforton capellanus, Ricardus Cappellanus filius eius, et plures alii.[e]

---

[a] Cum autem uenirent] *B*; Tunc autem uenerunt *MS*.
[b] rapacitatisque] rapacitatis quod *MS*.
[c] *The next entry runs on without a break.*
[d] Id est secundo anno et tempore guerre] In E secundo A et T G *MS*.
[e] *In margin in a contemporary hand* miraculum 2.

church were red with the blood of the slain and wounded. Then, when the sons of audacity and the servants of their rapacity arrived en masse, whatever could be found in the town that was valuable and desirable suffered plunder and spoliation.

2   Nothing is covered that should not be revealed, etc.[9]

3   One Richard, surnamed Badger,[10] from Evesham, was on his way to Stratford upon Avon[11] with his merchandise when a large army came into view, approaching from Kenilworth. In fear he turned back along the road and there he met Sir William Beauchamp[12] with all his retinue, among whom was Sir Piers Saltmarsh.[13] Richard said, 'Take care! Look, here come your enemies.' Sir William Beauchamp said, 'Turn the baggage train about,' and they halted in the place where the holy martyrs had fallen.[14] Then said Sir Piers, 'Nearly everybody is saying that Sir Simon the earl of Leicester is a saint. If we ourselves were to do that, we would disparage Jesus Christ and the holy mother of God, perhaps even mocking them by bending the knee [to the earl]. If he is a saint let him show his powers and give us some living water just here.' And he picked up a horse's shoulder blade and began to dig. O, the wonderful power of God! From the dry and stony earth the sweetest waters leapt forth on top of the hill. And this was a year later [than the battle of Evesham]; that is, in the second year and during the war.
[*In the margin*] miracle 1.

4   Henry the chandler, a prominent layman, had a gout in his side so that for nearly three days he was unable to walk without the aid of a stick. By chance, however, he met a man from Mickleton carrying a container with water from what was called 'Earl Simon's well'.[15] Henry asked him if he would give him some of the water, as much as he might keep in his hand. The man agreed and gave it to him, and after he had bathed the gouty place he recovered. The witnesses to this matter are John the chaplain of Bretforton, Richard Chaplain his son and many others.[16]
[*In the margin*] miracle 2.

---

[9] An allusion to the Sermon on the Mount (at Matt. 10: 26–8).
[10] A badger was a hawker.
[11] Fourteen miles north-east of Evesham.
[12] A royalist: *ODNB*, s.n. 'Beauchamp, William de, ninth earl of Warwick'. He died in 1269: *Cal. Inq. p.m.* 1236–72, p. 220. See also 9n.
[13] He witnesses William's charters in the 1260s: *Beauchamp Cart.* pp. 22, 27.
[14] On Green hill.
[15] Henry lived at Bretforton (see 55), about four miles east of Evesham and half-way to Mickleton.
[16] This is a version of 55.

5   Radulfus de Boklonde de Teneth ultra Cantuariam habens guttam per tres annos et septem septimanas nimis pungidiuam in sinistra gamba. Et iacuit continue in lecto in dextere parte. Mensuratus ad comitem et gamba lota de aqua fontis martiris multis uidentibus ad predictum fontem conualuit. Vnde hoc testatur tota insula de Teneth.[a]

6   Domina comitissa Glouernie habuit palefridum asmaticum, gallice porsif, per duos annos. In redeundo ab Eueshamia uersus Theukesbury, cabello hausto de fonte comitis et caput et facies lota, in presencia dicte comitisse conualuit. Et denario plicato in testimonio sanitatis et miraculi iterum misit armigerum suum Eueshamiam. Huius rei testes predicta comitissa cum tota familia sua.[b]

7   Alicia de Novereis Burton iuxta Leycestriam percussa paralisi in sinistra parte per tria annos, postea percussa in dextera per sex annos. Ista pernoctauit ad fontem [fol. 164r] comitis nocte sancte Eadburge uirginis et ibi sanitatem in omnis membris tam in dextera quam in leua gloriose recuparauit anno gracie †M°CC°lix°†. De hoc teste tota uillata de Novereis Burton.

8   Item Radulfus clericus de †Sepham Burland† claudus per nouem septimanas ad fontem comitis conualuit.

9   Mulier de Elmeley egrota misit puellam ad fontem comitis propter aquam. In redeundo a fonte ministrales castelli obuiam habuit. Interrogauerunt puellam quid haberet in pichero. Ait illa, 'Nouam seruiciam Eueshamie'. Qui dixerunt, 'Non. Habes aquam de fonte comitis' et hauserunt et inuenerunt sicut puella dixerat. Et

---

[a] *In margin in a contemporary hand* miraculum 3.
[b] *In margin in a contemporary hand* miraculum 4.

THE EVESHAM ABBEY MIRACLE BOOK

5   Ralph of Buckland from Thanet beyond Canterbury had had an extremely painful gout for three years and seven weeks in his left leg and had lain in bed all the time on his right-hand side. But after being measured to the earl and after the leg had been bathed with water from the martyr's well he recovered at the well in the sight of many people. The whole Isle of Thanet bears witness to this.
[*In the margin*] miracle 3.

6   The countess of Gloucester had a palfrey that had been asthmatic (*porsif* in French) for two years. On returning from Evesham in the direction of Tewkesbury,[17] after the horse had drunk from the Earl's well and its head and face had been bathed, it recovered in the countess's presence. And after a penny had been bent in recognition of the cure and miracle, she sent back her squire to Evesham. The witnesses to this matter are the countess together with her entire household.[18]
[*In the margin*] miracle 4.

7   Alice from Burton Overy near Leicester[19] had been stricken with paralysis on the left side for thirty years and had later been afflicted for six years on the right-hand side. But she spent the night at the Earl's well on the night of St Eadburh the virgin[20] and there she marvellously recovered the good health of all her limbs, on the right-hand side and on the left, in the year of grace †1259†. The whole township of Burton Overy bears witness to this.

8   Also Ralph the clerk from †Sepham Burland†,[21] who had been lame for nine weeks, recovered at the Earl's well.

9   A sick woman of Elmley Castle[22] had sent a girl to the Earl's well for some water. On her way back from the well she met some officials of the castle. They questioned the girl as to what she might have in the jug. 'Some new ale from Evesham', she said. They said to her, 'No, you have some water from the Earl's

---

[17] Thirteen miles south-west of Evesham.
[18] Identification of the lady is uncertain. The dowager Countess Maud (d.1289) was a Montfortian sympathizer and her daughter-in-law Countess Alice (d.1290) was not: Carpenter, *Henry III 1258–72*, pp. 394–6, 506. On the other hand, Alice was said to be a hypochondriac: *Complete Peerage* 5, p. 707.
[19] Burton Overy had been inherited by the daughters of Roger de Quincy earl of Winchester, one of whom was Margaret countess of Derby (d.1281) the widowed mother of William de Ferrers, an armed Montfortian: *Complete Peerage* 5, pp. 340–1; *VCH Leics.* 5, p. 71.
[20] 15 June at Evesham: *English Benedictine Kalendars after A.D. 1100* 2, ed. F. Wormald (Henry Bradshaw Soc. 81, 1946 for 1943–44), p. 32.
[21] *Recte* Teʒhe in Rutland? If so, this is Teigh, held by Eustace de Folville (d.1274) a rebel Montfortian: *VCH Rut.* 2, pp. 151–2.
[22] William Beauchamp held the castle at Elmley, five miles south-west of Evesham, and was succeeded there in 1269 by his son William earl of Warwick: *Complete Peerage* 12, pt 2, pp. 368–9. Both were royalists: *ODNB*, s.n. 'Beauchamp, William de, ninth earl of Warwick'. See also 3.

sic dimissa. Et cum ueniret ad infirmam iterum uersa uice est mutatus in aquam. Infirma hac gustata conualuit.

10   Henricus de Stodeley filius Isabelle de Stodeley Lamberd albuginem habens in oculis ambobis a natiuitate sua exeptis quatuor septimanis quibus clare uidebat. Ab illis quatuor septimanis penitus uisu oculorum priuatus fuit per duodecim annos et amplius. Hic ad comitem Simonem de Monteforti mensuratus uisum in oculo sinistro recepit in tantum quod uidimus ipsum de coloribus uere indicantem. De hoc testimonium perhibente Alicia mater Henrici et plures alii.

11   Willelmus de Sniteneford filius Henrici de Mitton habens quatuor digitos in sinistra manu per duodecim annos contractos. Apud Evesham ueniens meritis martiris nostri digitos predictos recepit extensos ita quod eos ad libitum suum mouere potuit et extendere. Huius rei testes sunt domina Margeria de Cantulupo et domina Iohanna de Cantulupo et tota uillata.

12   Rogerus Horsman de Buclande habens pedem dextrum [fol. 164v] [*blank*] contractum per annum et amplius. Ad comitem Simonem mensuratus die sancti Mathei circa uesperas. Et quod perdiderat per infirmitatem per merita sancti recuparauit. Ita quod uidimus eum incedentem ad libitum suum. Vnde tota uillata de Boclande perhibet testimonium.

13   Oliuia de Leministre per tres annos amisit potestatem eundi. Mensurata ad martirem et per noctes apud Evesham peruigilans conualuit. Vnde tota parochia perhibet testimonium.

14   Memorandum de manu sancti Simonis que cum adhuc esset ad quoddam castellum ad suscipiendam portitor manus iter habuit per quandam ecclesiam et audiuit pulsare ad missam et intrauit et adorauit. Et cum stetisset sacerdos ad eleuandum corpus Christi statim in birro iuuenis mouebatur et manus erecta sicut solebat uiua Iesum adorauit.

well,' and they took a drink of it, but they found that it was as the girl had said and so she was let go. And when she came to the sick woman it was turned back into water and the woman recovered after drinking some.

10 Henry of Studley, son of Isabel of Studley, from Sambourne,[23] had had a white film over both eyes since birth except in his first four weeks, during which he had been able to see clearly. From those four weeks onwards he had been nearly sightless for twelve years and more. But after being measured to Earl Simon de Montfort he got back the sight in his left eye to the extent that we saw him pointing out colours correctly. Alice, Henry's mother,[24] bears witness to this.

11 William from Snitterfield, son of Henry of Myton, had had the four fingers of his left hand crippled for twelve years. But on coming to Evesham he had the fingers straightened again through the merits of our martyr so that he could move and stretch them easily. The witnesses to this matter are Dame Margery Cantlow and Dame Joan Cantlow and the whole township.[25]

12 Roger Horseman from Buckland[26] had had a [*blank*] crippled right foot for a year and more. But after being measured to the earl on St Matthew's day[27] about the hour of Vespers, he recovered through the merits of the saint that which he had lost through his disability, in such a way that we saw him walking around easily. The whole township of Buckland bears witness to this.

13 Olive from Leominster had for three years lost the ability to walk. But she recovered after being measured to the martyr and keeping nightly vigils at Evesham. The whole parish bears witness to this.

14 A memorandum about St Simon's hand. While it was on its way to be received at a certain castle, the bearer of the hand was passing a church when he heard the bell for mass, and he went in and worshipped. And when the priest rose to elevate the body of Christ the hand immediately began to move in the young man's bag and, rising up, it worshipped Christ as it had used to do in life.[28]

---

[23] Sambourne manor (Warwickshire) belonged to Evesham abbey.
[24] Possibly stepmother.
[25] Margery (née Cumin) had married John Cantlow (fl.1257) who held Snitterfield manor by 1242: *VCH Warws.* 3, p. 168. His brother William (d.1254) had been a personal friend of Simon de Montfort: *ODNB*, s.n. Joan (d.1271) was William's daughter and had married Henry Hastings a leading rebel Montfortian: *Complete Peerage* 6, pp. 345–6.
[26] Possibly Buckland (Gloucestershire) because the county is not specified.
[27] 21 September.
[28] This is a version of **198**.

15 Mulier quedam [de] †oogredeford† habens brachium contractum ita quod brachium extendere non potuit per multa annorum curricula. Et cum pernoctasset circa tumulum martiris sanitatem recepit ita quod brachium extendere ad libitum suum potuit. De conualencia huius mulieris perhibet testimonium armiger domini Roberti de Colleworthe et parliamento ueniens colloquium habuit cum dicta muliere affirmante ipsam sanam effectam per merita martiris.

16 Iohannes de Broun miles de Traduncton paraliticus in una medietate totius corporis per annum. Ad comitem mensuratus candelam suam de mensura composuit et [cum] apud Evesham ueniret dictus infirmus de infirmitate qua tenebatur conualuit. De hoc perhibet testimonium rector ecclesie de Traduncton Eueshamiam personaliter accedens.

17 Quidam iuuenis [*blank*] circa sexdecim annos per patrem et matrem mensuratus ad sanctum Robertum Lincolniensem episcopum et ibidem ueniens cum patre et matre die sabbati proxima ante congressum belli die martis apud Evesham peracti cepit dormire et in dormitione illa perseuerauit per totam noctem [fol. 165r] et usque ad horam primam diei lune proxime sequentis. Qui tunc euigilans cepit loqui qui mutus et contractus fuerat toto tempore uite sue, dicendo patri et matri, 'Cur hic moram facitis?' Qui responderunt, 'Propter salutem uestram optinendam a sancto Roberto episcopo'. Qui dixit eis, 'Dictus sanctus episcopus non est hic, processit enim apud Evesham in adiutorium comitis Simonis fratris sui qui morietur apud Evesham die martis proximo sequente.' Et ita predictus iuuenis prius mutus et contractus conualuit. Qui de hiis perhibens testimonium adhuc uiuit perseuerans in ecclesia Lincolnensi.

18 Mabilia de †Belbeworth† per annum et amplius tantam sensit infirmitatem et debilitatem in gambis et tibiis quod ire non potuit nec usquam mouere. Hec apud

15 A woman from †oogredeford†[29] had an arm so crippled that she had been unable to extend it for many years. But when she had spent a night near the martyr's tomb she received a cure so that she could extend the arm easily. The squire of Sir Robert[30] of Culworth bears witness to the recovery of this woman and that, on coming from a parliament, he had a conversation with her in which she affirmed that she had been made well through the merits of the martyr.

16 John Brown, a knight from Tredington,[31] had been paralysed for a year in half of his entire body. But after being measured to the earl he made up his candle to the measurement, and when he came to Evesham he recovered from the disability to which he had been subject. The rector of Tredington church bears witness to this, having come to Evesham himself.

17 A youth [*blank*] about sixteen years was measured by his father and mother to St Robert the bishop of Lincoln.[32] The boy arrived there with his father and mother and he went to sleep on the Saturday[33] before the Tuesday on which battle was joined at Evesham. He stayed asleep all night and until the first hour of the following Monday.[34] Dumb and crippled all his life, on waking he began to speak, saying to his father and mother, 'Why are you staying here?' They replied, 'To obtain a cure for you from St Robert the bishop.' He said to them, 'The saintly bishop is not here, because he has gone to Evesham to help his brother Earl Simon who is going to die there next Tuesday.' So saying, the youth recovered, having previously been dumb and crippled. In witness to these things he now lives permanently in the church of Lincoln.

18 Mabel of †Belbeworth†[35] had experienced for a year and more an infirmity and debility in her thighs and lower legs so that she was unable to walk or move

---

[29] Possibly Mordiford (Herefordshire) because the county is not specified. Mordiford manor was held in 1243 by William de Ferrers earl of Derby: *Bk of Fees* 1, pt 2, p. 801. At his death in 1254 it presumably passed to his son Robert de Ferrers earl of Derby, a rebel Montfortian: *Complete Peerage* 4, pp. 198–202.

[30] *Recte* Richard? Richard of Culworth was a rebel Montfortian: *Cal. Pat.* 1258–66, pp. 540, 575; *Cal. Inq. Misc.* 1, pp. 189, 202. In 1267 during the Montfortian occupation of London he was made chief bailiff: *Cron. Maiorum*, p. 91. He died c.1286: *Cal. Close*, 1279–88, p. 387. See also **34n**.

[31] In the late thirteenth century Henry and William Brun were taxpayers at Newbold on Stour in Tredington parish: *Worcs. Subsidy*, p. 74. Tredington (including Newbold) was an estate of Evesham abbey.

[32] Robert Grosseteste (d.1253), a mentor to Simon de Montfort.

[33] 1 August.

[34] 3 August.

[35] *Recte* Kibbeworth? If so, the surname may refer to Kibworth Harcourt (Leicestershire), which was held by Saher de Harcourt, a Montfortian; he forfeited the manor after the battle of Evesham (*Cal. Inq. Misc.* 1, p. 102) but was pardoned in 1267 and retrieved it (*Cal. Pat.* 1266–72, pp. 150, 264). His brother William (below, **111n**) was another Montfortian: *ODNB* (online edn), s.n. 'Harcourt [de Harcourt] family'.

Evesham in †biba† adducta et ad comitem mensurata conualuit. Et hanc uidimus procedentem et ambulantem ad libitum suum. Hinc perhibent testimonium uicini ipsius qui infirmitatem ipsius uiderunt.

19   Felicia de Fladbury ita gambis et tibiis contracta per duos annos et dimidium quod nec sedere nec incedere poterat. Hec mensurata ad comitem conualuit. Huius testes sunt uicini eius.

20   Robertus filius Hugonis Boteler de Morton sub Maluernia sentiens molestiam lapidis per octo annos, mensuratus conualuit.

21   Aucipiter magistri Thome de Cantulupo per duos dies eiecit omnia alimenta que receperat quod est signum mortis huiusmodi auis. Mensuratus ad comitem conualuit.

22   Senescallus predicti magistri Thome nomine Nicholas per magnum tempus de quadam gutta laborauit. <Veniens>[a] ad comitem conualuit.

23   Willemus de †Sarle† monachus Wynchecumbe patiebatur tussim cum morbo idropico. Iste adductus Oxoniam et ibi multa in medicis inane expendebat. Mensuratus ad comitem astitit ei quadam nocte quidam senex in uisione dicens, 'Oportet te scarificari.' At ille, [fol. 165v] 'Scarificationem ullo modo sustinere non possum.' Senex apprehendens monachi †ataxam† et percussit eum sub plantis pedum. At ille euigilans cum clamore magno inuenerat lectum suum undique liquore fetidissimo plenum et brachia et pedes et etiam totum corpus gracile et delicatum et sic per merita martiris nobilissime curatus est. De hoc testificatus est abbas Wynchecumbe cum sacro conuentu.

---

[a] uenire *MS*.

around at all. But after being brought to Evesham on a †litter† and measured to the earl the woman recovered, and we saw her getting around and walking at will. Her neighbours who had seen her disability bear witness to this.

19   Felice of Fladbury had for two and a half years been so crippled in the thighs and lower legs that she had been unable to sit or walk but after being measured to the earl she recovered. Her neighbours are the witnesses to this.

20   Robert, son of Hugh Butler, from Castle Morton[36] under the Malverns, had suffered the discomfort of a stone for eight years but after being measured he recovered.

21   Master Thomas Cantilupe's[37] hawk had for two days regurgitated all the food it received, which is a fatal sign for that kind of bird, but after being measured to the earl it recovered.

22   The said Master Thomas's steward, called Nicholas,[38] had suffered for a long time from a kind of gout but on coming to the earl he recovered.

23   William of †Sarle†[39] a monk of Winchcombe had been suffering from a cough together with a dropsical illness. He was brought to Oxford and spent a lot of money there on doctors, but in vain. But after he was measured to the earl, an old man came to him one night in a vision, saying, 'You need to be scarified;' but William said, 'In no way could I bear scarification.' The old man, taking hold of the monk's †bedcover†, struck him under the soles of his feet. Whereupon, waking with a great yell he found that the bed was soaked all over with a really fetid liquid and that his arms, his feet and indeed his entire body were slender and fine. And thus through the merits of the martyr he was cured most splendidly. The abbot of Winchcombe[40] has attested to this together with the holy convent.

---

[36] Part of Castle Morton was held by John de Muscegros (fl.1276): *VCH Worcs.* 4, pp. 50, 113. He was an armed Montfortian: *Cal. Inq. Misc.* 1, p. 259.
[37] Thomas Cantilupe, the brother of John and William Cantlow (see 11n), had been chancellor of England during Simon de Montfort's regime but lived abroad after the battle of Evesham; he had returned to England by c.1272 and became bishop of Hereford in 1275; after his death many miracles were attributed to him: *ODNB*, s.n.
[38] On his deathbed Thomas made confession to his priest called Nicholas: *Acta Sanctorum*, October, vol. 1 (Paris and Rome, 1866), p. 578.
[39] *Recte* Farle?
[40] John of Yanworth 1247–82.

24 Rogerus capellanus et uicarius de Hide in Cantia habuit infirmitatem ignotam unde phisici desperati, item per alium annum quartanam. Mensuratus ad comitem sine mora conualuit. De hoc perhibet testimonium tota uillata de Hide.

25 Robertus de Malton canonicus cecidit super brachium sinistrum unde amisit utilitatem brachii. Die ueneris ante festum sancti Iohannis Baptiste mensuratus ad comitem et in eundo uersus Evesham apud Stretford super Auenam causa orationis intrauit quandam ecclesiam, habuit in memoriam sanctitatem martiris, conualuit. De hoc perhibent [testimonium] prior de Malton et totus conuentus.

26 Thomas filius Iordani de Botoleston in uigilia sancti Matthei anno gracie †M°CC°lviij°† priuatus subito uisu et loquela mensuratus ad comitem conualuit. Item Agnes de eodem loco quasi de sanitate desperata conualuit.

27 Item filius Iacobi de †Fancote† submersus in quodam fonte per dimidiam diem mensuratus conualuit.

28 Alicia de Herforde per quinque annos sine sustentatione duorum baculorum procedere non potuit. Mensurata ad comitem conualuit. Die sancti Egwini nobis uidentibus gloriose curata est. Testes huius rei tota ciuitas Herfordie.

29 Christiana Hibernie primo anno belli habens guttam per quinque annos. Ista sompniauit ut iret ad tumbam sancti Wlsini et acciperet de puluere et secum

24 Roger the chaplain and vicar of West Hythe in Kent had an unnamed illness for which physicians could offer no hope and which during its second year was recurring every fourth day, but after being measured to the earl he recovered straight away. The whole township of Hythe bears witness to this.[41]

25 Robert a canon of Malton[42] had fallen on his left arm and as a result had lost the use of the arm. On the Friday before the feast of St John the Baptist,[43] after being measured to the earl and on his way to Evesham, he entered a church at Stratford upon Avon to pray, reflected on the martyr's sanctity and recovered. The prior of Malton[44] and the whole convent bear witness to this.

26 Thomas, son of Jordan, from Boston,[45] had suddenly been deprived of sight and speech on St Matthew's eve[46] in the year of grace †1258†[47] but after being measured to the earl he recovered. Also Agnes from the same place, who had been virtually without hope of a cure, recovered.

27 Also the son of James of †Fancote† had lain drowned in a well for half a day but after being measured he recovered.[48]

28 Alice from Hereford had for five years been unable to walk without the support of two sticks but after being measured to the earl she recovered. On St Ecgwine's day[49] we saw that she was marvellously cured. The whole citizenry of Hereford are witnesses to this matter.[50]

29 Christian from Ireland, in the first year since the battle of Evesham, had had a gout for five years. She dreamt that she should go to the tomb of St Wulfsige[51] and should take some of the dust and carry it away with her, which she did and

---

[41] Hythe was one of the Cinque Ports; their inhabitants were active Montfortians: Maddicott, *Simon de Montfort*, pp. 263, 299, 317; Jobson, *First English Revolution*, pp. 67, 93, 154–5.
[42] The manors of Old and New Malton had descended in 1253 to Agnes de Vescy (d.1290): *VCH Yorks. NR* 1, pp. 532, 537. Her half-brother Robert de Ferrers earl of Derby and her son John de Vescy were rebel Montfortians: *Complete Peerage* 4, pp. 198–201; 12, pt 2, pp. 277–80; below, **199**.
[43] 24 June.
[44] John of 'Homerton' c.1257–1276.
[45] Thomas of Moulton held the manor of Boston in 1273: *Knights of Edward I* 3, ed. C. Moor (Harleian Soc. Visitations 82, 1930), p. 234. He had been a Montfortian: *Complete Peerage* 9, pp. 402–3.
[46] 20 September.
[47] *Recte* 1268?
[48] This is a version of **59**.
[49] 30 December. Ecgwine and the Virgin Mary were the joint dedicatees of Evesham abbey.
[50] The citizens had been Montfortians before the battle of Evesham and were afterwards heavily fined: *Cal. Pat.* 1258–66, pp. 444–5, 548; *Close R.* 1264–68, p. 165. See also **118**.
[51] His tomb was in the choir of the abbey church at Evesham, near Simon de Montfort's first grave: Cox, 'Tomb of Simon de Montfort', pp. 160–2.

asportaret, et ita fecit et conualuit. Et antequam ad propria ueniret puluis ille mutatus est salem. Huius testes Rogerus uir eius et Ricardus filius eius et plures alii.

30 Dominus Andreas rector de Keuelston de Norhamptonscire habuit calculum per quinque annos. Mensuratus ad comitem conualuit. Testes huius rei tota parochia de Keuelston.

31 Ricardus Feypo miles Hibernie habuit mulierem pregnantem et febricitantem et propter mesticiam et dolorem perdidit loquelam. [fol. 166r] Phisici desperauerunt et dixerunt, 'Aut peribit puer aut mater.' Post paululum uersa est ad uomitum et peperit masculum elegantem set abortiuum. Dictus Ricardus plicuit denarium ad martirem nostrum super matrem et puerum et reuixit puer et sanata est mater. Et dederunt nomen Simonis de Montfort. Item dictus Ricardus habens cardiacam passionem per annum simili modo conualuit. Testes huius rei dictus Ricardus cum tota familia sua.

32 Heliseus filius Willelmi de Middilton in Cantia habens †tracem† in sinistro oculo et sinistra maxilla per uiginti quatuor septimanas mensuratus ad comitem conualuit. De hoc perhibet testimonium uillata de Middelton.

33 Elisabet de Brome habens quinque uermes auriculi [*blank*] per annum et amplius in sinistra aure ad comitem mensurata et denario plicato super eam continuo exierunt et conualuit. Testes huius tota parochia de Budforde.

recovered. And before she had reached home the dust was turned into salt. Her husband, Roger, and her son Richard[52] and many others are the witnesses to this.

30   Sir Andrew the rector of Chelveston in Northamptonshire[53] had had a stone for five years but after being measured to the earl he recovered. The whole parish of Chelveston are the witnesses to this matter.

31   Richard Feypo a knight from Ireland had a wife who was pregnant and feverish and who had lost the power of speech on account of her distress and pain. The physicians had no hope and said, 'Either the child will die or the mother.' After a little while she began vomiting and gave birth to a boy who was handsome but stillborn. Over the mother and child the said Richard bent a penny to our martyr, and the boy came back to life and the mother was cured. And they named him after Simon de Montfort. Also Richard, who had had *cardiaca passio*[54] for a year, likewise recovered.[55] Richard with his entire household are the witnesses to this matter.[56]

32   Ellis, son of William, from Milton in Kent,[57] had had an †inflammation† of the left eye and of the left side of his jaw for twenty-four weeks but after being measured to the earl he recovered. The township of Milton bears witness to this.

33   Elizabeth of Broom had had five pestilent insects [called] earwigs in her left ear for a year and more but after being measured to the earl and a penny having been bent over her they immediately came out and she recovered. The whole parish of Bidford on Avon are the witnesses to this.[58]

---

[52] See also **31**.
[53] The manor and advowson were held in 1243 by William de Ferrers earl of Derby: *VCH Northants.* 4, pp. 8, 11. They seem to have descended to his son Robert earl of Derby, a rebel Montfortian whose estates were confiscated in 1266 and granted to the king's son: *Complete Peerage* 4, pp. 198–202; *Cal. Inq. p.m.* 1291–1300, p. 296. The Chelveston estate of Hugh de St Philibert, another Montfortian, was also confiscated: *Close R. (Suppl.)* p. 42.
[54] Heart pains and/or palpitations.
[55] He died c.1284 and his son Simon was living in 1297: E. Hickey, *Skryne and the Early Normans: Papers concerning the Medieval Manors of the de Feypo Family in Ireland in the 12th and early 13th Centuries* (Drogheda, 1994), pp. 10–11. I owe this reference to the kindness of Mr Paul Duffy.
[56] This seems to be a version of **87**.
[57] Possibly Milton (near Gravesend), a manor held by William de Munchensi: *Cal. Inq. Misc.* 1, pp. 117, 230. He was a rebel Montfortian: *Complete Peerage* 9, pp. 422–4; *ODNB*, s.n.
[58] By 1265 Bidford manor was held by Joan daughter and coheir of Robert de Quincy; she had married Humphrey de Bohun the younger, a Montfortian who died a prisoner in 1265 after the battle of Evesham; by 1280 the manor had passed to Joan's sister Hawis and her husband Baldwin Wake, a leading rebel Montfortian: *VCH Warws.* 3, p. 52; *Complete Peerage* 6, pp. 462–3; 12, pt 2, pp. 299–301.

34 Agnes de Scelgrave in Norhampton habuit conuenam pullorum inter quos unus casu cecidit in puteum aque et submersus est. Dictus Agnes extraxit pullum a puteo et dedit pueris ad ludendum. Tandem dixit, 'Commendo te Deo et beato Simoni' et continuo surrexit. In signum miraculi detulit predictum pullum apud Evesham. De hoc perhibet testimonium tota parochia de Selgrave.

35 Perrus Leycestre recitauit de filio fratris sui qui iacuit in fonte aque submersus per quatuor dies, silicet a die ueneris sancti Mathei apostoli usque ad [quartum] diem sequentem. Puer ab aqua extractus et ad comitem mensuratus statim apperuit oculos et respirauit. De hoc perhibet testimonium tota uillata de Glendon in Norhamptonshire anno gracie †M°CC°lix°†.

36 Maria de Chepingnorton amisit potestatem ambulandi per duos annos. Mensurata ad comitem conualuit. De hoc perhibet testimonium tota uillata de Chepingnorton.

37 Henricus capellanus de †Geddewolde† habuit cardiacam passionem per septimanam unde credidit expirare. Mensuratus ad comitem conualuit. De hoc perhibet testimonium tota parochia de †Geddewolde†.

34 Agnes from Sulgrave in Northamptonshire[59] had a brood of chicks, one of which accidentally fell into a well of water and was drowned. Agnes pulled the chick out of the well and gave it to the children to play with. But eventually she said, 'I commend you to God and the blessed Simon' and it immediately got up. As a token of the miracle she brought the chick to Evesham. The whole parish of Sulgrave bears witness to this.

35 Piers Leicester[60] gave an account of his brother's son who had fallen into a well of water and had lain drowned for four days, that is to say from the Friday of St Matthew the apostle[61] until the [fourth] day following. After the boy had been pulled from the water and measured to the earl he immediately opened his eyes and began to breathe. The whole township of Glendon in Northamptonshire bears witness to this in the year of grace †1259†.[62]

36 Mary from Chipping Norton[63] had for two years lost the ability to walk but after being measured to the earl she recovered. The whole township of Chipping Norton bears witness to this.

37 Henry the chaplain from †Geddewolde†[64] had had *cardiaca passio*[65] for a week, from which he thought he was going to die, but after being measured to the earl he recovered. The whole parish of †Geddewolde† bears witness to this.

---

[59] Hugh of Culworth held a manor at Sulgrave by 1258 (A. W. Hershey, 'An introduction to and edition of the Hugh Bigod eyre rolls, June 1258–February 1259: P.R.O. Just 1/1187 & Just 1/873' (London Univ. Ph.D. thesis, 1991) 1, pp. 290–1) and still in 1278 (G. Baker, *The History and Antiquities of the County of Northampton* (London, 1822–41) 1, p. 515). He was a rebel Montfortian and brother of Richard (*Cal. Pat.* 1258–66, pp. 354–5, 488), another rebel; Richard held an estate at Sulgrave in 1266 and in the early 1270s (*Cal. Pat.* 1258–66, pp. 540, 575; J. Bridges, *The History and Antiquities of Northamptonshire*, ed. P. Whalley (Oxford, 1791) 1, p. 127). See also 15n.

[60] A Piers of Leicester was among the rebel Montfortians pardoned after the surrender of Kenilworth castle: *Cal. Pat.* 1266–72, p. 16. A man of the same name was a burgess of Northampton in 1294 (*Rolls and Reg. Sutton* 2, p. 110) and c.1305 (TNA, SC 8/52/2589). The king had deprived the mayor and burgesses of Northampton of their powers until 1268 for having supported the Montfortians: *Cal. Pat.* 1266–72, p. 225.

[61] 21 September.

[62] *Recte* 1268? Between 1265 and 1270 that was the only year in which St Matthew's day was a Friday.

[63] Chipping Norton manor was held in 1260 by John FitzAlan: *Close R.* 1259–61, p. 99. He was an early supporter of the reform movement but had become a loyalist by 1264: *Complete Peerage* 1, p. 240. At his death in 1267 his heir was his son John (*Cal. Inq. p.m.* 1236–72, p. 216), who died in possession in 1272 (*Close R.* 1268–72, pp. 580–1).

[64] *Recte* Beddeworðe? If so, possibly Bedworth (Warwickshire): *PN Warws.* p. 97. The manor was held by Henry Hastings (d.1269): *Close R.* 1268–72, pp. 41–2. He was a leading rebel Montfortian: *Complete Peerage* 6, pp. 345–6.

[65] Heart pains and/or palpitations.

38   [fol. 166v] Symon Secher de la Ry morbo frenetico fatigatus per quinque septimanas. Iste apud Evesham adueniens et coram nobis in choro uinculis ferreis astrictus per merita comitis miraculose est curatus.

39   Radulfus de Sancto Nicolao ate Wode in Theneth simili morbo fatigatus per quinque septimanas mensuratus ad comitem et denario plicato conualuit. De hoc perhibet testimonium tota insula de Thenetlonde.

40   Filius Radulfi Barate de †Besseborne† puer cecidit in cloacam et per medium diem iacuit extinctus. Mensuratus ad comitem et denario conplicato statim surrexit et conualuit. De hoc testimonium perhibet tota uillata de †Besseborne†.

41   Margaria de la Burd de Werinton habens spasmum et disseniteriam et fantasma in capite per quinque septimanas unde pre dolore amisit memoriam mensurata ad comitem et denario plicato conualuit. De hoc perhibet testimonium tota uillata de Werinton.

42   Alyne de Samelesburye habens quandam infirmitatem ignotam per quinque septimanas mensurata ad comitem conualuit. Vnde predicta uilla perhibet testimonium.

43   Wyon de Werinton sensit guttam in gambam dexteram per duos annos. Iste sompniauit quod fuit in quodam loco ubi comes erat et uidebatur ei quod comes sufflauit super eum et tota infirmitas euanuit.

44   Gilbertus de Werynton habens guttam nimis pungitiuam per quatuor annos mensuratus ad comitem conualuit. De hoc perhibet testimonium tota uillata de Werington.

38 Simon Secher from Rye[66] had been afflicted for five weeks with a frenetic disorder. But he came to Evesham and here in the choir, bound in iron chains, he was miraculously cured in our presence through the merits of the earl.

39 Ralph from St Nicholas at Wood[67] in Thanet had been afflicted with a similar disorder for five weeks, but after being measured to the earl and a penny having been bent, he recovered. The whole Isle of Thanet bears witness to this.

40 The son of Ralph Barate from †Besseborne†,[68] a child, fell into a privy and lay lifeless for half a day, but after being measured to the earl and a penny having been bent, he immediately got up and recovered. The whole township of †Besseborne† bears witness to this.

41 Margery de la Burd from Warrington had for five weeks had cramp, dysentery, and delirium in the head, through which she had lost her mind on account of the distress, but after being measured to the earl she recovered. The whole township of Warrington bears witness to this.[69]

42 Aline of Samlesbury had had an unnamed illness for five weeks but after being measured to the earl she recovered. The whole of the said town [of Warrington] bears witness to this.

43 Guy from Warrington had suffered from a gout in his right leg for two years. But he dreamt that he was in some place where the earl was and it seemed as if the earl breathed on him, and all the disease vanished.

44 Gilbert from Warrington had had an extremely painful gout for four years but after being measured to the earl he recovered. The whole township of Warrington bears witness to this.

---

[66] Rye was one of the 'ancient towns' affiliated to the Cinque Ports, whose inhabitants were active Montfortians: see **24, 39**.

[67] For the identification of this place, also called Wood and now Woodchurch, I am indebted to Dr Paul Cullen. Woodchurch was a chapelry of Monkton parish and a 'limb' of Dover, one of the Cinque Ports: E. Hasted, *The History and Topographical Survey of the County of Kent*, 2nd edn (Canterbury, 1797) 10, pp. 310–11.

[68] *Recte* Wesseborne? If so, possibly Great Washbourne (Gloucestershire) or the adjoining Little Washbourne (Worcestershire). Great Washbourne was held by Tewkesbury abbey (*VCH Glos.* 6, p. 233), Little Washbourne by the loyalist Beauchamps of Elmley (*VCH Worcs.* 3, p. 471; see **9n**).

[69] Warrington manor was held by William Butler (d.1280): *Complete Peerage* 2, p. 230. He was a rebel Montfortian: *Close R.* 1264–68, pp. 71–2; *Cal. Pat.* 1266–72, pp. 19, 199.

45 James de Weryngton habuit guttam que dicitur fetre per nouem septimanas. Mensuratus ad comitem et denario plicato conualuit. Isti sex de uilla predicta super Merse hoc super illam aquam.

46 Alicia de †Weredech† habens quandam infirmitatem usque ad mortem longo tempore unde phisici desperati mensurata ad comitem et denario plicato conualuit. De hoc perhibet testimonium uir [fol. 167r] eius, Iohannes de la Ware frater Predicatorum et tota uillata de Derleston in Statfordeschire.

47 Robertus de Verell filius <Gileberti>[a] habens guttam per quindecim dies usque ad mortem mensuratus conualuit. Testes ut supra de Werynton.

48 Willelmus clericus de †Wistan† habuit ut phisici dicunt festum et cauernum et nouem aperturas in tibiis per biennium. Mensuratus ad comitem et denario plicato statim conualuit. De hoc perhibet testimonium tota uillata de †Wistan†.

49 Domina Christiana de Maule de Essex habens puerum etate quinque annorum puer iste habuit infirmitatem durissimam usque ad mortem per duas septimanas. Mensuratus ad comitem conualuit. In signum sanitatis fecit deferri puerulum de cera. De [hoc] perhibet testimonium tota uillata de Seringes.

50 Dominus Willelmus de Troy gallicus habuit guttam frigidam longo tempore in gambis et tibiis ultra modum pungitiuam. Mensuratus ad comitem Simonem conualuit. In signum sanitatis deferri fecit gambam cum pede de cera apud

---

[a] Gilel' MS.

45 James from Warrington had a gout called a *fetre*[70] for nine weeks, but after being measured to the earl and a penny having been bent, he recovered. The six from the forementioned town on the Mersey, that is to say beside that river, [bear witness to this].[71]

46 Alice of †Weredech†[72] had had a certain illness for a long time, to the point of death, and physicians could offer no hope for it, but after being measured to the earl and a penny having been bent, she recovered. Her husband bears witness to this and John de la Ware a Dominican friar and the whole township of Darlaston in Staffordshire.[73]

47 Robert of Wirral, son of Gilbert,[74] had had a gout for a fortnight to the point of death, but after being measured he recovered. The witnesses are as above, from Warrington.[75]

48 William the clerk from †Wistan†[76] had had for two years what physicians call a *festum*,[77] with a fissure and nine sores on the lower legs, but after being measured to the earl and a penny having been bent, he recovered. The whole township of †Wistan† bears witness to this.

49 Dame Christian de Maule[78] from Essex had a son aged five. For two weeks the boy had had a very severe illness to the point of death, but after being measured to the earl he recovered. In token of the cure she directed a little boy of wax to be sent. The whole township of Sheering bears witness to this.[79]

50 Sir Guillaume de Troyes, a Frenchman, had had a cold gout for a long time in the thighs and lower legs which was extremely painful, but after being measured to the earl he recovered. In token of the cure he directed a waxen leg, with its foot,

---

[70] An ulcer.
[71] The six are named in **41–5, 47**.
[72] *Recte* Meredech?
[73] Darlaston, held by Henry de Verdun a rebel Montfortian, had been forfeited by 1268; he died c.1272: 'Suits affecting Staffordshire tenants, taken from the Plea Rolls of the reign of Henry III', ed. G. Wrottesley, *Collections for a History of Staffordshire* 4 (William Salt Archaeological Soc. 1883), pt 1, pp. 1–215 (at pp. 165, 185, 201).
[74] Possibly Gilbert from Warrington (above, **44**).
[75] See **41n**.
[76] Possibly Whistones, in Claines (Worcestershire), which occurs as 'Wystan' in 1255: *PN Worcs.* p. 115.
[77] An ulcer.
[78] Christian (fl.1290) was a daughter of William de Valognes and had married Piers de Maule (fl.1256): *English Baronies*, pp. 12–13; *VCH Essex* 4, p. 251; 8, p. 243.
[79] This seems to be a version of **95**.

Evesham per Iohannem de Reans armigerum suum. Vnde idem Iohannes perhibet testimonium cum tota familia sua.

51 Domina Iuliana Grimbaud in partu premagno dolore credidit periclitari et sindi puerum ex uentre eius. Mensurata ad comitem infra breuem conualuit et peperit masculum elegantem. Vnde dicta Iuliana est testes cum pedisequa et familia sua.

52 Ricardus Cantuarie filius Gilberti <Bernard>[a] habens per tres annos gambam sinistram contractam ita quod sine sustentationem duorum baculorum incedere non potuit, hic cum per duos annos loca diuersa sanctorum uisitans causa salutis sue recuparande et nullum infirmitatis sentiret leuamen uel adiutorium, quadam nocte uidebatur ei cum esset apud Cantuariam in sompnis quod adiret locum ubi Symon de Monteforti occubuit et requiescit. Quo documento comperto surrexit cito et abiectis baculis de adiutorio diuino confidens baculos suos aliquando coadiutores super scapulas secum apud Evesham detulit et de conualencia sua nos certos redidit.

53 [fol. 167v] Philippus de Bretforton laicus infirmitate que tylys uocatur in tantum artabatur infirmitate predicta quod propter angustiam eiusdem passionis credebatur ab omnibus qui aderant uiam uniuerse carnis ingressurum. Qui ad comitem mensuratus conualuit. De [hoc] perhibet testimonium Iohannes capellanus de Bretforton et <Alexander le Bond>[b] et Alicia seruiens illius et uxor ipsius Philippi.

54 Agnes uxor Willelmi Alexandri de Bretforton acuta febre laborans et pregnans ad comitem Simonem mensurata conualuit. Huius rei testes Iohannes Bretfortone capellanus et Willelmus uir eius et Willelmus Saxi laicus.

---

[a] Berirard *MS.*
[b] Alexander le Bond] alicia h'ere bebond *MS.*

to be taken to Evesham by Jean de Reims his squire. The same Jean bears witness to this together with his entire household.

51 Dame Gillian Grimbald,[80] when she was in labour and in great distress, thought that she was in danger and that the child would need to be cut from her womb, but after being measured to the earl she recovered within a short time and gave birth to a handsome boy. The said Gillian is the witness to this together with her handmaid and her household.

52 Richard of Canterbury, son of Gilbert Bernard, had had a crippled left leg for three years so that he was unable to walk without the support of two sticks. He had found no relief or help for his infirmity from visiting the various shrines of the saints to recover his good health, but when he was at Canterbury one night it seemed to him in a dream that he ought to go to the place where Simon de Montfort died and rests. He took note of that guidance and got up quickly. He threw down the sticks and, putting his faith in divine help, carried them, his former assistants, on his shoulders with him to Evesham and convinced us of his recovery.

53 Philip from Bretforton, a prominent layman, had the illness called 'tylys'.[81] He was so burdened by it that everyone who was there thought, from the intensity of his suffering, that he was about to go the way of all flesh. But after being measured to the earl he recovered. John the chaplain of Bretforton, Alexander le Bond[82] and Alice his servant and the said Philip's wife bear witness to this.

54 Agnes, the wife of William Alexander, from Bretforton[83] had been struggling with an acute fever and was pregnant but after being measured to the earl she recovered. John the chaplain of Bretforton, William her husband and William Saxi,[84] a prominent layman, are the witnesses to this matter.

---

[80] Robert Grimbald was dead by 1265 when his heir was a ward of Henry Hastings, a leading rebel Montfortian (see **11n**): *Cal. Inq. Misc.* 1, p. 256. Robert's widow Gillian afterwards married William of 'Northburgh' and was living in 1288: *Rolls and Reg. Sutton* 2, p. 31; TNA, CP 25/1/285/23, no. 191.
[81] Possibly a skin ailment.
[82] A John le Bond was a taxpayer at Bretforton in the late thirteenth century: *Worcs. Subsidy*, p. 83.
[83] William was a tenant of Evesham abbey at Bretforton: *Mon. Angl.* 2, p. 32.
[84] The second-highest resident taxpayer at Bretforton in the late thirteenth century (*Worcs. Subsidy*, p. 83) and a tenant of Evesham abbey there (*Mon. Angl.* 2, p. 32).

55 Henricus Chanteler de Bretforton laicus guttam habens in renibus quod uix per tres dies incedere non potuit nisi cum sustentatione baculi. De hoc perhibet testimonium tota uillata de Bretforton.

56 Frater Iohannes dictus le Taylur de ordine Predicatorum et de conuentu fratrum de Norhamton habuit per mensem sinistram gambam usque ad poplites contractam. Qui spem et fiduciam ponens in comitem Simonem conualuit. Huius rei testis fuit frater Willelmus de Bannebury Predicator.

57 Matildis de uilla que appelatur Raddeston in comitatu Norhamton quadam gutta per multa tempora fatigata que nulla arte medicorum potuit curari licet magnas expensas fecisset pro sanitate recuparanda, mensurata ad comitem Simonem statim conualuit post mensurationem.

58 Agnes de eodem loco usque ad mortem infirmata que omnibus sacramentis ecclesiasticis inuncta postquam corpus eius tanquam mortuum in area collocatum, propinqui eius ad memoriam reduxerunt comitem Simonem et ipsam mulierem ad ipsum mensurauerunt. Statim infirma conualuit per merita comitis prout asserebat.

59 Filius Iacobi de †Fancote† submersus in quodam fonte mortuus [fol. 168r] extractus et per medium diem mortis uinculis detentus, tandem de consilio quorundam qui ad mortuum conuenerant ad comitem Simonem mensuratus a mortuis surrexit et se per merita comitis resuscitatum confessus est.

60 Willelmus Gullafre de Havekebore habens filium nomine Henricus undecim annos a natiuitate sua habens, hic Henricus infirmabatur per quindecim dies demum infirmitate grauante mortuus est. Pater et mater de consilio uicinorum

THE EVESHAM ABBEY MIRACLE BOOK

55 Henry the chandler from Bretforton, a prominent layman, had a gout in his side so that for nearly three days he was unable to walk without the support of a stick.[85] The whole township of Bretforton bears witness to this.[86]

56 Friar John Taylor of the Dominican order and from the Northampton friary had a left leg that for a month had been crippled as far as the knee-joint. But by putting his hope and trust in Earl Simon he recovered. Friar William of Banbury, a Dominican, was the witness to this matter.

57 Maud from the township called Radstone in Northamptonshire[87] had for a long time been afflicted with a gout. She could not be cured by any of the skills of doctors although she had spent a lot of money in seeking to recover her health. But on being measured to Earl Simon she recovered immediately afterwards.

58 Agnes from the same place was ill to the point of death and was anointed with all the sacraments of the church. After her body was set down in the churchyard like a corpse, her family and friends reflected upon Earl Simon and measured her to him, and the sick woman, so she declared, recovered immediately through the merits of the earl.

59 The son of James of †Fancote†[88] was drowned in a well, had been pulled out dead, and was bound in death's chains for half a day. But eventually on the advice of people who had gathered at the corpse he was measured to the earl. And he rose from the dead and acknowledged that he had been revived through the merits of the earl.[89]

60 William Gullafre from Hawkesbury[90] had a son called Henry, eleven years old. This Henry was ill for a fortnight and after the illness worsened he eventually died. His father and mother measured him to Earl Simon on the advice of neighbours

---

[85] Words about his recovery seem to be missing.
[86] This is a version of **4**.
[87] The manor was held by Isabel de Fors, countess of Aumale and Devon: Baker, *County of Northampton* 1, pp. 670–1. Unlike the inhabitants of Radstone (see **59n**) she may not have been a Montfortian sympathizer (see **160n**).
[88] *Recte* Faucote? If so, the surname may refer to Falcutt (Northamptonshire). In May 1265 the men of Astwell and Falcutt under Robert de Wauncy, who held a knight's fee in those townships in 1284 (*Feudal Aids* 4, p. 3), and the men of Radstone, Syresham and Whitfield, allegedly raided the Whistley park of Alan la Zouche (*Rot. Selecti*, pp. 187–8), an active royalist (*Complete Peerage* 12, pt 2, pp. 932–4; *ODNB*, s.n.).
[89] This is a version of **27**.
[90] Possibly Hawkesbury (Gloucestershire) because the county is not specified.

mensurauerunt ad comitem Simonem qui statim post mensurationem reuixit. Et surgens asseruit se resuscitatum meritis comitis Simonis.

61 Alexander de Ros filius Willelmi de Ros subito infirmatus et mortuus iacens et totaliter decoloratus estimaretur ut mortuus per diem. Iste ad comitem mensuratus post quandam respirationem paruam emissam conualuit et de resuscitatione sua meritis comitis facta narrauit hiis qui presentes aderant. Nomina autem eorum qui presentes aderant sunt hec silicet et qui resuscitationem uiderunt, Alexander Lutterel et Robertus sucarius eiusdem. Facta autem sunt prescripta in castello de Helmelling ubi est capella Petri et Pauli ad quam infirmus deportatus est et iacuit mortuus et postea suscitatus a mortuis. 'Per omnia benedictus Deus' qui per merita comitis talia operatur.

62 Memorandum de merilione Iohannis de †Culne† qui iacuit mortuus per diem et noctem. Et tandem posito in sporta et mensuratus ad martirem conualuit.

63 Magister Iohannes Crowolton per quindecim dies erat graui infirmitate [detentus] capitis et faucis sinistre usque ad dentes. Qui orationem fudit ad Dominum ut ipsum liberaret ab infirmitate quam patiebatur per merita comitis Simonis. [*blank*] post orationem factam liberatus fuit. Ecce mirum et admirandum. Quicquid infirmitatis recepit in sinistra qua curatus fuerat recepit in dextera fauce. Qui per merita dicti comitis Simonis recurrens conualuit uirtute diuina.

64 Willelmus Haymunde de Brack[l]ey clericus inflammationem [fol. 168v] habens per totum corpus per unam septimanam qui iudicatus fuit a diuersis medicine peritis fuisse ydropicus ad comitem mensuratus conualuit. Et hoc miro modo

and immediately after that he came back to life. Getting up, he declared himself revived through the merits of Earl Simon.

61   Alexander de Ros, son of William de Ros,[91] was suddenly taken ill, and lying lifeless and totally without colour he was thought for a day to be dead. But after being measured to the earl, and after he had given out a little breath, he recovered and told those who were present that his revival had been brought about through the merits of the earl. The names of those who were present there and had thus seen his revival were Alexander Luttrell[92] and his squire Robert. The above-written events took place in the castle of Helmsley, where there is a chapel of Peter and Paul to which the sick man had been carried and had lain dead and was afterwards raised from the dead. 'Blessed be God in all things,'[93] who performs such things through the merits of the earl.

62   A memorandum about the merlin of John of †Culne† which lay dead for a day and a night and eventually recovered after being placed in a basket and measured to the earl.

63   Master John Croughton[94] had for a fortnight been [taken] with a severe disorder of his head and in his left cheek as far as the teeth. But he uttered a prayer to the Lord that he would set him free through the merits of Earl Simon from the disorder that was troubling him, and [*blank*] after the prayer he was set free. And here is something miraculous and to be wondered at: he acquired the same disorder in his right cheek as he had had in his left, of which he had been cured. By appealing again he was cured by the divine power through the merits of Earl Simon.

64   William Haymunde from Brackley,[95] a clerk, had had an inflammation over his whole body for a week and was judged by various learned doctors to be suffering from dropsy, but after being measured to the earl he recovered. And it was in an

---

[91] William (probably d.1264) had been succeeded as lord of Helmsley by Alexander's elder brother Robert (d.1285), a prominent Montfortian: *Cal. Inq. p.m.* 1272–91, p. 344; *Complete Peerage* 11, pp. 93–6.
[92] Alexander left England for the Holy Land in 1270 (*Close R.* 1268–72, pp. 278–9) and is believed to have died there c.1273 (*Cal. Fine R.* 1272–1307, p. 5; H. Maxwell-Lyte, *A History of Dunster and of the Families of Mohun & Luttrell* (London, 1909), pp. 66–7).
[93] 2 Macc. 1: 17.
[94] A *magister* of this name witnesses an Oxford deed c.1270: *BRUO to 1500* 1, p. 520.
[95] Brackley manor was held by Alan la Zouche: Baker, *County of Northampton* 1, pp. 561–2. He was an active royalist: *Complete Peerage* 12, pt 2, pp. 932–4; *ODNB*, s.n. The advowson belonged to Leicester abbey: Baker, *County of Northampton* 1, p. 574.

quia tota inflatura quam habuit per aperturas quasdam gambarum decur[r]ebat quouscumque sanitati restituebat.

65   De quodam miraculo mirabili quod nobis recitauit Henricus de Pomery miles. Dicebat se enim fuisse in capella comitis Simonis ubi proposuit audire uesperas suas. Set recordatus propter diuersa negosia coram ipso recitata hora debita uenire non potuit. Tandem autem sero ueniens uidit duodecim cereos quos comes preparari iusserat diuinitus illuminatos. Quos dum ipse respexerat prohibuit comes dicto militi et aliis qui interfuerant id dictum miraculum alicui reuelarent.

66   Auicia filia Alani de Derebi certissime mortua mensurata ad comitem Simonem conualuit resuscitata.

67   Radulfus <primus>[a] filius Gilberti et Alicie de Dereby tam a sacerdote suo parochiali qui clausit oculos eiusdem quam ab aliis uicinis mortuus iudicatur. Ad comitem Simonem mensuratus statim conualuit resuscitatus.

68   Radulfus de Dereby parmentarius a pueritia sua in gamba dextra infirmitate grauatus per quam habuit gambam unam grossiorem alia et sensiens continue corosionem in osse ipsius gambe set non circa cor, grauatus infirmitate uidit in sompnis comitem Symonem sibi assistere et dicentem sic, 'Mortalibus infirmitatibus grauatus es. Set surge summo mane et adeatis locum apud Evesham in quo uiuus fui et mortuus et sanitatem plenam recuparabis.' Quod dum fecit conualuit de omnibus infirmitatibus suis.

69   Ricardus de Herforde carpentarius dum esset in reparationem stagni cuiusdam molendini quedam strues lignorum cecidit super pedes eius et eos ita contriuit quod se mouere non potuit. Vnde per alios fecit se deportari in domum quandam. Vnde eodem in lecto quodam collocato de consilio quorumdam apponi fecit emplastrum super pedes eius. Et cum ultra modum grauaretur post [fol. 169r] appositionem emplastri et dolorem sentiret quem ferre non posset de eorum consilio pedes suos fecit mensurari ad comitem Simonem. Et hoc facto dolor apparuit leuigatus. Vnde emplastro deposito apparuerunt pedes sui omnino sanitati restituti. Per quod surrexit et opera sua fecit sicut prius consueuit. Idem etiam Ricardus detulit quod

[a] pur' MS.

amazing way, for all the swelling that he had sustained flowed away through fissures in his legs until he was restored to health.

65   Concerning a wonderful miracle that Henry de la Pomeroy, a knight,[96] related to us. He said that he had been in Earl Simon's chapel where he had intended to hear Vespers but, on remembering to go to the earl about various items of business, he had been unable to be there at the prescribed hour. In due course, however, after arriving late he had witnessed twelve candles, which the earl had ordered to be prepared, being lit by divine agency. When Sir Henry remarked on them the earl forbade him, and the others who had been with him, to disclose that miracle to anyone.

66   Avice, daughter of Alan of Derby, was quite certainly dead but after being measured to the earl she recovered and was restored to life.

67   Ralph, the first son of Gilbert and Alice, from Derby, was judged to be dead both by his parish priest who closed his eyes and by other neighbours, but after being measured to the earl he recovered immediately and was restored to life.

68   Ralph of Derby, a parmenter,[97] had been troubled since boyhood with an infirmity of his left leg, as a result of which he had one leg thicker than the other and experienced a constant gnawing pain in the bone of that leg, though not around the heart. Oppressed by this infirmity, he saw Earl Simon in a dream standing beside him and saying, 'You are troubled with mortal infirmities but rise early tomorrow and go to the place at Evesham where I was alive and dead and you shall recover your full health,' and when he had done that he recovered from all his infirmities.

69   Richard of Hereford, a carpenter, had been doing repairs at a millpond when a pile of timbers fell on his feet and so crushed them that he was unable to move. He therefore had some others carry him into a house. After being laid on a bed, on people's advice he had a plaster put on his feet. But as he was extremely distressed after the application of the plaster and experienced pain that he could not bear, on their advice he had his feet measured to Earl Simon. After that was done the pain seemed to ease and when the plaster was removed his feet were seen to be completely mended, whereupon he got up and carried on with his work. The same

---

[96] A Montfortian: *Cal. Inq. Misc.* 1, pp. 198, 265–6. He died in 1281: *Cal. Inq. p.m.* 1272–91, p. 238. See also **165**.
[97] A furrier or tailor.

Agnes uxor Reginaldi Maniworde dum esset pregnans et de uita desperata propter dolorem continuum quem patiebatur ad comitem Simonem mensurata statim partum edidit et de periculo quod timebat euasit et hoc meritis predicti comitis.

70   Matildis uxor Willelmi filii Hugonis guttis laborabat in omnibus membris et hoc per multa tempora. Hec autem ad comitem Simonem mensurata conualuit et in huius rei testimonium locum in quo dictus comes uiuus fuit et mortuus humiliter requisiuit et uisitauit.

71   Memorandum quod cum comes Symon de Monteforti in sompnis appareret uicario de Wardon et eidem precipit ut Galfridum de Scalares militem ex parte sua moneret quod seditiones et machinamenta que contra comitem Symonem et suos complices apud Luddelow fecerat emendaret et idem uicarius bis premunitus preceptis comitis non obtemperaret, dictus comes apparens ei tertio cum comminatione precepit eidem ut diceret predicto militi quod nisi cum festinatione pretaxata machinamenta faceret emendari subito uel inopinata morte ab hac uita transiret. Verum cum miles auditis monitis non adquiesceret in prouictu itineris uersus London in quadam domo ubi fuerat hospitatus incendio periit cum domo et hernesio et tota familia sua ita quod nec minimum signum de omnibus predictis appareret post predictam combustionem.

72   Alicia soror Willelmi rectoris ecclesie de Werinton subito in dextra parte capitis et per faucem dextram usque ad collum inflaturam sustinens per quam dubitabatur eam morte [fol. 169v] subitanea extingui, hec autem de consilio quorumdam eidem assistentium et [ad] comitem Simonem mensurata conualuit. Huius rei testimonium perhibuit dictus Willelmus qui candelam mensuratam apud Evesham detulit.

73   Memorandum quod dictus Willelmus quoddam mirabile nobis retulit dicens quod cum ipse post bellum apud Evesham commissum de terra ubi comes iacuit in

Richard stated that Agnes, the wife of Reynold Maniword,[98] had been pregnant and in despair of her life from the constant pain that she was suffering. But after being measured to Earl Simon she had given birth immediately and escaped the danger that she had feared, and it was through the merits of the earl.

70   Maud, wife of William son of Hugh, had suffered for a long time from gouts in every part of her body but after being measured to Earl Simon she recovered. And in witness to this matter she humbly sought out and visited the place in which the earl had been alive and dead.

71   A memorandum that Earl Simon de Montfort had appeared to the vicar of Whaddon in a dream and had commanded him that, on his behalf, he should warn Geoffrey Deschalers, a knight, that he should make amends for the treachery and plotting that he had perpetrated at Ludlow against Earl Simon and his allies.[99] And when the vicar had not complied after being twice given notice, the earl appeared to him a third time with a threat. He commanded him that he should say to the knight that, unless he quickly made amends for the forementioned plotting, he would pass from this life by a sudden or unexpected death. But, since the knight would not accept the warnings that he had heard, while making a journey towards London he perished in a fire at a house where he was lodging, together with the house and his belongings and his entire retinue, so that after the blaze not the slightest trace of anything was to be seen.[100]

72   Alice the sister of William the rector of Warrington[101] was suddenly afflicted by a swelling on the right-hand side of her head and down the right cheek as far as her neck, and from it she was expected quickly to expire. She recovered, however, after being measured to the earl on the advice of people who were there. The said William who carried the measured candle to Evesham bore witness to this matter.

73   A memorandum that the said William told of a marvellous thing, saying that after the battle had taken place at Evesham he had carried away with him some of

---

[98] Reynold was a bailiff of Hereford in 1285: *Registrum Ricardi de Swinfield, episcopi Herefordensis, A.D. MCCLXXXIII–MCCCXVII*, ed. W. W. Capes (Canterbury and York Soc. 6, 1909), p. 94. He also occurs there in 1287: *Placita de Quo Warranto Temporibus Edw. I, II, et III in Curia Receptae Scaccarii Westm. Asservata*, ed. W. Illingworth (Record Commissioners, 1818), p. 252.
[99] Probably a reference to the anti-Montfortian alliance formed at Ludlow after Edward's escape from Hereford on 28 May 1265: see Maddicott, *Simon de Montfort*, p. 334.
[100] Geoffrey Deschalers the elder held the manor of Whaddon by 1260: *Cal. Pat. 1258–66*, p. 117. He died in 1284 some years after the miracle book was finished, so the fire victim was probably his son and heir Geoffrey the younger, who was dead by January 1267: *Cal. Pat. 1266–72*, p. 30; *Cal. Inq. p.m. 1272–91*, p. 309.
[101] See 41n.

campo secum asportasset, et quidam laicus nomine [*name omitted*] infirmabatur usque ad mortem ita quod ecclesiastica sacramenta recepisset et sine loquela per biduum iacuisset, comes Symon eidem infirmo apparens ut sibi uidebatur dixit ei quod precaret dictum Willelmum ut aliquam particulam eidem donaret de terra memorata quam habuit in sua potestate et quod misceret in aqua et eam uteretur uel declutiret. Quod dum factum fuisset dictus infirmus sanitatem recuparauit.

74 Quidam monachus de Burgo Sancti Petri quoddam mirabile narrauit quod unus de conuentu fratrum consueuit detrahere comiti Symoni una cum quodam clerico fratre suo nec bonum audire uel dicere potuit. Contigit quadam nocte quod contentio erat inter fratres pro dicte comite. 'Quidam eorum dixerunt quia bonus fuit alii non sed seducebat turbas.' Tandem lite sopita petierunt strata. Media nocte apparuit dicto religioso quidam miles armatus habens gladium in dextra manu et portinunculam suillam in leua. Et ait, 'Comede. Aut gustabis aut interibis. Melius est comedere carnes crudas quam uiuas.' Et comedit ut uidebatur usque ad medietatem. Et dixit miles, 'Sufficit, sed uade et defer aliam dimidietatem fratri tuo' et nominauit illum et sic disparuit. Iste euigilans perterritus ut de contentione et uisione ablueret manus[a] surrexit. Inuenit os suum intus et extra sanguine maculatum. Hec uidentes fratres mirabantur et crederunt eum ab aliquo percusse. Dictus religiosus recognescens [fol. 170r] ueritatem et petens ueniam a martire penitentia ductus omnis macula faciei euanuit. De hoc perhibet testimonium totus conuentus loci illius.[b]

75 Thomas de †Crest† narrauit de rectore de †Pytylton† paralici percusso die qua cantauit suam nouam missam. Et in reda apud Evesham deportatus statim et sine mora conualuit. De hoc perhibet testimonium tota parochia et dictus Thomas qui uidit dictum rectorem postea celebrantem et Deum clara uoce laudantem.

---

[a] de contentione et uisione ablueret manus] \a/ ablueret manus \b/ de contentione et uisione MS.
[b] *In margin in a contemporary hand* Nota bene istud miraculum.

the earth from where the earl had lain on the battlefield, and for safe-keeping had stored it in a cloth. An unlettered person called [*name omitted*] had been sick to the point of death so that he had received the sacraments of the church and lain speechless for two days. But Earl Simon, who seemed to this invalid to appear to him, said that he should ask this William to give him some of the earth that was in his possession, and should mix it with water and apply it or drink it. And after that had been done the patient recovered his health.

74   A monk of Peterborough told of something marvellous about one of the convent of brothers who, together with his own brother, a clerk, had often disparaged Earl Simon and could not hear or speak any good of him. One night it came to pass that there was an argument among the monks. 'Some said he was a good man. And others said: No, but he seduced the people.'[102] When the dispute had eventually subsided they went to their beds. But in the middle of the night there appeared to that monk an armed knight who had a sword in his right hand and a piece of pork in the left, and the knight said, 'Eat it. You shall either taste it or die. It is better to eat raw meat than living flesh.' And the monk ate as much as half of it, so it seemed. And the knight said, 'That is enough, but go and take the other half to your brother' and he named him, and thereupon he vanished. Waking in terror, the monk got up to wash his hands of the argument and of the vision and found that his mouth was bloodstained inside and out. The brothers were amazed at seeing this and thought that he had been beaten by someone. When the monk admitted the truth and, driven by remorse, sought forgiveness from the martyr, all the bloodstains on his face disappeared. The whole convent of that place bears witness to this.[103]

[*In the margin*] Heed this miracle well.

75   Thomas of †Crest† told of the rector of †Pytyltone†[104] who was stricken with paralysis on the day when he sang his first mass but after being carried to Evesham in a cart he recovered immediately and quickly. The whole parish bears witness to this together with the said Thomas, who afterwards saw the rector celebrating mass and praising God in a clear voice.

---

[102] An allusion to Christ. Cf. John 7: 12.
[103] Peterborough abbey was heavily fined for supporting Simon de Montfort, and Abbot Robert of Sutton (1263–74) was accused of sending men to fight for him: *VCH Northants.* 2, p. 88; Fernandes, 'Northamptonshire assize jurors', pp. 49–50. In the late fourteenth or the fifteenth century the abbey possessed a *Vita Simonis de Monteforti rithmice* (The Life of Simon de Montfort in Verse): *Peterborough Abbey* (CBMLC), p. 158, no. BP21.285f.
[104] *Recte* Fytyltone? If so, possibly Fittleton (Wiltshire): 'Fitilton' in 1303 (*Cal. Close*, 1302–27, p. 19). The living was a rectory: *VCH Wilts.* 11, p. 147.

76   †Gelbreda† Belle de Phyleby casu confregit brachium dextrum que tanto grauata dolore non habuit requiem neque per diem neque per noctem. Tandem mensurata ad comitem Simonem et denario plicato super eam omnis ille dolor euanuit. De hoc perhibet testimonium tota uillata de Phileby [et] ille Iohannes qui uidit dictum brachium contractum et hoc narrauit.

77   †Cutting'† de Norþ[u]mbarland de abbatia Penmoster percussus quodam ferro quod gallice dicitur gayne inclusum habuit in pectore per duos dies et duas noctes. Hic mensuratus in [die] sancti Bartholomei ad comitem Simonem sine mora conualuit, unde uidimus propriis oculis. Et illum ferrum remanet penes nos. Testes huius rei abbas de Penmoster et conuentus loci illius.[a]

78   Eadmunde Kokerell rector ecclesie de Þerne iuxta Sanctum Benedictum de Holm graui infirmitate detentus unde phisici sui desperauerunt, iste habuit in memoria comitem Simonem et mensuratus conualuit. De hoc perhibet testimonium dictus infirmus et Iohannes de Phileby qui detulit candelam suam apud Evesham.

79   Willelmus cognomento Child constabularius de Brugges habens puerum fere mortuum dictus Willelmus <tantum>[b] dolorem concepit in mente quod nullum gaudium uel letitiam potuit habere. Casu superueniente uenit quidam Predicator socius ab antiquo. Vidit nimiam anxietatem et dolorem. Voluit ab illo declinare. Vltimo dictus Predicator quesiuit si contrarius fuit aliquando comiti Simoni. At ille, 'Sic [fol. 170v] quia priuauit me multis bonis.' Cui ille, 'Pete ueniam a martire et recuparabis filium tuum.' Interim infans expirauit et ecce dolor super dolorem,

---

[a]   *In the MS this entry runs on from* 76 *without the usual line-break or display initial.*
[b]   tantem MS.

76 †Gelbreda†[105] Belle from Filby[106] had accidentally broken her right arm. She was suffering such pain that she had no rest by day or night. But eventually, after being measured to Earl Simon and a penny having been bent over her, all the pain disappeared. The whole township of Filby bears witness to this, [as does] that John[107] who saw the injured arm and told us about this matter.

77 †Cutting'†[108] of Northumberland from the abbey of Newminster had been struck by an iron object, called a *gayne* in French.[109] He had it lodged in his chest for two days and two nights but after being measured to Earl Simon on St Bartholomew's [day][110] he recovered straight away. Afterwards we saw the scars from the wound with our own eyes, and the iron object remains in our possession. The abbot of Newminster and the convent of that place are the witnesses to this matter.[111]

78 Edmund Cockerel the rector of the church of Thurne[112] near St Benet of Holme had been taken with a grave illness for which his physicians had no hope. But he reflected upon Earl Simon and after being measured he recovered. The patient bears witness to this as does John of Filby[113] who brought his candle to Evesham.

79 William Child the constable of Bridgnorth[114] had a young son who was virtually dead. William experienced such anguish of mind that he could have no joy or gladness. But as chance would have it, a Dominican friar who was an old friend arrived, saw his extreme anxiety and anguish and wanted to relieve him of it. In due course the Dominican asked him if he had ever been an opponent of Earl Simon. He said, 'Yes, because he deprived me of many valuable things.' The friar said to him, 'Ask the martyr for forgiveness and you shall recover your son.'

---

[105] *Recte* Albreda (Aubrey in English)?
[106] From 1263 part of Filby manor was held by the king's 'alien' half-brother Willam de Valence who died in 1296: *Cal. Inq. p.m.* 1236–72, p. 170; *Cal. Pat.* 1258–66, p. 299; *Cal. Close*, 1264–68, p. 540. Another part was held in 1243 by John de Warenne (d.1304) earl of Surrey. They were brothers-in-law and active royalists: *ODNB*, s.nn. Portions of the manor were held under them throughout by the families of Filby and Holme: TNA, CP 25/1/156/60, no. 666; *Feudal Aids* 3, p. 470; *Bk of Fees* 1, pt 2, p. 905.
[107] Probably John of Filby (as in 78).
[108] *Recte* Cuddy (a pet-form of Cuthbert)?
[109] An arrowhead or a crossbow bolt.
[110] 24 August.
[111] Posthumous miracles had been attributed to the first abbot of Newminster, St Robert (d.1159): *ODNB*, s.n. 'Robert [St Robert]'.
[112] The advowson and the manor were held by St Benet's abbey: C. Parkin, *An Essay towards a History of the County of Norfolk* (London, 1805–10) 11, p. 79.
[113] Probably the John in 76.
[114] He occurs as royal constable there in 1267/8: R. W. Eyton, *Antiquities of Shropshire* (London, 1854–60) 1, p. 288.

et iacuit se super lectum et parum obdormiuit. Et uidit in sompnis Christum descendere de celis. Et tetigit eum dicens, 'Quicquid petieritis in honore comitis mei dabitur tibi.' Et surgens cum festinatione mensurauit puerum et denario plicato super eum statim apperuit oculos. Et sic per merita comitis sanus et incolumis redditur patri suo. De hoc perhibet testimonium constabularius de Slopesbury Clemens Londoniarum una cum patre predicti mortui.

80   David de †Cordebrege† de Berkeshire ydropicus per septem septimanas in tantum inflatus quod uix incedere uel uidere potuit, hic mensuratus ad comitem Simonem sine mora conualuit. De hoc perhibet testimonium tota uillata de †Cordebregge†.

81   Willelmus frater illius David surdus per tres annos simili modo mensuratus gloriose conualuit.

82   Domina Mabilia sanctimonialis de Stodeley iuxta Oxoniam grauata ex magna infirmitate circa cor per nouem annos quam medici cardiacam passionem uocant, hec mensurata et super eam denario plicato ad comitem statim conualuit anno gracie †M°CC°viij°† circa Assumptionem Beate Virginis. De hoc perhibet testimonium conuentus de Stodeley.

83   Galfridus de Say miles de Essex graui infirmitate in tibiis et gambis per octo septimanas detentus ita quod uix incedere potuit, mensuratus ad comitem Simonem sine mora conualuit. De hoc perhibet testimonium Iohannes de †Hyke† qui candelam suam apud Evesham detulit.

84   Prior Sancti Crucis de Waltham graui infirmitate detentus sicut ipse narrauit priori nostro usque ad mortem, fratres circumstantes fleuerunt et dixerunt, 'Bonum est ut sis mensuratus ad comitem Simonem.' At ille negauit dicens, 'Absit aliquo religioso facere uotum sine precepto prelati.' Nocte media uidebatur ei in sompnis

But meanwhile the child died, which caused sorrow upon sorrow. William lay down on his bed and went to sleep for a short while and in a dream he saw Christ come down from the heavens, and he touched him, saying, 'Whatever you ask in honour of my earl, I shall grant you.' Rising in haste, William measured the boy and, a penny having been bent over him, he opened his eyes immediately. And in that way he was restored to his father, well and unharmed, through the merits of the earl. Clement of London the constable of Shrewsbury bears witness to this together with the father of the dead boy.

80   David from †Cordebrege†[115] in Berkshire had been suffering from dropsy for seven weeks and was so swollen that he could hardly walk or see but after being measured to Earl Simon he recovered straight away. The whole township of †Cordebregge† bears witness to this.

81   William, brother of that David, had been deaf for three years but after being measured in the same manner he recovered splendidly.

82   Dame Mabel, a nun of Studley near Oxford, had been troubled for nine years by a great malady about the heart which doctors call *cardiaca passio*.[116] But after being measured and a penny having been bent over her to the earl, she recovered immediately; that was around the Assumption of the Blessed Virgin[117] in the year of grace †1208†.[118] The convent of Studley bears witness to this.

83   Geoffrey de Say a knight from Essex[119] was afflicted with a serious infirmity in the lower legs and thighs for seven weeks so that he could hardly walk, but after being measured to Earl Simon he recovered straight away. John of †Hyke†,[120] who brought his candle to Evesham, bears witness to this.

84   The prior of Waltham Holy Cross had been taken seriously ill to the point of death, so he told our prior. The brothers standing round him begged him and said, 'It would be a good thing if you were to be measured to Earl Simon.' But he refused, saying, 'Far be it from any man of religion to pray for something without the command of his superior.' In the middle of the night, however, it seemed to him

---

[115] Possibly Coldridge in Great Shefford parish.
[116] Heart pains and/or palpitations.
[117] 15 August.
[118] *Recte* 1268?
[119] Geoffrey de Say lord of Rickling (Essex) is said to have died in or before 1271; in 1265 the Montfortian government had granted him free warren in Rickling manor: Maddicott, 'Follower, leader, pilgrim, saint', p. 651.
[120] *Recte* Ryke'? If so, the surname may refer to Rickling.

quod [fol. 171r] uidit comitem Simonem inter multitudinem pauperum sibi occurrentem et dulciter amplectentem. Euigilans habuit quandam eructationem et fecit uomitum et sic conualuit.

85   Frater laycus de eodem cenobio paralisi in dextra parte percussus mensuratus simili modo conualuit. Cocus eiusdem loci freneticus per merita martiris gloriose sanatus est. Testis dictus prior eiusdem loci.

86   Iohannes de Coventre cognomento Forbeor graui infirmitate detentus et ex toto mortuus, mulier sua uidens uirum mortuum mora mulieris exclamauit, 'O Simon de Mounteforti! Si aliquod \bonum/ fecisti pro Deo et sicut nos credimus te martirizatum pro iusticia, ostende uirtutem tuam in homine isto.' Et statim respirauit et denario plicato et deaurato miraculose resuscitatus conualuit. De hoc perhibet testimonium uillata de Coventre.

87   Quidam nobilis Hibernie habens mulierem pregnantem et morbo ydropisi laborantem unde amici illius desperauerunt, adueniente tempore parturitionis peperit masculum elegantem set abortiuum. Interim uoluit dominus eius recedere a loco donec uideret finem. Quidam ex consodalibus quasi ludendo dixit, 'Bonum est ut domina uestra sit mensurata ad comitem Simonem,' etc. Ab obstetricibus facta sine mora conualuit. Hec audiens dictus dominus uoluit uidere uxorem. Et cum respexit uidit morbum undique sedatum. Quesiuit de puero. Negauit se non habere puerum nec unquam infirmitatem. Tandem perscrutatur. Inuenit ut superius dictum est silicet abortiuum. Denario super eum plicato confestim apperuit oculos et dedit uagitus. 'Per omnia Deus benedictus' unde tria sunt miracula hec perpetrata: mulier a morbo ydropico sanata, a puero liberata, a morte gloriose resuscitatus. De hoc perhibet testimonium magister Iohannes de Wychio hoc audiente a Minoribus et ceteris personis ualde fidedignis.

in his dreams that he saw Earl Simon amidst a multitude of poor people running to meet him and tenderly embracing him. On waking he belched and vomited and so recovered.

85   A lay brother of the same religious house was stricken with paralysis on his right-hand side but after being measured he recovered in a similar way. Also the deranged cook of that place was splendidly cured through the merits of the martyr. The witness is the said prior of that place.

86   John Furber[121] from Coventry had been taken seriously ill and was absolutely dead. His wife, on seeing her husband, exclaimed like a woman, 'O Simon de Montfort! If you ever did anything good for God, and as we believe that you were martyred for justice, exert your power upon this man,' and he immediately began to breathe. And after a penny had been bent and gilded he recovered and was miraculously revived. The town of Coventry bears witness to this.

87   A nobleman from Ireland had a wife who was pregnant and afflicted with the illness of dropsy, for which his friends had no hope. When the time for delivery came she gave birth to a baby boy, handsome but stillborn. Meanwhile her husband had chosen to leave the room until he should see what the final result would be. One of his comrades said, almost frivolously, 'It would be a good thing if your lady were to be measured to Earl Simon,' etc. And when the midwives did that, she recovered straight away. Hearing of this, the lord wanted to see his wife, and when he looked at her he saw that her disorder had altogether abated. He asked about the boy but she denied having had a boy or having been ill. In due course he made a search and found him to be as described above, that is to say stillborn. But after a penny was bent over him the baby immediately opened his eyes and gave a cry. 'Blessed be God in all things,'[122] for there were these three miracles performed: the woman was cured of a dropsical disorder, she was delivered of a boy, and he was splendidly brought back from the dead. Master John of Wich[123] bears witness to this, having heard it from Franciscan friars and other really trustworthy people.[124]

---

[121] A furber was a polisher of metal.
[122] 2 Macc. 1: 17.
[123] Possibly the brother of Richard of Wich (d.1253) bishop of Chichester, who was canonized in 1262: *BRUO to 1500* 3, p. 2099; *ODNB*, s.n. 'Wyche, Richard of'.
[124] This seems to be a version of 31.

88   [fol. 171v] Hugo Peverell de Devenchire habens filiam lactantem nomine Iohannam, hec per duos dies et duas noctes iacuit sine anelitu. Mensurata ad comitem Simonem et denario plicato surrexit et lac de nutrice auide siuit. De hoc perhibet testimonium dictus Hugo una cum uxore nobilissima et tota familia.

89   Domina Margareta de Heydon iuxta Castrum Nouum uxor Nicholai de Screngham egrota graui infirmitate quam mulieres flores uocant per annum, hec sua expendit in medicis et nichil preualuit. Tandem mensurata ad comitem statim conualuit. Testes huius rei tota uillata de Heydon et Hawysa que detulit candelam suam usque Evesham.

90   Quidam nobilis de Derebeschire fecit magnum conuiuium conuicaneis suis. Affuerunt inter eos duo detractores qui et dixerunt uniuersa mala de comite. At dominus conuiuii quod bonus fuit, at ille, 'Domine Iesu Christe, sicut credo comitem Simonem pro iusticia terre et ueritate martirizatum, ostende magnificenciam tuam in me.' Et inuoluit manum in birro. Interim rediit mensam. O mira Dei uirtus! Post prandium aperuit manum. Nichil aparuit nisi cicatrix circa policem. Hec uidentes detractores statim fiebant Dei laudatores.

91   Thomas clericus Cantuarie filius Roberti Yve habens morbum caducum per quadraginta dies mensuratus ad comitem conualuit. Nec infirmitas ultra ad eum rediit. De hoc perhibet testimonium Iohannes uicarius de †Sellinge† in Cantea et plures alii.

92   Alicia de Chileam de Cantea mulier fidedigna narrauit de quodam puero quadrennio filio †Wolkokani†[a] Cantuarie nomine Alexander quod in conflictu seruientium casu cecidit in ignem et iacuit ibidem fere per dimidiam horam et quatuor rybaldi super eum, et sic fuit in oculis et ceteris membris fere adustus.

[a] *Or* Wolkokam MS.

88   Hugh Peverel from Devon[125] had an unweaned baby daughter called Joan. She lay without breathing for two days and two nights, but after being measured to Earl Simon and a penny having been bent, she recovered and eagerly sucked from the nurse. Hugh bears witness to this together with his very excellent wife and the entire household.

89   Dame Margaret from Heddon near Newcastle, wife of Nicholas of Scrayingham,[126] had been ill for a year with a serious complaint that women call 'flowers'.[127] She had spent money on doctors but to no avail. But eventually, after being measured to the earl she recovered immediately. The witnesses to this matter are the whole township of Heddon, and Hawis who brought Margaret's candle to Evesham.

90   A nobleman of Derbyshire held a great feast with his neighbours. Among them were two detractors and they said all sorts of evil things about the earl. But the lord of the feast said something good. He said, 'Lord Jesus Christ, since I believe Earl Simon was martyred for justice on earth and for the truth, show forth your greatness in me.'[128] And he wrapped his hand in his cloak. He then returned to the table. O, the wonderful power of God! After the meal he uncovered his hand. There was nothing to be seen but a scar about the thumb. When the detractors saw this they immediately began to praise God.

91   Thomas, a clerk of Canterbury, son of Robert Yve, had the falling sickness for forty days, but after being measured to the earl he recovered and had no further attacks. John the vicar of †Sellinge† in Kent bears witness to this as do many others.

92   Alice of Chilham from Kent, a trustworthy woman, told of a four-year-old boy called Alexander, son of †Wilcock† of Canterbury. He had accidentally fallen into a fire during an argument between servants, and lay there for half an hour with four louts on top of him. And thus he was almost burnt away about his eyes and on other parts of his body. But after being measured to Earl Simon he was

---

[125]   Active in Devon in support of the Montfortian regime 1264–65: *Cal. Pat.* 1258–66, pp. 393, 420, 434; *Close R. (Suppl.)* p. 38. He died in 1296 and his wife Margery survived him: *Cal. Inq. p.m.* 1291–1300, pp. 207–8.
[126]   Margaret (who sometimes occurs as Margery) and Nicholas were living 1257–72: J. Brand, *The History and Antiquities of the Town and County of the Town of Newcastle upon Tyne* (London, 1789) 1, p. 212n; *Three Early Assize Rolls for the County of Northumberland, saec. XIII* [ed. W. Page] (Surtees Soc. 88, 1891 for 1890), pp. 161, 202, 217; *Northumb. Pleas*, pp. 255, 299, 304, 312–13.
[127]   A menstrual disorder.
[128]   The MS seems to omit here a clause about a deliberate injury to his hand.

Hic mensuratus ad comitem Simonem statim gloriose curatus est sine omni lesura. Testes huius [fol. 172r] rei uniuerse multitudo Cantuarie.

93   Frater <Guarinus>[a] Bossoun de ordine Minorum uidit sompnia post mortem comitis sicut recitauit presente fratre suo eiusdem ordinis Odone Hanseotico. Videbatur ei esse in magno campo et lato et uidit duas scalas siue acies ut milites dicunt, unam magnam et aliam minorem, in minori Iesum sedentem et dicentem, 'Si est aliquis qui aliam uictoriam in hoc seculo fecerit propter nomen meum, surgat in medio.' Et ecce Simon comes detulit capud suum in manibus et optulit ei. At Iesus, 'Magna est oblatio.' Dictus frater euigilans reuoluebat intra se quid potest esse, sompnia an reuelatio. Et iterum obdormiuit et astitit ei quidem ei manifesta reuelatio, cui demonstrata est modo cuidam monacho Eueshamie. Vnde prior bone memorie sepe narrauit quod tunc temporis aperte uidit.

94   Rogerus fullo molendinarius de Wychio habens filiam lactantem et reptantem, ista sine custodia casu cecidit in aquam rapidoque meatu fluminis absorta et uoluentis rote hauritoriis excepta statim extinguitur. Hec ab aqua eleuata et ad comitem Simonem mensurata aperuit oculos et sic per merita martiris uita restituta. O mira Christi clemencia! Et que numquam gressus stando ad terram misit recte super pedes postea ambulauit. Istud contigit primo anno set motu regalium parentes noluerunt nec potuerunt probare. Testis huius rei tota uillata de Wichio.

95   Willelmus de Maule nobilis puer de Essex habens infirmitatem ab infancia quasi dementia et priuatus sensu hominis mensuratus ad comitem Symonem conualuit. Vnde in signum sanitatis detulit capud cere apud Evesham et candelam sue longitudinis et latitudinis. De hoc perhibet testimonium tota parentela sua nobilissima.

96   Reginaldus de †Besseforde† habuit brachium contractum [fol. 172v] per duos annos. Mensuratus ad comitem die Exaltationis Sancti Crucis conualuit. De hoc perhibet testimonium tota uillata de †Besseforde†.

[a] Gaprinus MS.

immediately healed, splendidly and with no sign of injury. A crowd of people from the whole of Canterbury are the witnesses to this matter.

93   Friar Guarin Bossoun of the Franciscan order had a dream after the death of the earl, which he described in the presence of his brother of that order Otes Hansard. It seemed to him that he was in a large, broad field and saw two escheles or battle-lines, as soldiers call them, one big and the other smaller. Jesus was seated in the smaller one, saying 'If there is anyone who will achieve a second victory in this world for my name's sake, let him stand forth in your midst.' And behold, the saintly earl brought his head in his hands and offered it. Then Jesus said, 'This is a great offering.' The said friar on waking wondered to himself what it could have been, whether it had been a dream or a revelation. He went to sleep again and a clear revelation indeed came to him, which was shown to him and later to a monk of Evesham. The prior of happy memory often talked about that which he had witnessed clearly at the time.

94   Roger the fuller, a miller from Droitwich, had a daughter who was unweaned and crawling. While unsupervised she accidentally fell into the water and was overwhelmed by the fast-flowing stream. Caught by the revolving blades of the mill-wheel, she was killed instantly. On being lifted out of the water and after being measured to Earl Simon she opened her eyes and so was restored through the merits of the martyr. O, the wonderful mercy of Christ! And she, who had never put a foot to the ground, afterwards walked upright on her feet. This occurred in the first year,[129] but the parents would not and could not declare it because of the stance of the royalists. The whole town of Droitwich is the witness to this matter.

95   William de Maule a noble boy from Essex had had a malady since infancy, a kind of dementia, and had no human reason, but after being measured to Earl Simon he recovered. And so, in token of his cure he took a waxen head to Evesham and a candle of his height and width. All of his most noble kindred bear witness to this.[130]

96   Reynold from †Besseforde†[131] had had a crippled arm for two years but after being measured to the earl at the Exaltation of the Holy Cross[132] he recovered. The whole township of †Besseforde† bears witness to this.

---

[129] 1265/6.
[130] This seems to be a version of 49.
[131] Possibly Besford (Worcestershire) because the county is not specified.
[132] 14 September.

97 Ricardus de Berewyk habens puerum masculum duorum annorum, die lune post sanctam Pascham casu cecidit in puteum aque et iacuit ibi mora trium horarum. Mensuratus ad comitem statim surrexit. De hoc perhibent testimonium omnes conuicanei loci illius de Berewyk in parochia de Neuwenton.

98 Reginaldus Angeuinus habens quandam infirmitatem unde phisici desperauerunt mensuratus ad comitem simili modo conualuit. Testes tota uillata de Holecombe.

99 Ricardus Neirun nobilis cognatus domini Walteri de Cantulupo habens quandam infirmitatem circa cor uix respirare potuit. Mensuratus ad comitem et denario plicato conualuit et ut dixit apparuit bis in sompnis dictus Symon.

100 Richard Pepre de Scelegrave ultra Bannebury quinque leucas habens puerum nomine Robertum, cum quandam die silicet le Hokeday numerasset animalia <patris>[a] sui ad pasturam in quodam loco non debito obdormiuit. Euigilans non habuit memoriam hominis et sic remansit sine sensu per duos dies. Mensuratus ad comitem Symonem statim sensum recuparauit. De hoc perhibet testimonium tota parochia de Selegrave.

101 Leticia Palmer de Oxonia habens brachium inutile et manum inualidam per annum et dimidiam mensurata ad comitem conualuit. Et in signum sanitatis detulit [brachium] cere apud Evesham. De hoc perhibet testimonium tota parochia sancte Abbe uirginis Oxonie.

---

[a] fratris *MS*.

97 Richard from Berrick Prior[133] had a two-year-old son. On the Monday after Easter he had accidentally fallen into a well of water and he lay there for a period of three hours, but after being measured to the earl he got up immediately. All the neighbours there at Berrick Prior in the parish of Newington bear witness to this.

98 Reynold Angevin[134] had a malady for which physicians could offer no hope, but after being measured to the earl he recovered in a similar way. The witnesses are the whole township of Holcombe.

99 Richard Neirun,[135] a noble kinsman of Sir Walter Cantlow,[136] had a malady around his heart so that he could scarcely breathe, but after being measured to the earl and a penny having been bent, he recovered. And, so he said, Simon appeared to him twice in his dreams.

100 Richard Pepre from Sulgrave,[137] five leagues beyond Banbury,[138] had a son called Robert. While counting his father's livestock at pasture one day, that is to say at Hock-day,[139] he had fallen asleep in what was an unsuitable place. On waking he had no human understanding and he remained witless like that for two days, but after being measured to Earl Simon he came to his senses immediately. The whole parish of Sulgrave bears witness to this.

101 Lettice Palmer from Oxford[140] had a useless arm and a feeble hand for a year and a half but after being measured to the earl she recovered. And in token of the cure she brought a waxen [arm] to Evesham. The whole parish of St Ebbe the virgin in Oxford bears witness to this.[141]

---

[133] In 1279 he was a freeholder at Berrick Prior, having succeeded his father Hugh c.1271: *VCH Oxon.* 18, p. 316.

[134] In 1279 Reynold was living at Holcombe (Oxfordshire), where he had held the manor since c.1271: *VCH Oxon.* 18, pp. 315, 326.

[135] Possibly Richer Neyrnut, who was lord of Ufton Nervet (Berkshire) by 1243 (*Bk of Fees* 1, pt 2, pp. 845, 849, 854) but had gone by 1274 (*Rot. Hund.* 1, p. 17).

[136] Possibly Walter Cantilupe the Montfortian bishop of Worcester who had died in February 1266: *ODNB*, s.n.

[137] Hugh of Culworth held a manor at Sulgrave by 1258 and in 1278; his brother Richard also held an estate there; both were rebel Montfortians: above, **34n**.

[138] Sulgrave is about eight miles north-east of Banbury.

[139] The second Tuesday after Easter.

[140] In 1278 Lettice the widow of Simon Palmer lived at Oxford in St Ebbe's parish where she held eight other houses and two cottages: *Rot. Hund.* 2, pp. 790, 808.

[141] In 1266 a large fine was imposed on the burgesses of Oxford for having supported the Montfortians: *Cal. Pat.* 1258–66, p. 576.

102 Gregorius de Grandun rector ecclesie de Sapecote habens totam faciem inflatam una cum collo ultra modum mensuratus ad comitem die martis post Theophaniam conualuit.

103 Idem narrauit cum esset in castello de Kenelingworth post bellum accidit ei guttam pungitiuam. Recolens de loco ubi comes sedere solebat accessit et ibi adorauit et [fol. 173r] gutta statim euanuit.

104 Item idem de bouo suo dixit qui non comedit per quindecim dies. Denario plicato ad comitem statim auide comedit et conualuit.

105 Item narrauit de quadam aue domine de Grandon mortua dilacerata et medietate commesta. Mensurata et merita comitis gloriose sine lesura resuscitata est.

105 Rogerus de Estwell de Norhamtonshire conduxit puellam nomine Iohannam apud Evesham priuata uisu per nouem septimanas. Mensurata ad comitem confestim uisum recepit. De hoc perhibet testimonium tota uillata de Evesham.

107 Vxor Iohannis de †Hicclebury† nomine Rosa habens quandam infirmitatem die sancti Pauli in itinere uersus uillam tanta fuit grauata quod inter brachia uiri sui expirauit. Mensurata ad comitem et super eam denario plicato statim respirauit et conualuit. Et mirum contigit de denario plicato perdito et quesito et tertia nocte in

102   Gregory of Grendon the rector of the church of Sapcote[142] had his whole face extremely swollen together with his neck, but after being measured to the earl on the Tuesday after Epiphany[143] he recovered.

103   The same man told us that a painful gout had come upon him when he was in Kenilworth castle after the battle of Evesham. Remembering the place where the earl had used to sit, he had approached it and had worshipped there and the gout had immediately disappeared.[144]

104   Also the same man spoke of his ox which had not eaten for a fortnight. After a penny was bent to the earl it ate eagerly straight away and recovered.

105   The same man told of a fowl belonging to the lady of Grendon,[145] which had been dead, carved up and half eaten. After being measured, it was splendidly brought back to life through the merits of the earl and without any sign of injury.[146]

106   Roger of Astwell from Northamptonshire[147] brought to Evesham a young daughter called Joan who had been without sight for nine weeks. After being measured to the earl she quickly got her eyesight back. The whole town of Evesham bears witness to this.

107   The wife of John of †Hicclebury†,[148] called Rose, had some kind of illness and on St Paul's day[149] was so afflicted on the way to town that she expired in the arms of her husband. But after being measured to the earl and a penny having been bent over her, she immediately began breathing again and recovered. And a wonder occurred concerning the bent penny, which was lost and was searched for

---

[142]   Ralph Basset lord of Sapcote had been a leading Montfortian before the battle of Evesham: *ODNB*, s.n.
[143]   6 January.
[144]   This must have occurred before 14 December 1266, when the rebel garrison at Kenilworth surrendered.
[145]   Possibly Scholace, the second wife of Robert of Grendon (d.1269×1273) lord of Grendon (Warwickshire): H. S. Grazebrook, 'Shenstone charters', *William Salt Archaeological Soc. Collections for a History of Staffordshire* 17 (1896), pp. 239–98 (at p. 295); *VCH Warws.* 4, p. 76; *Close R.* 1268–72, p. 43. He was a Montfortian until, it seems, shortly before the battle of Evesham: R. Cassidy, 'Simon de Montfort's sheriffs, 1264–5', *Historical Research* 91 (2018), pp. 3–21 (at p. 20).
[146]   It is tempting to read this story as a joke devised by some mischievous sceptic, and it may not have been the only one.
[147]   The inhabitants of Astwell were probably Montfortians: see 59n.
[148]   *Recte* Hildebury? If so, the surname may refer to Hillborough (Warwickshire): 'Hyldeberewe' in 1312 (*PN Warws.* p. 210).
[149]   30 June.

lecto suo mirabiliter inuento. De hoc perhibet testimonium capellanus parochialis una cum tota uillata de †Donninton†.

108 Abbas Hugo de la Dale ordinis Premonstratensis percussus paralisi die saboti post festum sancti Marci euangeliste coram iusticiariis domini regis tunc sedentibus in uilla de Dereby et sic detentus infirmitate per quatuor dies, concilio prudentium mensuratus ad comitem conualuit sine mora in presencia totius congregationis. In signum sanitatis dictus abbas misit candelam suam apud Evesham per Iohannem canonicum suum de Baþekewell anno gracie M°CC° sexagesimo <ix°>.[a]

109 Robertus Aleyn de Bruell ultra Oxoniam habens uxorem nomine Matildam, hec patiebatur febribus et ualla dura capitis et colli per tres annos. Mensurata ad comitem conualuit.

110 Item quidam narrauit de filio suo nomine Radulpho laborante febribus per septem annos tantum noctibus simili modo. Mensuratus ad comitem conualuit. De hoc perhibet testimonium tota uillata de Bruell.

111 [fol. 173v] Leticia de Heyleston iuxta Leycestriam ydropica per septem annos mensurata ad comitem in eundo uersus Evesham cum sternutatione et ructuatione et uomitu conualuit. Et que tumida et aquosa fuit uidimus propriis oculis gracilem et delicatam. De hoc perhibet testimonium tota uillata de Heyleston cum ceteris uillulis adiacentibus.

---

[a] ix°] xx MS.

and on the third night was miraculously found in her bed. The parochial chaplain bears witness to this together with the whole township of †Donninton†.[150]

108 Hugh[151] the abbot of Dale of the Premonstratensian order was stricken with paralysis on the Saturday[152] after the feast of St Mark the evangelist in the presence of the king's justices then sitting in the town of Derby,[153] and for four days he was afflicted with infirmity in that way. But after being measured to the earl on the advice of some wise people, he recovered straight away in the presence of the whole community. In token of the cure the abbot sent his candle to Evesham by means of his canon John of Bakewell in the year of grace 1269.[154]

109 Robert Aleyn[155] from Brill[156] beyond Oxford had a wife called Maud. She had suffered for seven years from fevers and hard lumps on her head and neck but after being measured to the earl she recovered.

110 Also someone told of Robert Aleyn's son called Ralph who had been afflicted with night-time fevers for seven years. After being measured to the earl in a similar way he recovered. The whole township of Brill bears witness to this.

111 Lettice from Aylestone[157] near Leicester had suffered from dropsy for seven years. But after being measured to the earl she recovered on her way to Evesham with sneezing, belching and vomiting. And we saw with our own eyes that she who had formerly been swollen and full of water was slender and attractive. The whole township of Aylestone bears witness to this together with the neighbouring hamlets.

---

[150] Possibly Dunnington, in Salford Priors (Warwickshire): 'Donynton' in 1332 (*PN Warws*. p. 221) and about six miles from Hillborough.
[151] Hugh of Lincoln.
[152] 26 April.
[153] The justices in eyre were sitting at Derby from 7 April to 8 May 1269: D. Crook, *Records of the General Eyre* (London, 1982), p. 137.
[154] Hugh was dead by 21 March 1271: *Heads* 2, p. 499.
[155] Probably related to John Alan, a potter at Brill in 1254: see M. Farley and B. Hurman, 'Buckinghamshire pots, potters and potteries, c.1200–1910', *Records of Buckinghamshire* 55 (2015), pp. 161–234 (at p. 181).
[156] On Brill's Montfortian stance before and after 1265 see Jacob, *Studies*, pp. 44–7, 290–1, 344–9.
[157] William de Harcourt lord of Aylestone was a Montfortian and forfeited the manor after the battle of Evesham, but it was restored to the family in 1267: *Cal. Pat*. 1266–72, p. 120; *Cal. Close*, 1272–79, p. 436. William (d.1270) was the brother of Saher de Harcourt (above, **18n**) another Montfortian: ODNB (online edn), s.n. 'Harcourt [de Harcourt] family'. William is also said to have been brother-in-law to Henry Hastings (Eyton, *Antiquities of Shropshire* 2, p. 223) a leading rebel (above, **11n**).

112 Agnes de †Deneburne† habens guttam et spasmum in toto corpore mensurata et confricata de terra ubi comes occubuit mox conualuit. De hoc perhibet testimonium Alicia Malherbe et cetere mulieres.

113 Alicia de †Chaddelee† habens in capite infirmitatem unde fere amisit oculum dextrum per septendecim septimanas, mensurata ad comitem Simonem conualuit. De hoc perhibet testimonium tota uillata de †Chaddelee†.

114 Quedam domina fidedigna narrauit de pullo suo pauonis quod casu pede conculcato unde per ambas partes capitis sanguis exiuit. Mensuratus ad comitem Simonem sine mora et lesione conualuit. In signum miraculi et sanitatis detulit bona mulier apud Evesham caudam predicti pauonis.

115 Willelmus de la Horste de Bulne narrauit de quodam uicino suo Roberto diacono. Secundo anno post bellum Eueshamie contigit quod dictus Willelmus fecit magnum conuiuium. Inter conuiuantes lis mota est de comite unde dictus Robertus ultra mensuram uituperauit comitem et uniuersa mala proposuit. At dominus domus silicet dictus Willelmus, 'Nolite detrahere comitem.' Inter hec dictus Robertus perdidit loquelam nec potuit mouere manum uel pedem set sedit quasi mortuus. Cum orationibus conuiuantium parum respirauit et concilio dicti Willelmi promisit quod de cetero numquam aduersa de dicto comite diceret et sic de periculo euasit.[a]

116 Idem Willelmus recitauit de clerico nomine Willelmo de †Hylamtre† habens sanguinis passionem. Mensuratus et denario plicato conualuit. Testes huius rei dictus Willelmus et plures alii.

---

[a] *In margin in a contemporary hand* Nota miraculum.

112 Agnes of †Deneburne† had a gout and cramp in her whole body but after being measured and being rubbed with earth from where the earl had fallen she recovered. Alice Malherbe[158] and other women bear witness to this.

113 Alice from †Chaddelee†[159] had had a malady in her head for seventeen days, from which she almost lost her right eye, but after being measured to Earl Simon she recovered. The whole township of †Chaddelee† bears witness to this.

114 A trustworthy lady told of her young peacock which had been accidentally trodden underfoot so that blood issued from both sides of its head. After being measured to Earl Simon it recovered straight away and without any sign of injury. In token of the miracle and cure the good woman brought the peacock's tail to Evesham.

115 William of the Hurst from Bell[160] told of a neighbour of his, Robert the deacon. In the second year after the battle of Evesham it came to pass that this William held a great feast. Among the guests an argument began about the earl, during which the said Robert castigated the earl immoderately and alleged all sorts of wicked things. But the master of the house, namely William, said, 'Do not denigrate the earl.' At that, the said Robert lost the power of speech and could move neither hand nor foot but sat as if he were dead. But eventually, through the prayers of his fellow-guests, he began to breathe a little. On William's advice he promised that he would never say anything against the earl in future, and in so doing he escaped from danger.
[*In the margin*] Heed the miracle.

116 The same William told of a clerk called William of †Hylamtre†. He had had a blood disease, but after being measured and a penny having been bent, he recovered. William and many others are the witnesses to this matter.

---

[158] Probably the widow of Robert of Gatton. Alice Malherbe was lady of the manor of Boughton Malherbe (Kent) at some time before 1243: T. Willement, *Historical Sketch of the Parish of Davington in the County of Kent* (London, 1862), p. 61. By 1243, however, Boughton Malherbe and Wormshill (also in Kent) were being held by Robert of Gatton (*Bk of Fees* 1, pt 2, pp. 665, 677), whom she had probably married. Robert died in 1264 (*Cal. Inq. p.m.* 1236–72, p. 182) and Alice of Gatton was holding Wormshill manor in 1275 (ibid. 1272–91, p. 108).

[159] Possibly Chadley, in Wellesbourne (Warwickshire). One of the leading Montfortians, Piers de Montfort (*ODNB*, s.n.), held the manor of Wellesbourne Mountford in the same parish; he was killed at Evesham (*VCH Warws.* 5, p. 194).

[160] In the late thirteenth century William (fl.1275–92) was a taxpayer at Brians Bell, in Belbroughton: *Worcs. Subsidy*, p. 11; *VCH Worcs.* 3, pp. 16–17. His surname refers to the present Hurst Farm: *PN Worcs.* p. 277.

117 Iohannes Benedist de Tortynton de Suþsex habens filium mutum et claudum longo tempore. Mensuratus ad comitem media nocte clamauit ad matrem, 'Perduc me ad ecclesiam de Evesham.' Illa [fol. 174r] turbata ait, 'Potes loqui!' At ille, 'Sic, quia astitit michi senex dicens, "Quia habes nomen meum sanaberis."' De hoc perhibet testimonium domina Hawysa de Nevile et domina Iohanna de la Mare nobiles mulieres.

118 Sthephanus de Holle et Nicolaus de Hulle, Iohannes Godde, Walter Sypard, ciues Herefordie narrauerunt quoddam mirabile de Philippo capellano de Brenteles qui uituperauit comitem. Inter uerba conuiciosa ait, 'Si Symon comes est sanctus ut dicitur, uolo ut diabolus frangat collum meum uel aliquid miraculum antequam domum ueniam.' Et sicut petiit ita contigit, nam in redeundo uersus domum casu obuiam habens leporem et in saltum post eum de caballo cecidit. Seruiens illius pro conuiciis <areptus>[a] a demonio more Walencium clamauit, 'Ob-Ob!' Insanuit iste, apprehensus et ligatus, et sic permansit in uinculis a festo sancti Iohannis Baptiste usque ad translationem sancti Benedicti. De hoc perhibet testimonium tota ciuitas Herefordie.

119 Dominus Heliseus decanus de Werynton priuatus uisu per tres annos mensuratus ad comitem conualuit. De hoc perhibent testimonium omnes conuersantes inter Ribbel et Merse, hoc est inter illas duas aquas.

120 Memorandum de ceco apud Norhampton qui unum oculum recuparauit. De hoc perhibet testimonium clericus domini episcopi Lincolniensis.

---

[a] areptis *MS*.

117 John Benedist from Tortington in Sussex had a son who had been dumb and lame for a long time. But after being measured to the earl, in the middle of the night he called out to his mother, 'Take me to the church of Evesham.' Thrilled, she said, 'You can speak!' And he said, 'Yes, because an old man was standing beside me and said, "Because you have my name you shall be cured."' The noble ladies Dame Hawis de Neville[161] and Dame Joan de la Mare[162] bear witness to this.[163]

118 Stephen Hill and Nicholas Hill, John Godde and Walter Syward, citizens of Hereford, told of a miracle concerning Philip the chaplain from Bronllys[164] who had castigated the earl. Among his insulting words he had said, 'If Earl Simon is a saint as they say, I wish the Devil to break my neck, or for any other miracle, before I get home.' And as he asked, so it happened, for in returning towards home he came by chance upon a hare and in leaping after it he fell from his horse. In return for the insults his servant was seized by an evil spirit and shouted like a Welshman, 'Ob-Ob!'[165] He went insane, was arrested and bound, and remained in chains like that from the feast of St John the Baptist[166] until the translation of St Benedict.[167] The whole city of Hereford bears witness to this.[168]

119 Sir Ellis the dean of Warrington[169] had been without his eyesight for three years but after being measured to the earl he recovered. All the people who live between those two rivers, the Ribble and the Mersey, bear witness to this.

120 A memorandum about a blind man at Northampton who recovered his sight in one eye. A clerk of the bishop of Lincoln[170] bears witness to this.[171]

---

[161] Hawis de Courtenay (d.1269) had married John de Neville (d.1246) and afterwards John of Gaddesden (d.1262); her sons Hugh de Neville (d.1269) and John de Neville (d.1282) were both rebel Montfortians: *Complete Peerage* 9, pp. 481–4.
[162] Joan was Hawis's daughter by John de Neville. She was the widow of Henry de la Mare who died c.1256; she had afterwards married Walter de la Hyde: M. S. Giuseppi, 'On the testament of Sir Hugh de Nevill, written at Acre, 1267', *Archaeologia* 56 (1899), pp. 351–70 (at pp. 357–61); *Complete Peerage* 9, pp. 482–3; *Cal. Pat.* 1247–58, p. 478; *VCH Surr.* 3, p. 248.
[163] This seems to be a version of **179**.
[164] Bronllys (Breconshire) was held from 1263 by Maud Longespee (née Clifford); she married c.1271 John Giffard who fought against Simon de Montfort at Evesham: *English Baronies*, p. 36; *Complete Peerage* 5, pp. 639–44; *ODNB*, s.n. 'Giffard, John, first Lord Giffard'. Bronllys is three miles from Pipton where Simon de Montfort made a treaty with Llywelyn ap Gruffudd prince of Wales in 1265.
[165] 'Oh! Oh!' in English: *Geiriadur Prifysgol Cymru: A Dictionary of the Welsh Language* (Cardiff, 1964–in progress, and at the 'GPC Online' website), s.v. 'ob-ob'.
[166] 24 June.
[167] 11 July.
[168] See **28**n.
[169] Dean by 1250: W. Beamont, *Warrington Church Notes: The Parish Church of St Elfin, Warrington, and the Other Churches of the Parish* (Warrington, 1878), p. 27. See **41**n.
[170] Probably Richard of Gravesend 1258–79, a prominent Montfortian: *ODNB*, s.n.
[171] Northampton supported the Montfortians in the civil war: see **35**n.

121 Willelmus de †Braddewell† habens quandam infirmitatem ignotam per annum, mensuratus ad comitem continuo conualuit. De hoc perhibet testimonium tota uillata de †Braddewell†.

122 Reginaldus Rigon Oxonie recuparauit uisum per merita comitis in oculo sinistro die mercurii proxima ante festum decollationis sancti Iohannis Baptiste anno gracie millesimo CC°lxv^{to}. De hoc perhibent testimonium prior Sancte Freþewþe Oxonie, Willelmus de Crofta, Robertus de Stratforde.

123 Puer quidam de Glousestria filius [*name omitted*] per septem annos pedibus et manibus contractus, et ad comitem mensuratus conualuit anno gracie [fol. 174v] predicto circa Assumptionem Beate Marie Virginis. De hoc perhibet testimonium Robertus de †Aldewik† tunc temporis prior Sancti Petri Gloucestrie.

124 Quedam sanctimonialis de Acornebury diligebat multum comitem Symonem. Que nimio dolore constricta pro eo quod audierat dictum comitem adeo enormiter detrunccatum, unde blasphemare Deum et sanctos multipliciter cepit, asserendo ipsum esse iniustum eo quod proderet iustos et innocentes malos autem et preuaricatores saluaret. Vnde propter dolores et angustias quas patiebatur innumeras non potuit recipere consolationem. Set amens efficiebatur ita quod uinculis constringebatur tanquam amens effecta. Postea aliquantulum sedata et sui compos effecta sequebatur conuentum. Set utrum aliquid de Deo diceret uel non ignorabatur. Tandem exclamauit dicens se habere capud comitis in gremio suo quod sibi arridebat et applaudebat. At illa monialibus astantibus ostendit oculos et nasum et nares et os eius quod et osculabatur circumquaque et in hoc recepit sensum quem amiserat.

125 Checheley de †Romesey† grauedinem capitis per dimidium annum et amplius sustinuit. Que ueniens ad tumulum comitis Simonis mensurauit se et statim conualuit.

THE EVESHAM ABBEY MIRACLE BOOK

121 William from †Braddewell†[172] had had an unnamed illness for a year but after being measured to the earl he recovered immediately. The whole township of †Braddewell† bears witness to this.

122 Reynold Rigon from Oxford recovered the sight of his left eye through the merits of the earl on the Wednesday before the feast of the decollation of St John the Baptist[173] in the year of grace 1265.[174] The prior of St Frideswide's at Oxford[175] and William of Croft and Robert of Stratford bear witness to this.

123 A boy from Gloucester, son of [*name omitted*], had been crippled for seven years in his feet and hands but after being measured to the earl he recovered in the same year of grace around the Assumption of the Blessed Virgin Mary.[176] Robert of †Aldewik†, at that time prior of St Peter's, Gloucester, bears witness to this.[177]

124 A nun of Aconbury greatly loved Earl Simon and had been afflicted with intense sorrow for the earl on hearing that he had been so grievously mutilated. As a result she had begun to blaspheme repeatedly against God and his saints, asserting that he was unjust because he had betrayed the just and innocent and had saved the wicked and the transgressors. And thus, on account of the innumerable sorrows and miseries that she was suffering she had been unable to find any solace. But an improvement was brought about in that she was bound in chains until improvement had been made. Afterwards she became a little more calm and composed and more obedient to the convent. But it was unknown whether or not she would be saying things about God. Eventually she exclaimed that she had the earl's head in her embrace and that it was smiling at her and praising her. And to the nuns who were present she showed his eyes and nose and nostrils, and his mouth which she was kissing all over, and in doing so she got back the sanity she had lost.

125 Cecily of †Romesey†[178] had suffered for half a year and more from a heaviness in her head, but on coming to the tomb of Earl Simon she measured herself and recovered immediately.

---

[172] Possibly Broadwell (Gloucestershire), an estate of Evesham abbey.
[173] 29 August.
[174] If the year is correctly copied the event would have occurred less than four weeks after the battle of Evesham.
[175] Robert of Olney 1260–78.
[176] 15 August.
[177] The burgesses of Gloucester had supported Simon de Montfort before the battle of Evesham and had been heavily fined: Carpenter, *Henry III 1258–72*, p. 383.
[178] The surname may refer to Romsey (Hampshire).

126 Memorandum de quodam puero de Gloucestrie mortuo. Qui postquam classica que pulsantur pro mortuis in parochia sancti Audoeni fuissent †deportata† et pulsata notale pro dicto puero mortuo dictum fuit matri eiusdem ut mensuraret puerum ad comitem Symonem. Quod cum mater fecisset surrexit a mortuis qui adhuc uiuit. De hoc perhibent testimonium pater et mater pueri et plures alii qui interfuerunt et predicta uiderunt.

127 Willelmus de Uffenham capellanus filius Willelmi Margerie dum esset in loco quodam et transitum faciens super equum suum casu cecidit de equo et lesionem unius pedis habuit ita quod pedem mouere non potuit per duas septimanas. Vnde cum audisset a quibusdam uicinis de miraculis que Deus operatus est apud Evesham per merita comitis Simonis plicauit unum denarium [fol. 175r] soluendum pro sanitate recuparanda. Statim sanitatem recepit in pede et nichil sensit de aliqua molestia quam prius habuit. Huius rei testis est qui scripta retulit iuratus.

128 Quidam frater Minor de conuentu Herefordensi febrium molestia grauatus per mensem et amplius, ad dictum comitem mensuratus statim conualuit. De hoc perhibent testimonium fratres Minores qui interfuerunt et predicta uiderunt iurati.

129 Robertus de <Darlingestok>[a] guttam habuit per dimidium annum et amplius. Qui mensuratus ad sanctum Robertum et ad alios sanctos non sensiens conualescenciam, postquam audiuit comitem Symonem bello mortuum censuit ipsum martirem. Vnde supplicauit Deo ut per merita dicti martiris eidem subueniret et statim liberatus fuit a dicta gutta. Idem de ipso testimonium perhibet.

130 Quidam [*word omitted*] apud Hawekesbury mutus et contractus per septem annos mensuratus ad comitem statim conualuit in omnibus que patiebatur. De hoc testimonium perhibet abbas de Persore et plures alii.

---

[a] Carlingestok *MS*.

126 A memorandum about a dead boy from Gloucester. After the bells that are rung for the dead in the parish of St Owen had been †brought out† and rung to announce the boy's death, his mother was told that she ought to measure him to Earl Simon. When she did that, he rose from the dead and he is living still. The boy's father and mother, and many others who were present and saw those events, bear witness to this.[179]

127 William the chaplain from Offenham,[180] son of William Margary,[181] had been passing through some place on horseback and had accidentally fallen off his horse and injured one of his feet so that he was unable to move it for two weeks. But when he heard from some neighbours about the miracles worked by God at Evesham through the merits of Earl Simon, he bent a penny to purchase from God the recovery of his good health. He immediately got back the good condition of his foot and did not feel any of the discomfort that he had previously had. He is the witness to this, having delivered a written account on oath.

128 A Franciscan friar of the Hereford convent had been troubled by distressing fevers for a month and more but after being measured to the earl he recovered immediately. The Franciscan friars who were present and saw these things bear witness to this on oath.

129 Robert of Darlingscott had had a gout for half a year and more and had not felt any improvement in health after being measured to St Robert[182] and to other saints. But after he had heard about Earl Simon's death in battle, he considered him a martyr. And so he begged God to bring him relief through the merits of this martyr and he was immediately freed from the gout. He himself bears witness to this.

130 A [*word omitted*] at Hawkesbury[183] had been dumb and crippled for seven years but after being measured to the earl he recovered from everything that he had been suffering from. The abbot of Pershore[184] bears witness to this as do many others.

---

[179] The burgesses of Gloucester had supported Simon de Montfort before the battle of Evesham and had been heavily fined: Carpenter, *Henry III 1258–72*, p. 383.
[180] Offenham was an estate of Evesham abbey.
[181] William Margary of Offenham was dead by 1275 when his son Richard was chaplain there: *The Worcester Eyre of 1275*, ed. J. Röhrkasten (WHS, new ser. 22, 2008), pp. 23–4, 41–2.
[182] Possibly Robert Grosseteste (cf. **17**) or Robert of Knaresborough (cf. **196**).
[183] An estate of Pershore abbey: *VCH Worcs.* 2, p. 129.
[184] Probably Henry of 'Bideford' 1264–c.1274.

131 Osbertus Giffard febribus diu fatigatus sompniauit quod comes Symon apparuit sibi dicens ei quod aciperet 'le gambilem quod habuistis de me in bello et ponatis super uos et sanabitis'. Euigilans dixit ministris suis ut inuestigarent de armaturis que iacebant ad pedes lecti sui. Qui inuestigantes inuenerunt le gambilem posueruntque super eum et sic sanus factus est. De hoc perhibet abbas de Evesham qui prescripta audiuit de ore eius qui curatus fuit.

132 Ricardus de parochia de Inteberg filius Iohannis <Fillot>[a] contractus a natiuitate qui gambas et pedes habuit per quinquennium bifurcatas nullo modo ualens incedere, per Aliciam matrem suam ad comitem Symonem mensuratus et in reda quadam Eueshamiam adductus sero in uigilia Sancte Crucis anno gracie M°CC°lxv°, cum mater ipsius predicta cum puero ad sepulcrum comitis Simonis usque ad mediam noctem in uigiliis et orationibus perseuerasset dictus puer meritis martiris surrexit et in omnibus membris suis sanus factus est [fol. 175v] ita quod ad uoluntatem suam incessum habuit. Huius rei testes sunt mater pueri, <et Nicolaus Grate, Iohannes Herteber et Sara uxor illius>,[b] et tota uillata Inteberg.

133 Rosa Tholus passionem quandam sustinuit in capite cuius omnia organa sensuum doloribus contringebantur tantum quod dubitabat sensu priuari. Cuius oculus habuit tumorem et grossidiorem ad mensuram oui. Mensurata ad comitem statim conualuit.

134 Alicia uxor Nicolai Grate de Inteberg per dimidium annum et amplius in gambis pedibus et tibiis tantam sensit debilitatem et molestiam quod predicta membra mouere non potuit. Que ad comitem Simonem mensurata et in reda quadam apud Evesham aduecta et usque fere mediam noctem uigiliis et orationibus insistens tantam de infirmitate sensit alleuationem quod baculo sustentata potuit incedere. Testes huius rei sunt qui scribuntur in curatione Iohannis consequente.

---

[a] Fillot] fili et MS.
[b] et Nicolaus Grate, Iohannes Herteber et Sara uxor illius] et Sara uxor et Nicolaus Grate et Sara uxor illius Iohannes Herteber MS.

131 Osbert Giffard,[185] who had long been wearied by fevers, dreamt that Earl Simon appeared to him, telling him to take up 'the gambeson[186] that you had off me in the battle of Evesham; put it on yourself and you shall be healed'. On waking he told his servants to search through the armour that lay at the foot of his bed. On making a search they found the gambeson and put it on him and thus was he healed. The abbot of Evesham[187] bears witness to this, having heard these things from the mouth of the one who was cured.

132 Richard from the parish of Inkberrow,[188] son of John Fillot,[189] had been crippled since birth and his legs had been bent outwards for five years so that he was in no way fit to walk. But after being measured to Earl Simon by his mother Alice he was brought to Evesham on a cart late on the eve[190] of the Holy Cross in the year of grace 1265. After his mother had stayed with the boy watching and praying at the grave of Earl Simon until the middle of the night, the boy stood up through the merits of the martyr and was made so well in all his limbs that he could walk easily. The witnesses to this matter are the boy's mother and Nicholas Grate, John Hartlebury and Sarah his wife and the whole township of Inkberrow.

133 Rose Tholus[191] had suffered from an illness in her head. All her mental faculties had been afflicted by the pains, so much so that she thought she would lose her mind, and her eye had a swelling that had enlarged it to the size of an egg. But after being measured to the earl she recovered immediately.

134 Alice, wife of Nicholas Grate of Inkberrow, had experienced weakness and discomfort in her thighs, feet and lower legs for half a year and more, so that she was unable to move those limbs. But after being measured to Earl Simon and being conveyed to Evesham on a cart, and after staying up nearly half the night watching and praying, she felt so much relief from her infirmity that she could walk with the aid of a stick. The witnesses are those whose names are recorded in relation to the following cure of John.

---

[185] Osbert Giffard (b.1237, fl.1304) had fought for Simon de Montfort at Lewes but against him at Evesham: *Complete Peerage* 5, pp. 649–53.
[186] A padded jacket or tunic usually worn under chain mail.
[187] William of Whitchurch 1266–82.
[188] Inkberrow manor had been forfeited by William de Munchensi (*VCH Worcs.* 3, p. 421) a rebel Montfortian (*Complete Peerage* 9, pp. 422–4; *ODNB*, s.n.).
[189] A Christine Fillote was a taxpayer at nearby Feckenham in the late thirteenth century: *Worcs. Subsidy*, p. 20.
[190] 13 September.
[191] A Godfrey Tolas was a taxpayer at Hanbury (adjacent to Feckenham and Inkberrow) in the late thirteenth century: *Worcs. Subsidy*, p. 33.

135 Iohannes de Fekham filius Thome Adelard per duos annos et dimidium gambis et tibiis contractus et apud Evesham in reda adductus qui sine duorum baculorum adiutorio per dictum tempus incedere non potuit meritis et adiutorio martiris nostri conualuit ita quod baculos abiectis omnino sanus abcessit. Idem de seipso testimonium perhibet una cum uillata de Fekham et specialiter hii Ricardus Hunte, Ricardus de †Odebury†, Hugo Hunte, Ricardus Chyldessonne, Adam clericus de †Odebury†. Prescripta autem quatuor miracula uidimus et personas singulorum.

136 Adam de Habelench capellanus habuit neruos suos in poplite contractos ita quod per sex septimanas incedere non potuit. Qui monitionem in sompnis accepit ut tumulum comitis Symonis uisitaret. Qui uisioni predicte paruit sanusque factus est. Idem apud Evesham ueniens testimonium perhibuit de seipso.

137 Henricus de †Lesseberge† habens dissinteriam per duos annos, mensuratus ad comitem conualuit. Hinc perhibent testimonium [fol. 176r] uicini illius una cum illo capellano de Bench qui mensurauit illum.

138 Rogerus de †Peytun† comitatu Lincolniensis habens guttam in capite immo pungitiuam mensuratus ad comitem Symonem conualuit. Ipsemet perhibet testimonium de seipso.

139 Rogerus decanus de Werinton tanta infirmitate in genu dextro detentus die dominica proxima ante Natiuitatem Domini anni presentis quod a loco ubi sedebat mouere non potuit nec sustinere quod aliquis manum adiutricem apponeret nec unguentum nec emplaustrum, tandem ad memoriam passionem reduxit comitis Symonis statimque conualuit ita quod die Natali Domini diuina sine impedimento officia expleuit nec hucusque in aliqua parte infirmitatis signum sentiuit. De hoc

135 John from Feckenham, son of Thomas Adelard, had been crippled for two and a half years in his thighs and lower legs and was brought to Evesham on a cart. He had been unable to walk for that period of time except with two sticks, but he recovered through the merits and assistance of our martyr so that he threw down the sticks and walked away completely well. He bears witness to this himself together with the township of Feckenham and especially Richard Hunte,[192] Richard of †Odebury†,[193] Hugh Hunte,[194] Richard Chyldessonne, and Adam the clerk from †Odebury†. Indeed we ourselves saw the above four miracles and the persons involved in each.

136 Adam the chaplain from Ab Lench[195] had had the sinews of his knees so crippled that he had been unable to walk for six weeks. In a dream he received instruction that he should visit the tomb of Earl Simon. He obeyed the vision and was made well. On coming to Evesham he bore witness for himself.[196]

137 Henry of †Lesseberge†[197] had had dysentery for two years but after being measured to the earl he recovered. Hence his neighbours bear witness to this together with the chaplain of Bengeworth[198] who measured him.

138 Roger of †Peytun† from Lincolnshire had an extremely painful gout in his head but after being measured to Earl Simon he recovered. He bears witness for himself.

139 Roger the dean of Warrington[199] was taken with such an infirmity in his right knee, the Sunday before Christmas[200] in the present year, that he could not move from where he was sitting or bear anyone to put a helping hand on the knee or an ointment or a poultice. But eventually he reflected upon the suffering of Earl Simon and immediately recovered so that on Christmas Day he performed the divine offices without difficulty. Nor has he felt any symptom of the infirmity to

---

[192] In the 1240s a Richard Hunte was accused of unlawfully building a house in Feckenham forest: *Records of Feckenham Forest, Worcestershire, c.1236–1377*, ed. J. Birrell (WHS, new ser. 21, 2006), pp. 13, 23.
[193] A taxpayer at Feckenham in the late thirteenth century: *Worcs. Subsidy*, p. 20.
[194] The surnames of Richard and Hugh Hunte may refer to Hunt End in the same parish: *PN Worcs.* p. 319.
[195] Ab Lench was an estate of Evesham abbey.
[196] This event may be dated before April 1269 when one Robert was instituted to the chaplaincy of Ab Lench: *Reg. Giffard* 1, p. 7.
[197] *Recte* Wasseburne?: see *PN Worcs.* p. 176. The family of Washbourne was prominent at Bengeworth by the sixteenth century: E. A. B. Barnard, *Some Notes on the Evesham Branch of the Washbourne Family* (Evesham, 1914).
[198] An estate of Evesham abbey.
[199] See **41n**.
[200] 25 December.

perhibet testimonium Ricardus dictus heremita qui candelam suam detulit apud Evesham.

140 Robertus capellanus et uicarius de Evesham habens spasmum in gambis et tibiis longo tempore mensuratus ad comitem Symonem statim conualuit, hiis presentibus domino abbate de Evesham, Fratre Willelmo de Hekelingos librario monasterii tunc confessor illius Roberti, et toto conuentu.

141 Item idem Robertus recitauit de quodam monacho Bruerie paralitico per septem annos. Iste monachus uidit in sompnis Iohannem abbatem suum iam defunctum una cum milite quodam circuente infirmariam. Et cum ad lectum uenissent infirmi dixit abbati miles, 'Quis est iste?' At abbas, 'Nobilis psalmicinos fuit.' Miles accessit ad eum et tetigens dicens, 'Surge in nomine Iesu et fac officium tuum.' Et statim surrexit sanus laudens Deum et comitem Symonem. De hoc perhibet testimonium totus conuentus Bruerie cum abbate.

142 Ricardus Hercy emit pullum equi ad nundinas de [fol. 176v] Scotia. Pullus indomitus ad nauem adductus et ligatus et pre sonitu maris ita perteritus coram nautis et ceteris aspicientibus cecidit mortuus. Consilio facto ad comitem Symonem mensuratus cum tribus denariis et super eum plicatis breui interuallo surrexit sanus et tandem cum oblatione apud Evesham adductus. De hoc perhibet testimonium una cum naui commorantibus.

143 Iohannes de Blanchewelle Lincolnie habens quandam infirmitatem et iacuit contra lectum per sex septimanas non manducans et uix bibens. Mensuratus ad comitem Symonem statim conualuit. Huius rei testes Thomas de Blanchewelle et Symon Luwerk.

144 Willelmus de †Lewerk† de uilla que uocatur †Shendeworthe† in comitatu de <Herteforde>[a] priuatus uisu per nouem septimanas, mensuratus ad comitem

---

[a] Hereforde *MS*.

this day. Richard, surnamed Armitt,[201] who brought his candle to Evesham, bears witness to this.

140 Robert the chaplain and vicar of Evesham had had a cramp in his thighs and lower legs for a long time but after being measured to the earl he recovered immediately in the presence of the abbot of Evesham,[202] the librarian of the monastery Brother William of Atch Lench (Robert's confessor at the time) and the whole convent.

141 Also the same Robert told of a monk of Bruern who had been paralysed for seven years. In his dreams this monk saw John his abbot, now deceased,[203] walking round the infirmary with a knight. And when they came to the patient's bed the knight said to the abbot, 'Who is this?' And the abbot said, 'He was an excellent psalm-singer.' The knight went up to him, touched him and said, 'Arise in the name of Jesus and perform your office,' and he immediately got up, cured and praising the Lord and Earl Simon. The whole convent of Bruern bears witness to this together with the abbot.

142 Richard Hercy had bought a colt at a fair in Scotland. When the untamed colt was taken to a ship and tethered, it was so greatly terrified by the sound of the sea that it fell dead in front of the sailors and other onlookers. But some advice was taken and in a short while the colt, after being measured to Earl Simon and after three pennies had been bent over it, got up restored. And later on it was taken to Evesham with an offering. He bears witness to this together with people who had been on the ship.

143 John of Brauncewell from Lincoln[204] had some kind of illness and had lain on his bed for six weeks, not eating and scarcely drinking, but after being measured to Earl Simon he recovered immediately. Thomas of Brauncewell and Simon Luwerk are the witnesses to this matter.

144 William of †Lewerk† from the township called †Shendeworthe† in the county of Hertford had been without sight for nine weeks but after being measured to the

---

[201] Possibly from the house of Austin (or Hermit) friars at Warrington, on which see D. Knowles and R. N. Hadcock, *Medieval Religious Houses: England and Wales*, 2nd edn (London, 1971), p. 244.
[202] William of Whitchurch 1266–82.
[203] He died between August 1265 and January 1274 (*Heads* 2, p. 266).
[204] In 1267 the citizens of Lincoln had recently been fined for their support of the Montfortian cause: *Cal. Pat.* 1266–72, pp. 28, 34, 152.

Symonem statim lumen recepit. Huius rei testes domina Matildis de Childresley et Margeria filia eius et Nicolaus de Childesley.

145 Frater Laurencius Cornubiensis ordinis fratrum Minorum contra festiuitatem Beate Virginis a discretis phisicis in annua febre adiudicatus, in passione sua predicta comitis merita ad memoriam reducens statim de infirmitate conualuit. Testis frater fuit Nicolaus de †Gulac†.

146 Frater Nicolaus de †Gulak† de eodem ordine habens calculum et grauissimum dolorem sentiens ita ut suus cyrurgicus eum incidere proposuisset et idem frater de salute et uita desperatus nullatenus incidi permisisset. Conuertit tandem se ad Dominum ut meritis sui martiris Symonis comitis eum curare dignaretur. Mira res! In crastino circa horam tertiam cum surrexisset a lecto ut commederet[a] cecidit calculus ad pedes eius nullo dolore precedente aut sequente plene curatus die martis in septimana Pasche anno gracie M°CC°lxix°. De hoc perhibet testimonium totus conuentus Oxonie.

147 [fol. 177r] Willelmus de la Rye miles in Norhamtonshire habens acutam febrem mensuratus ad comitem et sequente nocte prorsus conualuit.

148 Matildis Sherlonde frenetica per duos dies et ligata, mensurata ad comitem Simonem omnino conualuit.

149 Walter le Forde piscator de Fisherestrete Londonia commorans <sinistre>[b] habens duos lucios quorum unus mortuus per totam noctem, hic concilio plicato denario ad comitem Symonem crastino inuenit illum uiuum et cum cauda in panerio ludentem. Testes huius rei omnes conuicanei loci illius.

150 Quidam sacerdos de Welles nomine Benedictus aliquo tempore comiti contrarius cum quadam die celebraret diuina in celebratione misse uisu parumper

---

[a] ut comederet] *Halliwell emends this to* ut commingeret *(in order to urinate): Miracles, p. 96.*
[b] sinistre] s. in uistre MS.

earl he immediately had his eyesight back. The witnesses to this matter are Dame Maud of Childerley and Margery her daughter and Nicholas of Childerley.[205]

145 Friar Lawrence Cornish of the Franciscan order was judged by expert physicians to have an annual fever, just before the feast of the Blessed Virgin.[206] While suffering from it he reflected upon the merits of the earl and recovered from his illness immediately. The friar who witnessed this was Nicholas of †Gulac†.

146 Friar Nicholas of †Gulak† of the same order had a stone and was experiencing such very severe pain that his surgeon proposed to cut him open. The friar, fearing for his safety and his life, would on no account allow himself to be cut open. But eventually he turned for help to the Lord, that he would allow him to be cured through the merits of his martyr Earl Simon. What a marvellous thing! On the morrow about the third hour on the Tuesday[207] in Easter week in the year of grace 1269 he rose from his bed to eat and the stone fell at his feet quite harmlessly and without pain either before or after. The entire Oxford convent bears witness to this.[208]

147 William of Rye a knight from Northamptonshire had an acute fever but after being measured to the earl he recovered completely the following night.[209]

148 Maud Sherlonde had been raving for two days and had been tied up but after being measured to Earl Simon she recovered completely.

149 Walter le Forde a fisherman from Fisher Street, a resident of London, had two pike but unfortunately one of them lay dead all night. He took some advice, however, and a penny was bent to Earl Simon; and on the morrow he found it alive and flipping its tail in the basket. The witnesses to this matter are all the neighbours in that locality.

150 A priest from Wells[210] called Bennet had once been opposed to the earl. One day when performing divine service he lost some of his eyesight while celebrating

---

[205] Perhaps relatives of Henry of Childerley, lord in 1274 of Little Childerley (Cambridgeshire), where a Nicholas of Childerley was one of his tenants: *Rot. Hund.* 2, p. 408. Henry had been an armed Montfortian: *Cal. Pat.* 1266–72, p. 61.
[206] 25 March.
[207] 26 March.
[208] Adam Marsh (d.1259), eminent Franciscan theologian at Oxford, had been one of Simon de Montfort's mentors: *ODNB*, s.n.
[209] This seems to be a version of 153.
[210] Possibly Wells (Somerset) because the county is not specified.

amisit. Post celebrationem uero uisum penitus amisit et loquelam. Mensuratus ad comitem Symonem statim uisum et loquelam manifeste recuparauit. Huius rei tota parochia perhibet testimonium.

151 Iohannes de Herlow de Norþhamburland habens in memoria comitem Simonem in mente ante diem ireticum conualuit ita ut die lune sequenti equitauit sex miliaria. De hoc perhibent testimonium omnes consedales de Norþhamburlande.

152 Matildis Farun de Neubery iuxta Ungerford habens guttam ita pungitiuam unde adiudicata est a uicinis suis mortua, mensurata ad comitem Symonem statim conualuit. De hoc perhibent testimonium omnes uicini eius de Neubury.

153 Willelmus de la Rye iuxta Norþhampton habens acutam [febrem] mensuratus ad comitem Symonem conualuit. Vnde perhibent testimonium omnes conuicanei sui.

154 Willelmus de Pikeringes Cantuarie puerum infirmatum habuit usque ad mortem. Mensuratus ad comitem Symonem conualuit. Et in signum sanitatis detulit puerum apud Evesham de cera. De hoc perhibet testimonium tota parochia sancti Andree Cantuarie.

155 [fol. 177v] Idem Willelmus de Pikeringes eiusdem uille habens puerum unum genu sinistrum ita inflatum quod uix articuli pedis apparerent, mensuratus ad comitem Symonem statim tota inflatio euanuit. In signum sanitatis detulit alium puerum de cera. Testes ut supra.

156 Emma de Dene paralisi percussa per quatuor dies, ista mensurata est ad diuersa loca sanctorum. Tandem mensurata ad comitem Simonem conualuit ita ut

mass. When the celebration was over he lost his eyesight completely, and his speech, but after being measured to Earl Simon he recovered all of his sight and speech immediately. The whole parish bears witness to this matter.

151   John of Harlow[211] from Northumberland reflected upon Earl Simon before his brain fever reached its crisis, and he recovered so well that on the following Monday he rode six miles. All his associates in Northumberland bear witness to this.[212]

152   Maud Farou[213] from Newbury near Hungerford[214] had so painful a gout that she was judged by her neighbours to be dead, but after being measured to Earl Simon she recovered immediately. All her neighbours in Newbury bear witness to this.

153   William of Rye from near Northampton had an acute [fever] but after being measured to Earl Simon he recovered. All his neighbours bear witness to this.[215]

154   William of Pickering from Canterbury had a young son who was ill to the point of death but after being measured to Earl Simon he recovered. And in token of the cure William brought a waxen boy to Evesham. The whole parish of St Andrew at Canterbury bears witness to this.

155   This William of Pickering from Canterbury had a young son whose left knee was so swollen that his toes could hardly be seen but after he had been measured to Earl Simon all the swelling disappeared immediately. In token of the cure William brought a second waxen boy. The witnesses are those above.

156   Emm of Dene[216] had been stricken with paralysis for four days and had been measured at various saints' resting-places. Eventually, after being measured to Earl Simon, she recovered to the extent of being able to cross herself but she did

---

[211] In 1267 John was complicit with Gilbert de Umfraville in a raid on the manor of Fawdon: *Northumb. Pleas*, pp. 270–2. Umfraville, the lord of Harlow, had been a Montfortian: *Complete Peerage* 1, pp. 147–8. John died c.1276: TNA, CP 40/14, m. 6; E 372/119.
[212] Cf. **199**.
[213] The surname occurs frequently in medieval Newbury: W. Money, *History of the Ancient Town and Borough of Newbury, in the County of Berks.* (Oxford and London, 1887), pp. 116, 126, 144–6, 181–2.
[214] The manor and borough of Newbury were held by Simon de Montfort in right of his wife: Maddicott, *Simon de Montfort*, p. 50.
[215] This seems to be a version of **147**.
[216] Perhaps related to Richard of Dene (fl.1253–79) lord of the manor of Dene, in Wingham (Kent). See A. Hussey, *Chronicles of Wingham* (Canterbury, 1896), pp. 72, 75.

habuit potestatem se imprimere signo Sancte Crucis. Set non multum superuixit. De hoc perhibet testimonium Ricardus uicarius de Wingeham cum tota parochia.

157 Christiana de Lullingeston habens guttam pungitiuam a scapula usque ad manum, a manu usque ad plantam pedis longo tempore, ista mensurata ad comitem Simonem conualuit. Testes ut supra de parochia sancti Andree Cantuarie.

158 Walter de †Lydeham† in comitatu Oxonie habens policem contractum per octo dies, lauatis manibus ad fontem comitis Simonis conualuit. Vnde qui affuerunt cum eo in presencia nostra testimonium perhibent.

159 Guido de Pynele iuxta Warrewyk inutilis et paralisi per decem annos, mensuratus ad comitem Symonem conualuit. De hoc perhibet testimonium tota parochia sancti Laurencii de Rorynton.[a]

160 Henricus Bounde habens in dextro brachio infirmitatem ignotam per tres annos et dimidium annum et amplius, et hic cito post mortem comitis ipsum brachium ad dictum comitem Symonem mensurauit et infra tempus trium horarum diei plene conualuit. Idem habens aliud brachium inutile cum ceteris infirmitatibus per dimidium annum et amplius unde cum a peritis medicis iudicaretur pro paralitico, a quibusdam pro ydropico, a quibusdam pro leproso tum propter scabiem et tumorem cutis quam habebat, hic iterum mensuratus per merita comitis conualuit. De hoc perhibet testimonium dominus Iohannes filius Iohanni cum domina comitissa de Aubomarle cum tota familia sua.

161 Robertus de Gamages de Netrewent habens filium quinque annorum, puer iste ex quadam infirmitate ab omnibus uicinis mortuus est adiudicatus. Concilio facto ad comitem Simonem mensuratus et denario plicato statim respirauit et conualuit. De hoc perhibet testimonium tota patria de Netrewent.

---

[a] *In the MS this entry runs on from* **158** *without the usual line-break or display initial.*

not survive for long. Richard the vicar of Wingham bears witness to this together with the whole parish.

157 Christian of Lullingstone had had a painful gout for a long time from her shoulder to her hand and from her hand to the sole of her foot but after being measured to Earl Simon she recovered. The witnesses, as above,[217] are from the parish of St Andrew at Canterbury.

158 Walter from †Lydeham† in Oxfordshire had had a crippled thumb for eight days but by washing his hands at Earl Simon's well he recovered. Those who were with him have borne witness to this in our presence.

159 Guy from Pinley[218] near Warwick had been disabled with paralysis for ten years but after being measured to Earl Simon he recovered. The whole parish of St Lawrence at Rowington bears witness to this.

160 Henry Bounde had had an unnamed infirmity in his right arm for three and a half years and more, but soon after the earl's death he measured the arm to Earl Simon and within the space of three hours he recovered fully. This man's other arm was disabled with other infirmities for half a year and more. Thus, when he was judged by learned physicians to be paralytic, and by some to be dropsical, and by some to be leprous because of the roughness and swelling of his skin, after being measured again he recovered through the merits of the earl. Sir John fitz John[219] bears witness to this together with the countess of Aumale[220] and her entire household.

161 Robert de Gamages from Netherwent had a five-year-old son who, on account of some illness, was judged by all the neighbours to have died. But advice was taken and, after being measured to Earl Simon and a penny having been bent, he immediately began to breathe again and he recovered. The whole district of Netherwent bears witness to this.

---

[217] In **154–5**.
[218] Part of Pinley was held by the nuns of Pinley priory: *VCH Warws*. 3, p. 151. Their patron until 1265 was Piers de Montfort. He was killed at Evesham on the side of Earl Simon and was succeeded as patron by his son Piers, a fellow-Montfortian: *VCH Warws*. 2, pp. 82–3; *ODNB*, s.n.
[219] John (d.1275) had been a prominent rebel Montfortian: *Complete Peerage* 5, pp. 433–5; *ODNB*, s.n.
[220] Isabel de Reviers (b.1237) had married William de Fors (d.1260) count of Aumale; she succeeded to the earldom of Devon in 1262 and lived until 1293; she may not have been a Montfortian sympathizer and in 1264 Simon de Montfort the younger tried unsuccessfully to gain her hand in marriage: *Complete Peerage* 4, pp. 321–3; *ODNB*, s.n.; Carpenter, *Henry III 1258–72*, pp. 394–5. In 1266 she undertook to reconcile John fitz John to the king and to produce him if he should cause further offence: *Cal. Pat.* 1258–66, p. 545.

162 [fol. 178r] Reginaldus de Geynesbury in comitatu Lincolnie habens puellam mortuam ab omnibus iudicatam, mensurata ad comitem Simonem et denario plicato statim respirauit et plene et gloriose resuscitata. De hoc perhibet testimonium tota uillata de Geynesbury.

163 Iohannes de Ardelle surdus per dimidium annum, mensuratus ad comitem Symonem et denario plicato statim auditum recepit. De hoc perhibet testimonium tota parochia sancti Dunstani Londoniarum.

164 <Prepes>[a] †cum tibiis† aucipitris cuiusdam militis per casum inflatus infirmabatur usque ad mortem. Mensuratus ad comitem Symonem statim conualuit. De hoc perhibet testimonium, etc.[b]

165 Henricus filius Henrici de la Pomere militis de Devenshire graui infirmitate detentus usque ad mortem a uicinis iudicatus, mensuratus ad comitem Symonem statim conualuit. Iterum idem Henricus postea infirmitatem fluxus patiebatur. Mensuratus autem ad comitem Simonem sine mora conualuit. Huius rei tota familia sua perhibet testimonium.

166 Walter de †Bokyngeham† aliquo tempore comiti contrarius infirmitatem habens oculorum pre graui apostemate in corpore infirmabatur ita quod nullus medicus sibi sanitatem promiserat set mortem. Hic mensuratus ad comitem Symonem ex utraque egritudine plenarie conualuit. De hoc perhibent testimonium uicini sui.

167 Quedam mulier nomine Agnes per sex septimanas omnium membrorum suorum officium et possibilitatem amiseret ita quod sine sustentamento neque ambulare neque mouere se poterat. Mensurata ad comitem Simonem statim conualuit. De hoc perhibet testimonium, etc.

---

[a] Perpes *MS*.
[b] *Between this entry and the next there are three or more words in a contemporary hand in the inner (left) margin but they are partly hidden in the binding and I have not tried to make out more than the last word:* miraculum.

162   Reynold from Gainsborough in Lincolnshire had a young daughter who was judged by all the neighbours to have died. But after being measured to Earl Simon and a penny having been bent, she immediately began to breathe again and was fully and splendidly revived. The whole township of Gainsborough bears witness to this.[221]

163   John de Hardel[222] had been deaf for half a year, but after being measured to Earl Simon and a penny having been bent, he immediately got his hearing back. The whole parish of St Dunstan[223] in London bears witness to this.

164   A bird †with the lower legs† of a hawk belonging to a certain knight, had by chance become swollen and was ill to the point of death, but after being measured to Earl Simon it recovered immediately. Those who bear witness to this are, etc.[224]

165   Henry,[225] son of Henry de la Pomeroy, a knight from Devon,[226] was taken seriously ill and was judged by the neighbours to be at the point of death but after being measured to the earl he recovered immediately. Moreover Sir Henry suffered later on from an attack of the flux but after being measured to Earl Simon he recovered straight away. His entire household bears witness to this matter.

166   Walter of †Bokyngeham†, who had at one time been an opponent of the earl, had an ailment of the eyes and became ill with an extremely grave abscess on his body, such that no doctor would promise him a cure other than death. After being measured to Earl Simon, however, he recovered fully from both conditions. His neighbours bear witness to this.

167   A woman called Agnes had lost the use and capabilities of all her limbs for six weeks so that she was unable to walk or move without being supported. But after being measured to Earl Simon she recovered immediately. Those who bear witness to this are, etc.[227]

---

[221] In 1257 the king had granted Gainsborough manor to William de Valence (d.1296): *Cal. Chart. R.* 1257–1300, p. 1; *Cal. Inq. p.m.* 1291–1300, pp. 220–1. William was an 'alien' half-brother of Henry III, whom he supported actively: ODNB, s.n.
[222] His will was enrolled in 1279: *London Wills* 1, p. 40. He may have been the moneyer of that name who occurs 1247–56: ODNB (online version), s.v. 'Moneyers'.
[223] St Dunstan in the East or St Dunstan in the West.
[224] Possibly those in **165**.
[225] Born c.1265, he died in 1305: *Cal. Inq. p.m.* 1272–91, pp. 238, 400; 1300–7, p. 200.
[226] See **65**.
[227] Those mentioned in **168**.

168 Quedam mulier nomine Matildis de †Blyþe† graui infirmitate diu detenta tandem infirmitate grauante mortua est. Facto concilio mensurata ad comitem Simonem statim reuixit et conualuit. De utroque miraculo omnes uicini sui perhibent testimonium.

169 Margareta uxor Willelmi Mauncell de comitatu Glouernie aliquo tempore comiti contraria et inimica incidit in [fol. 178v] quandam infirmitatem que uocatur frenesis ita quod sensum penitus amisit per duos dies. Cui comes Simonem apparuit per uisionem et dixit sibi, 'Cur michi detrahis et semper de me loqueris malum?' At illa penitencia ducta de maladictis petiit ueniam. Comes concessit. Illa uero dictum comitem interrogauit quid eueniret de suis aduersariis et inimicis. At ipse dixit, 'Quidam penitent, quidam penitebunt, et quidam mala morte sine penitencia morientur.' Hec autem ad comitem Symonem mensurata statim conualuit. De hoc uicini sui perhibent testimonium.

170 Sthephanus filius Symonis Badbyry iuxta Malberge subito graui infirmitate detentus ita quod a uicinis suis pro mortuo fuerat iudicatus, facto concilio mensuratus ad comitem Simonem statim reuixit et conualuit. De hoc perhibent testimonium omnes uicini sui.

171 Michaell uicarius de Wychyndon iuxta Salusbury habuit tibiam inflatam ita quod per maximam inflationem pellis tibie fuerat dirupta et adhuc remanente passione tumoris. Hic mensuratus ad comitem Symonem statim conualuit. De hoc omnes uicini sui perhibent testimonium.

172 Willelmus †Ayse† de Forneyse habuit cancrum in utroque pede ita quod sine sustentatione uix incedere potuit. Fuit etiam paraliticus ita quod in dextera parte sui corporis potestatem penitus amiserat. Veniens ad ecclesiam sancte Marie et sancti Egwini Eushamme et ibi per paucos dies moram faciens ex utraque infirmitate plenarie conualuit. Huius rei testes congregatio conuentualis Eueshamme.

THE EVESHAM ABBEY MIRACLE BOOK

168 A woman called Maud of †Blythe† had long been afflicted with a grave illness and eventually, after her illness had worsened, she died. But some advice was taken, and after being measured to Earl Simon she immediately came to life and recovered. All her neighbours bear witness to both miracles.[228]

169 Margaret, wife of William Mauncelle,[229] from Gloucestershire, had at one time been an opponent and enemy of the earl. She began to suffer from that kind of illness called a 'frenzy', so that for two days she lost her wits completely. But Earl Simon appeared to her in a vision and said to her, 'Why do you disparage me and always speak ill of me?' Moved to penitence, she asked forgiveness for the abusive words that she had spoken. The earl granted it. She then enquired of Earl Simon what would happen to his adversaries and enemies. He said, 'Some are penitent, some will be penitent and some without penitence will die a bad death.' After being measured to Earl Simon she recovered immediately. Her neighbours bear witness to this.

170 Stephen, son of Simon Badbury,[230] from near Marlborough, was suddenly taken so gravely ill that he was judged by his neighbours to have died. But some advice was taken, and after being measured to Earl Simon he recovered immediately. All his neighbours bear witness to this.

171 Michael the vicar of Over Winchendon near Aylesbury[231] had a lower leg so swollen that the skin of the leg was split by the enormous swelling, and his suffering from the distension continued. But after being measured to Earl Simon he recovered immediately. All his neighbours bear witness to this.

172 William †Ayse†[232] from Furness had a canker in each foot so that he could scarcely walk without support. He was also so paralysed that he had completely lost capability on the right-hand side of his body. But after coming to the church of St Mary and St Ecgwine at Evesham[233] and staying there for a few days he recovered completely from both infirmities. The conventual community of Evesham are the witnesses to this matter.

---

[228] **167** and **168**.
[229] A William Maunsel, with his wife Margaret, quitclaimed their interest in the manor of Tortworth (Gloucestershire) in 1300: TNA, CP 25/1/9/36, no. 6.
[230] The surname refers to Badbury, in Chiseldon (Wiltshire).
[231] Salusbury MS.
[232] *Recte* Ayre?
[233] Evesham abbey.

173   Thomas Walding de †Tuddenham† habuit guttam in sinistra manu ualde grauidam ita quod non potuit mouere manum illam. Que quidam gutta assendebat in sinistra parte capitis et ita inflatum fuit caput quod uix potuit uidere aut loqui. Demum inspirante Dei gracia et denario super eum plicato [fol. 179r] ad sanctum Symonem statim ab illa grauissima infirmitate conualuit. De hoc perhibent testimonium tota familia sua et tota prouincia sua.

174   Quedam mulier de Donechirche iuxta Donesmore Auicia nomine ita contracta fuit in manibus et pedibus et in omnibus aliis membris quod nullo modo ire aut se mouere potuit et hoc durauit per diem et dimidium et per duas noctes. Gaudium! Ista mensurata ad comitem Symonem statim conualuit uel pristinam recuparauit sanitatem. De hoc perhibent testimonium omnes uicini sui.

175   Emma mulier de uilla de Auburne de comitatu Lincolnie habuit filiam nomine Elianore de etate fere duorum annorum que casu die Sancte Trinitatis anno gracie M°CC° septuagesimo secundo cecidit in quodam uiuario et submersa est et mortua. Mater reperiens postea filiam suam ita submersam statim extraxit eam de aqua et mensurauit ad comitem Symonem. Statim puella pristine sanitati diuina gracia opitulante restituitur. De hoc omnes uicini sui perhibent testimonium.

176   Quedam mulier Cantuarie Agnes nomine uxor Henrici medici quadam graui gutta percussa in manu dextra et detenta per annum et dimidium ita quod eandem manum mouere non potuit se penitus illam amisisse credebat, ista statim manu ad comitem mensurata pristinam recuparauit sanitatem. Et in signum huius rei apud Evesham ad dictum comitem Symonem unam manum de cera transmisit. Huius testimonium perhibent omnes uicini sui.

177   Thomas Atteheye quidem uir Cantuarie habuit frigidam guttam in omnibus suis membris ita quod nec ambulare nec in aliquo membro se mouere potuit et hoc per annum durauit. Iste ad comitem Symonem mensuratus statim [fol. 179v] conualuit et itinere apud Evesham arrepto personaliter ibidem cum multis uicinis suis accessit. Et huius rei testimonium de uisu omnes plene perhibebant.

173 Thomas Walding from †Tuddenham†[234] had had a very severe gout in his left hand so that he could not move that hand, and the gout had risen up into the left side of his head which was so swollen that he could scarcely see or speak. But eventually, after being inspired by God's grace and a penny having been bent over him to St Simon, he recovered immediately from that very grave illness. His entire household and his whole neighbourhood bear witness to this.

174 A woman from Dunchurch near Dunsmore[235] called Avice had been so crippled in her hands and feet and in all her other limbs that she could not walk or move at all. And this had lasted for a day and a half and two nights. But what joy! After being measured to Earl Simon she recovered immediately and got back her former good health. All her neighbours bear witness to this.

175 Emm, a woman from the township of Aubourn in Lincolnshire,[236] had a daughter called Eleanor who was nearly two years old. On Trinity Sunday[237] in the year of grace 1272 she fell by accident into a fishpond and drowned and was dead. Later the mother, finding her daughter drowned, pulled her out of the water straight away and measured her to Earl Simon. With the help of God's grace the girl was immediately restored to her former good health.

176 A woman from Canterbury called Alice, wife of Henry the leech, had been stricken with a severe gout in her right hand and had been so afflicted for a year and a half that she was unable to move that hand and thought that she would lose it completely. But as soon as the hand was measured to the earl she recovered her former good health. And in token of this matter she sent a waxen hand to Earl Simon at Evesham. All her neighbours bear witness to this.

177 Thomas Atteheye from Canterbury had had a cold gout[238] in all his limbs so that he had been unable to walk or to move any of them. And this had gone on for a year. But after being measured to Earl Simon he recovered immediately. Setting out in person for Evesham, he reached there with many of his neighbours and they all bore ample witness to this matter from personal observation.

---

[234] Possibly Todenham (Gloucestershire) because the county is not specified.
[235] Dunchurch manor had been held by Simon de Montfort's son Henry 1260–5 during the minority of the heir: *VCH Warws.* 6, p. 80.
[236] The manor was held by Walter de Coleville (d.1277) a Montfortian: *Complete Peerage* 3, p. 374. He was taken prisoner at Kenilworth before the battle of Evesham: *Cal. Pat.* 1266–72, pp. 280–1; *Close R.* 1268–72, p. 279; above, 1.
[237] 19 June.
[238] A gout attributed to an excess of cold humours.

178   Agnes de Sutton et filia sua Douce nomine tantam cecitatem oculorum per triduum annum patiebantur quod nichil penitus uiderunt. Tandem inuocato Dei auxilio mensurate sunt ad comitem Symonem et pristinum uisum receperunt. De hoc uicini perhibent testimonium.

179   Symon filius Iohannis Bundiht de Tartrintone iuxta Arundell grauissima in omnibus membris suis per duos annos et dimidium detentus infirmitate ita quod penitus nullum corporis sui membrum mouere potuit, iste mensuratus ad comitem Symonem omnium membrorum suorum statim recuparauit sanitatem. Et accedens apud Evesham cum multorum uicinorum suorum testimonio huius rei ueritatem affirmauit. Et de hoc perhibunt testimonium domina Iohanna de la Mare et domina Awysa de Newylle et plurimi.

180   Willelmus filius Willelmi de Weston iuxta Norþhampton tam graui infirmitate detentus quod a die iouis mane usque ad diem sabboti proximum sequentem omnibus circumstantibus et eum uidentibus tanquam mortuus reputabatur, iste ad comitem Symonem post triduum mensuratus statim diuina opitulante gracia pristine sanitati [restituitur]. Huius rei testimonium [perhibent] Thomas frater, Allexander Noverei prior de ordine Predicatorum Leycestrie et Robertus Novery frater suus et tota <familia>[a] eiusdem Willelmi.[b]

181   Allexander de Suffolchia ciuis Londoniarum qui manet in parochia Sancti Martini Inter Tabernas per qinqinnium tantam in testiculis patiebatur infirmitatem ita quod uix mingere potuit quia tamen inflati fuerunt testiculi quod nullus locus habilis fuit ad urinam faciendam. Iste ope medici credens sanari posuit quandam tentam in quadam apertura que aperuit in [fol. 180r] testiculo et nodauit filum in fine illius tente quo melius eandem cum necesse fuerit extrahere posset. Postea accidit quod philum cum dicta tenta in eodem membro retracta est quod <nondum>[c] per biennium uideri potuit. Tandem accessit quidam monens infirmum ut quereret aquam de fonte comitis Symonis apud Evesham et lauaret membrum sic inflatum. Quod ita factum est et statim apparuit pristina apertura, et dictus infirmus uidens tentam cum quodam cultello eandem extraxit cum toto philo et iterum lauit membrum suum cum eadem aqua et sanata est dicta apertura et totum membrum

---

[a] familia] familia sua MS.
[b] *In margin in a contemporary hand* notabile.
[c] uent' MS.

178 Agnes of Sutton and her daughter called Dowse had suffered for three years from such poor eyesight that they could see nothing at all. But eventually after invoking God's help they were measured to Earl Simon and got back their former sight. Their neighbours bear witness to this.

179 Simon, son of John Benedict, from Tortington near Arundel, had been afflicted for two and a half years by a very severe infirmity in all his limbs so that he had been quite unable to move any part of his body. But after being measured to Earl Simon he recovered the good health of all his limbs. Reaching Evesham, and with the testimony of many of his neighbours, he affirmed the truth of the matter. Dame Joan de la Mare and Dame Hawis de Neville bear witness to this matter as do many other people.[239]

180 William, son of William, from Weston Favell near Northampton,[240] had been afflicted with so grave an illness that from dawn on a Thursday until the following Saturday he was thought to be as good as dead by everyone there who saw him. After the three days, however, he was measured to Earl Simon and with the help of the divine grace was immediately [restored] to his former good health. Thomas a friar, and Alexander Noveray prior of the Dominican friars of Leicester and Robert Noveray his brother and William's entire household bear witness to this matter. [*In the margin*] Something noteworthy.

181 Alexander of Suffolk, a citizen of London[241] who dwells in the parish of St Martin Vintry, had suffered for five years with such an ailment of the testicles that he could scarcely urinate; the testicles were so swollen that there was no adequate space through which to pass urine. Thinking to be made better by medical intervention, he had put a plug into a hole that he had opened in †a testicle†[242] and had knotted a thread to the end of the plug, the better to pull it out when necessary. Later it so happened that the thread, with the plug, was retracted into that organ and for two years it was no longer to be seen. But eventually someone came forward to urge the patient to seek water from Earl Simon's well at Evesham and to bathe the swollen organ. When that was done the original hole immediately opened and the patient saw the plug and extracted it with a knife together with all the thread. He bathed the organ again with the same water and the hole healed

---

[239] This seems to be a version of **117**.
[240] The manor was held, probably from 1263 (*Cal. Inq. p.m.* 1236–72, p. 171) and still in 1284, by Robert de Crevequer (*VCH Northants.* 4, p. 108). He was an armed Montfortian: *Rot. Selecti*, p. 137; *Cal. Inq. Misc.* 1, pp. 224, 314.
[241] His will was enrolled in 1277: *London Wills* 1, pp. 28–9.
[242] Anatomically improbable; some misunderstanding seems to have occurred.

suum in pristinam reddit sanitatem. Huius rei testimonium perhibuit Michael Tovi cum tota familia sua, Rogerus Marescallus, Robertus Corbe, et Robertus filius Roberti Herdell et alii multi qui hoc uiderunt, etc.

182 Philippus Pecche de uilla de Corbi in comitatu Lincolnie graui detentus infirmitate ita quod per totum diem mortuus reputabatur, tandem inito amicorum consilio mensuratus fuit ad comitem Simonem et statim reuixit et sanus factus est. De hoc perhibent testimonium conuicanei sui.

183 Richardus de Wycumbe ciuis Londoniarum percussus paralisi in dextera parte per tres septimanas ita quod nichil potuit mouere dexteram partem, iste mensuratus ad comitem Simonem statim pristinam recuparauit sanitatem. Inde perhibent testimonium omnes uicini sui.

184 Willelmus de Hales ciuis Londoniarum graui infirmitate detentus per octo septimanas ita quod de uita sua penitus despirauit demum ad comitem Symonem mensuratus statim conualuit et de illa infirmitate curatus est.

185 Idem Willelmus de Hales in breui postea percussus paralisi in parte dextera ita quod tibiam dexteram mouere non potuit set penitus illam amisisse credebat, iterum mensurauit se ad comitem Simonem et statim pristinam optinuit sanitatem. De hoc perhibent testimonium omnes uicini sui.

186 Magister Gilbertus de Sancto Leofardo habuit quandam infirmitatem que ipsum per uices inuasit ineffabili cruciatu [fol. 180v] cuius insultus sustinuit

up, and the whole organ got back its former good health. Michael Tovey,[243] with his entire household, Roger Marshal,[244] Robert Corby, and Robert, son of Robert Hardel,[245] and many others who saw this, etc.

182 Philip Pecche[246] from the township of Corby in Lincolnshire was taken so gravely ill that for a whole day he was believed to be dead. But on the advice of some friends he was measured to Earl Simon and he immediately came back to life and was made well. His neighbours bear witness to this.

183 Richard of Wycombe a citizen of London had been stricken with paralysis on his right-hand side for three weeks so that he had been unable to move anything on that side. But after being measured to Earl Simon he immediately recovered his former good health. All his neighbours bear witness to this.

184 William of Hales a citizen of London had been afflicted for eight weeks with an illness so grave that he had completely despaired of his life. But after eventually being measured to Earl Simon he recovered immediately and was cured of his illness.

185 The same William of Hales was shortly afterwards stricken with paralysis on his right-hand side so that he was unable to move his lower right leg and thought he would lose it completely. But he measured himself again to Earl Simon and regained his former good health immediately. All his neighbours bear witness to this.

186 Master Gilbert de St Leofard[247] had an illness which from time to time assailed him with unspeakable torment, and he had suffered its attacks for eight

---

[243] Michael Tovey (fl.1240–66) goldsmith and alderman of London was active there in the Montfortian cause: J. McEwan, 'The aldermen of London, c.1200–80: Alfred Beaven revisited', *Transactions of the London and Middlesex Archaeological Soc.* 62 (2011), pp. 177–203 (at p. 193); *Cron. Maiorum*, p. 79; *Beauchamp Cart*. pp. xliii, 199–201.

[244] He remained a Montfortian sympathizer in 1267: *Cron. Maiorum*, p. 91. His will was enrolled in 1276: *London Wills* 1, p. 27.

[245] The will of Robert Hardel, living in the parish of St Magnus the Martyr (in Bridge ward), was enrolled in 1280; he was a rentier on a large scale: *London Wills* 1, pp. 46–7. He may have been son of Robert Hardel an important royal merchant (G. A. Williams, *Medieval London: From Commune to Capital*, 2nd edn (London, 1970), pp. 64–5) who occurs as alderman of Bridge ward 1244–57 (McEwan, 'Aldermen of London, c.1200–80', p. 192).

[246] Possibly a relative of Gilbert Pecche (d.1291). Gilbert held an estate at Corby of the bishop of Lincoln by 1243 (*Bk of Fees* 1, pt 2, pp. 1049, 1075) and in 1271; Gilbert was a royalist but his brothers Robert and Hugh were Montfortians (*Complete Peerage* 10, pp. 335–6).

[247] A canon lawyer and probably a Montfortian sympathizer, he became bishop of Chichester in 1288 and died in 1305; he too was said to have produced posthumous miracles: *ODNB*, s.n.

proculdubio octo annos et amplius. Et ipsum semper tempore nocturno est aggressa, ipsum aliquando usque ad meridiem aliquando usque ad nonam aliquando prolixius ac si dente canina frustratim circa regionem spiritualium dilaniaretur lamentabili penalitate corrodendo. Cuius infirmitatis acerbitas quamdiu durauit amaritudo passionis ipsum compulit in terra prostratum aliquando more parturientis uel dementis de loco ad locum uoluntare, aliquando se erigere sursum et in uarias partes domus saltando currere pre corrosione morbi qui ipsum ab inferiori parte cordis usque ad cerebrum compressit et secuit circumquaque, ita quod miraculum uidebatur patienti fragilitatem sue nature tante passionis uehementiam posse euadere sine morte. Et licet frequenter ad mitigationem morbi usus fuisset ope et opera medicorum magis tum obfuit quam prefuit proculdubio quod fecerunt. Tandem inualescente morbo cum simul ipsum aliquantulum grauius et prolixius arriperet quam solebat, cubicularius suus locutus est ei dicens, 'Domine, dicitur quod multa miracula fiunt per Symonem de Mounteforti et sociis suis. Bonum esset uouere uos sibi ut uidetur.' Cui respondit languidus, 'Placet michi quod sic fiat. Plica sibi et sociis denarium qui apud Evesham secum requiescunt, et si contingat me huius passionis amaritudine expirare deferas illuc denarium uice mea. Si uero possum euadere ipsos personaliter uisitabo.' Et ecce hoc facto stimulus cruciatus tanti subito molescit et infirmus se transferens ad lectum suauiter incidit in soporem. Cui uidebatur in sompno quod quidam apparuit ei tradens sibi tria paria litterarum que sub sigillis clause erant quarum una utrinque gibbosa fuerat habens interius grossum aliquid inuolutum prout sibi uidebatur. Locutus est infirmo sic, 'Frange et lege.' Et cum languidus ille fregisset et apperuisset primam plicaturam illius littere que sic gibbosa uidebatur inuenit in ea pixidem pulcherimam de metallo inuolutam in cuius fundo [fol. 181r] oleum fuerat ualde purum et serenum. Et dixit languido baiulus littere, 'Aperi litteram totam et lege eam.' Languidus rogauit illum quod ipse eam aperiret. Qui cum eam apertam ante faciem languidi ostentaret apparuerunt in ea milites armati equis suis insidentes filo serico subtilissime consuti et ualde delectabiles in aspectu. In superiori ordine linealiter una comitiua militaris, in inferiori alia, in tertia ordine tertia, et sic ulterius per totam membranam que mirabiliter creuerat in latum et longum inter manus ostendentis. Et dixit baiulus languido, 'Lege has que inter ceteras picturas in hac membrana sunt conscripte.' Quas cum languidus inspexisset et legisset, scripta

years and more, without a doubt. And it always came upon him at night, lasting sometimes until midday, sometimes until the ninth hour, and sometimes longer, as if he were being torn to pieces all around the heart and lungs by the teeth of a dog and was being ravaged with lamentable torment. As long as the severity of an attack lasted, the sharp pain forced him sometimes to lie on the ground and roll around all over the place like a woman in labour or a lunatic, or sometimes to stand up and run and leap to various parts of the house on account of the gnawing of the illness. It pressed on him from the lower part of the heart to his brain and stabbed him all over, so that it seemed to the patient to be a miracle that his weak constitution was able to endure such violent suffering and not die. And although he had often embraced the resources and services of doctors in mitigation of the disease, whatever they did had undoubtedly harmed him more than it had helped. But eventually as the illness became worse and at the same time assailed him rather more severely and for longer periods than it had used to, his servant of the bedchamber spoke up, saying, 'Sir, it is said that many miracles are performed in the name of Simon de Montfort and his companions.[248] It would seem to be a good thing for you to pray to him yourself.' The patient answered him, 'I would like that to be so. Bend a penny to him and his companions who rest with him at Evesham, and if it should happen that I die from the harshness of this suffering take the penny there in my place; but if I can get free of it I shall visit them in person.' And behold, when this was done the sharpness of such torment suddenly became more gentle and the patient took to his bed and went sweetly to sleep. In a dream it seemed as if someone appeared to him, carrying with him three letters closed with seals. One of the letters was bulging on either side, apparently having something large wrapped inside it. And the man spoke to the patient thus, 'Break it open and read it.' And when the patient had broken it open and unfolded the first fold of the letter that had seemed so bulging, he found wrapped in it a small and very beautiful metal container, in the bottom of which was a very pure and clear oil. And the bearer of the letter said to the patient, 'Open the whole letter and read it.' The patient asked him to open it himself. When he displayed it open to the patient's face, there appeared on it to be some armed knights seated on their horses, clad in the finest silk and very handsome in appearance. In the top row was a knightly company formed up in rank, in the next was another, in the third row was a third, and so on throughout the whole sheet, which miraculously grew in width and length in the hands of the man displaying it. And the bearer said to the patient, 'Read what is written between the pictures on this sheet.' When the

---

[248] Chiefly Henry de Montfort and Hugh le Despenser, both killed at Evesham and buried next to Earl Simon at Evesham abbey ('Annales monasterii de Waverleia', *Ann. Monastici* 2, pp. 129–411 (at p. 365)) where they were posthumously credited with miracles (*Chron. Melrose* (1835), pp. 200–1; *Chron. Canterbury–Dover*, p. 243).

fuerant ibidem ista uerba, 'Ista utere et nulla preparatione.' Quibus lectis euanuit baiulus ille. Et languidus ille expergefactus intellexit quod ad conualescenciam infirmitatis sue sufficere sibi deberet pro medicinam memoria passionis Symonis de Mountforti et aliorum militum qui apud Evesham martirium sunt perpessi. Quod et factum est. Ab illo tempore ab infirmitate supradicta meritis dicti sancti [et] sociorum suorum penitus est curatus.

187   Quedam mulier Isabella nomine manens super pontem Londoniarum per dimidium annum detenta graui infirmitate ita durante morbo contracta facta in omnibus membris eius in tantum quod nullum membrum corporis mouere potuit, tandem inualescente morbo penitus priuata est usu loquendi per spacium trium dierum et inter omnes uicinos pro mortua reputebatur. Demum habito quorumdam amicorum suorum concilio die ueneris in festo sancti Dunstani anno gracie M°CC°lxx° tertio mensurata fuit ad comitem Symonem. Statim de utroque morbo curata est et officium lingue incontinenti per Dei graciam et merita sancti Symonis gloriose recuparauit. Et die dominica proxima sequenti scilicet in Pentecoste cum uicinis suis ecclesiam corporaliter uisitauit et in signum sue conualescencie quendam ymaginem cere apud Evesham destinauit. Huius rei testimonium omnes uicini perhibent.

188   Quidam puer Iohannes nomine filius Philippi de Sancta Maria in Crei de Kent cecidit in torrentem et submersus mortuus [fol. 181v] est. Pater pueri gemens et lacrimans extraxit illum de torrente et reposuit in domum suam mortuum custodiens usque ad uesperam. Postea dictum puerum ad sanctum Symonem mensurauit et statim conualuit, quem corporaliter pater et mater apud Evesham adduxerunt. De hoc testimonium perhibent omnes conuicanei sui.

189   Symon de Patteshulle miles dominus de Blechesho in comitatu de Bedforde oppressus grauissima infirmitate et subitanea circa cor die Assencionis Domini anno gracie M°CC° septuagesimo tertio, mane mortem metuens superuenientem omnia iura ecclesiastica festinenter sibi dari precepit. Et factum est. Qui statim usu loquendi priuatus ab omni populo circumstanti mortuus reputebatur usque ad horam meridianam. Postea mensuratus ad comitem Symonem statim reuixit et de omni morbo salubriter est curatus et modum loquendi plenarie recuparauit. Et

invalid looked and read, these words had been written there, 'Use these and no medication,' and after the words had been read the bearer vanished. The patient understood on waking that, for him to recover from his illness, reflection upon the suffering of Simon de Montfort and of the other knights who had endured martyrdom at Evesham ought to be medicine enough. That is what he did, and from that time he was completely cured of that illness through the merits of the saint and his companions.

187   A woman called Isabel who dwelt on London bridge had been afflicted with a grave disorder for half a year, so that while it lasted she was crippled in all her limbs and was unable to move any part of her body. Finally, with the condition worsening, she had been completely without the power of speech for three days and was thought by all her neighbours to be dead. But eventually on the advice of some of her friends she was measured to Earl Simon on the Friday of the feast of St Dunstan[249] in the year of grace 1273. Through God's grace and the merits of St Simon she was immediately cured of both conditions and splendidly recovered the free use of her tongue. And on the next Sunday, namely Whit Sunday,[250] she went to church in person with her neighbours, and in token of her recovery she sent a wax image to Evesham. All her neighbours bear witness to this matter.

188   A boy called John, son of Philip of St Mary Cray, from Kent, fell into a rushing stream, drowned and died. The boy's father, moaning and weeping, pulled him out of the stream and laid him down in his house and watched over the dead boy until the evening. But he afterwards measured the boy to St Simon and he recovered immediately. The father and mother brought him in person to Evesham. All his neighbours bear witness to this.

189   Simon of Pattishall[251] the lord of Bletsoe in Bedfordshire was afflicted with a very grave and sudden illness around the heart on the morning of Ascension Day[252] in the year of grace 1273. Fearing that death would supervene, he ordered all the rites of the church to be given him. In fact he had been immediately deprived of the power of speech, and until midday everyone in attendance believed him to be dead. But later, after being measured to Earl Simon, he immediately came back to life, was safely cured of his entire affliction, and fully recovered his usual

---

[249]   19 May.
[250]   28 May, i.e. a week *after* the next Sunday.
[251]   A rebel Montfortian after the battle of Evesham; he died around Easter 1274, not long after the events reported here: *ODNB*, s.n.
[252]   18 May.

apud Evesham postmodum personaliter accedens oblatio sua ibidem reportauit. Huius rei testes sunt omnes familiares sui cum tota prouincia.

190 Dominus Willelmus de London capellanus rector ecclesie de †Hekynton† aduersa ualitudine detentus ita quod ire non potuit set in grabato iacens a media Quadragesima usque festum Sancte Trinitatis, postea mensuratus ad comitem Symonem Deo opitulante recuparauit sanitatem. Et in signum sue sanitatis destinauit Eueshamie ymaginem cere indutam alba et casula ad modum sacerdotis. Datum anno Domini millesimo ducentesimo septuagesimo quarto.

191 Sthephanus Aungevin de Donestaple habuit quendam filium qui nominabatur Iohannes qui graui infirmitate et subito circa cor detinebatur quadam [die] ante horam nonam. Et morbo ita ingrauescente ab illa hora usque ad uesperam quasi mortuus ab omnibus reputabatur. Et accessit qui quidam portans aquam de fonte comitis. Guttatim perfudit circa labia pueri uti puer aquam baiulans et postea hauriens et astantes oculos eius lauabant et eundem postea ad comitem Simonem mensurauerunt. Et apertis oculis eius membra sua cepit mouere scilicet manus et pedes et statim conualuit. [fol. 182r] Postea pater et mater dictum puerum apud Evesham adduxerunt ad tumbam beati Simonis cum uicinis suis testimonium inde perhibentibus.

192 Henricus filius Gunnulde de Ketene iuxta Staunforde percussus morbo paralitico in parte dextera ita quod usuram dextri brachii per tres septimanas penitus amisit nec quicquam manum ac brachium mouere potuit set ligatum circa collum suum portauit, qui tandem ad tumulum beati Simonis ueniens et accepto puluere de dicta tumba brachium suum fricuit et statim sanus effectus est coram multis astantibus et hoc aperte uidentibus.

way of speaking. Afterwards he came in person to Evesham, bringing his offering with him.

190   Sir William of London, chaplain, the rector of the church of †Hekynton†, had been so afflicted with ill-health that he was unable to walk and he lay on his sick-bed from mid-Lent[253] until Trinity Sunday.[254] But eventually after being measured to Earl Simon he recovered his health with God's help. And in token of his cure he sent to Evesham a waxen image clothed in an alb and chasuble in the manner of a priest. Given in the year of our Lord 1274.[255]

191   Stephen Angevin[256] of Dunstable[257] had a son named John who was stricken with a grave and sudden illness around the heart one day, before the ninth hour. And when the sickness worsened from that hour until the evening, everyone thought that he was as good as dead. But someone arrived carrying water from the Earl's well. Drop by drop they wiped it round the boy's lips and then the boy raised the water and drank some. And those who were present bathed his eyes and afterwards measured him to Earl Simon. He opened his eyes and began to move his limbs, namely his hands and feet, and he recovered immediately. And later the father and mother brought the boy to Evesham to the tomb of the blessed Simon, bearing witness to this with his neighbours.

192   Henry, son of Gunnell, from Ketton[258] near Stamford, was stricken with a paralytic condition on his right-hand side so that for three weeks he completely lost the use of his right arm. He was unable to move the hand at all or the arm, which he carried in a sling tied round his neck. But eventually he came to the tomb of the blessed Simon, and taking dust from the tomb he rubbed the arm and was immediately cured in the presence of many bystanders who saw this clearly.

---

[253]   11 March.
[254]   17 May.
[255]   The final clause suggests the dating of a formal document.
[256]   A substantial wool merchant living in 1273: T. H. Lloyd, *The English Wool Trade in the Middle Ages* (Cambridge, 1977), p. 56.
[257]   The manor was held by Dunstable priory: *VCH Beds.* 1, p. 371. The priory had admitted Simon de Montfort to its confraternity in 1264 and its contemporary annalist extolled his aims and deeds: L. Kjær, 'Writing reform and rebellion', in A. Jobson (ed.), *Baronial Reform and Revolution in England 1258–1267* (Woodbridge, 2016), pp. 109–24 (at pp. 113–17).
[258]   The parish lay in two manors. One had been held by the loyalist John de Grey, who died in 1266. It may then have passed to his brother Richard de Grey of Codnor an active Montfortian (d. by 1272) and to Richard's son John another Montfortian: *VCH Rut.* 2, p. 258; *Complete Peerage* 6, pp. 134–5 n. (a), 171; *ODNB*, s.n. 'Grey, Richard de'.

193   <Angareta>[a] uxor Willelmi le[b] Boteler de Merston peperit filium quendam Willelmum nomine qui a natiuitate brachium dextrum habuit longo tempore dorso recuruatum quem nutrix toto tempore caute abscondit ne a domino uel matre uel familia pro dolore uideret. Tandem uolente et precipiente matre puerum uidere oblatus est ei puer, quo uiso mater cum familia dolore repleta dictum puerum et brachium ita retortum ad sanctum Simonem mensurauit. Hoc facto puer brachium suum mobiliter erexit et reflexit. Et hoc cunctis intuentibus patenter innotuit.

194   Willelmus Colston de Tadcastre in comitatu Eboracensi contractus ita enormiter in parte sinistra ita quod tibia sinistra uentri reflexa, brachio etiam eiusdem partis miro modo curuato, capite terre inclinato, sic ut orribile monstrum appareret intuentibus. Et tali detinebatur infirmitate a Pentecoste anno gracie M°CC° septuagesimo quarto usque sextam feriam ante festum Annunciationis anno eiusdem gracie septuagesimo sexto. Qui ueniens apud Evesham quarta feria precedente et ibidem in ecclesia conuentuali feria sexta circa horam tertiam coram magno altare dormiens apparuit ut uidebatur in sompnia ei quedam formosa domina cum duobus armigeris albis quasi descendentes per fenestras uitreas ultra magnum altare ad locum ubi iacebat et excitentes ipsum ut surgeret, nec potuit. Tandem dicta domina accipiens ipsum [fol. 182v] per humerum dextrum precepit ei ut leuaret et ipse statim brachiis et tibiis extensis conuentu et populo hoc uidente sanus effectus est circa horam diei tertiam.

195   Anno Domini M°CC° septuagesimo octauo die ueneris proxima post festum beati Petri ad uincula Lecia la Mede Machare nomine de parochia sancte Brigide de uico de Fletebrigge Londoniarum manens infirmitatem grauem recepit ita quod uiribus corporalibus fere destituebatur et ex parte sinistra a planta pedis usque ad †armillas† turgida fuit quasi ydropyca. Nec potuit a predicto die usque Natale proximum sequens ecclesiam adire nisi baculo et alio fulcomento sibi subueniretur. Tandem adueniente Nathali tantum predicta grauabatur infirmitate quod de uita sua desperabatur. Dicta uero mulier tam graui infirmitate detenta uouit quod ad

[a]   Margareta *MS*.
[b]   de *MS*.

193 Angaret,[259] wife of William Butler,[260] of Butlers Marston, had given birth to a son called William.[261] For a long time after the birth his right arm was twisted backwards and the nurse carefully hid him all that time lest the lord, the mother, or the household should be distressed to see him. When the mother eventually wanted, and asked, to see the boy he was handed over to her. On seeing him the mother was full of sorrow together with the household and measured the boy and his twisted arm to St Simon. When that was done the boy raised his arm flexibly and twisted it back again. And that was clearly apparent to all the onlookers.

194 William Colston from Tadcaster in Yorkshire was so grievously crippled on his left side, with his lower left leg bent towards his belly, his arm on that side strangely curved and his head bent toward the ground, that to onlookers he seemed like a horrible monster. And he was afflicted with that condition from Whit Sunday[262] in the year of grace 1274 until the Friday[263] before the feast of the Annunciation in the year of grace 1276. But he had come to Evesham on the previous Wednesday, and while asleep on the Friday in front of the high altar at about the third hour, he dreamt that a beautiful lady with two squires in white appeared to him, as if coming down through the glass windows beyond the high altar to the place where he was lying and encouraging him to rise. But he was unable to, and the lady eventually grasped him by the right upper arm and commanded him to get up. And about the third hour, with the convent and people looking on, he was immediately made well again with his arms and lower legs straight.

195 In the year of our Lord 1278 on the Friday[264] after the feast of Peter's Chains, Lece Meadmaker who dwelt in the parish of St Bride Fleet Street in London had contracted such a serious illness that she had lost nearly all the strength in her body. And on her left side from the sole of her foot to her †arm-pit† she had become swollen as if dropsical. And from that day until the following Christmas[265] she had been unable to go to church without supporting herself on a stick or some other kind of crutch. Eventually she was so burdened by the infirmity that, as Christmas approached, her life was despaired of. But since she was afflicted with so serious

---

[259] Her forename is confirmed by *Cal. Inq. p.m.* 1272–91, p. 320; *Cal. Pat.* 1292–1301, p. 46.
[260] A Montfortian: *Close R. (Suppl.)* p. 48. Lord of the manor in 1279: *VCH Warws.* 5, p. 24. He died in 1283: *Cal. Inq. p.m.* 1272–91, p. 319.
[261] This William was a minor in May 1293: *Cal. Pat.* 1292–1301, p. 46. He was therefore born in or after 1272. He died in 1334: *Cal. Inq. p.m.* 1327–36, p. 406.
[262] 20 May.
[263] 20 March.
[264] 5 August.
[265] 25 December.

crucem et ad beatum Simonem apud Evesham personaliter accederet sue sanitatis imploratura suffragium. Ipsa uero langore sic consistens in septimana Pentecostes anno sequenti turgide et contracta per uirum suum ducebatur Eueshamiam in quadam cinera cum una rota et duobus pedibus. Quia cum uenisset ibidem die beati Petri ad uincula et in ecclesia per totum diem se orasset in crastino ducebatur in dicta cinera ad fontem beati Symonis et ibidem se orauit et ex aqua bibit et corpus suum lauit. Quibus peractis mox sanitatem recepit et statim erecta et sana sine aliquo fulcimento ad ecclesiam sancte Marie et beati Eggwini peruenit et ibidem de sanitate recuparata Deum laudauit.

196 Henricus diaconus de Bourton super Trent sedens in capella sita super ponte ultra fluminem quod uocatur Trent in eadem uilla scribens et subito inflatu miserandi uenti insoliti cecus factus et uanitate in cerebro percussus cecidit in terram quasi mortuus et sic permansit omnino cecus per triennium. Set in misericordia Dei sperans adductus [est] ad Robertum de Cnaresborg et ad sanctum Thomam Cantuarie et alibi per totam Angliam ubi ulla spes fuerit alicuius sancti. Atque quodam die cepit [fol. 183r] animo inuoluere ut adduceretur ad comitem Simonem apud Evesham. Et cum adductus esset stans in coro ubi sepultus fuerat comes orans deuote, monachis eiusdem loci missam matutinalem audientibus omnibus astantibus, diuina gracia redditus est ei uisus perspicuus.

197 Memorandum quod quidam homo de Lewe in Lyndessey nomine Robertus le Stormy habebat quendam puerum nomine Nicholaum qui die lune proxima ante Natiuitate Beate Marie anno Domini M°CC° septuagesimo octauo cecidit in quodam puteo in curia dicti Roberti circa horam tertiam et ibi mortuus exstitit usque post nonam. Eodem die predicto Robertus uenit de Essex. Quesiuit de uxore sua nomine Constantina ubi erant pueri sui. Illa autem quasi dormiens, 'Nescio.'

a condition this woman vowed in fact that she would go in person to the rood[266] and the blessed Simon at Evesham to beg help for her health. She remained ill like that until, in Whit week[267] the following year, her husband took her to Evesham, swollen and crippled, in a hand-cart with a wheel and two feet. When she had got there on the day of Peter's Chains[268] and had prayed all day in the church, on the morrow she was taken in the hand-cart to the blessed Simon's well and there she prayed, drank some of the water and bathed her body. After taking those steps she soon got her health back and, upright and well and without any crutch, she went immediately to the church of St Mary and the blessed Ecgwine[269] at Evesham and there praised God for her restored health.

196 Henry the deacon from Burton upon Trent had been sitting and writing in the chapel above the bridge beyond the river Trent in that town when he was suddenly blinded by an unusual bloating of appalling gas, and stricken with dizziness he had fallen to the ground as if dead. He had remained totally blind like that for three years and, hoping in God's mercy, was taken to Robert of Knaresborough,[270] to St Thomas of Canterbury and to other places all over England where there was any hope to be had from some saint. But one day he began to think about being taken to Earl Simon at Evesham. After he had been taken there and was standing in the choir where the earl had been buried, and was praying devoutly while all the monks of that place were standing nearby and hearing the morrow mass, he was given back clear eyesight by the divine grace.

197 A memorandum that a man from Louth in Lindsey[271] called Robert Sturmy[272] had a son called Nicholas. Around the third hour on the Monday[273] before the Nativity of the Blessed Mary in the year of our Lord 1277 the boy fell into a well in Robert's courtyard where he lay dead until after the ninth hour. On the same day Robert arrived from Essex and asked his wife, called Custance, where his sons were. She was nearly asleep, however, and said, 'I don't know.' So Robert and his

---

[266] At Evesham abbey the rood stood above the altar of the Holy Cross at the east end of the nave: Marlborough, *Hist.* p. 506.
[267] 21–7 May.
[268] 1 August.
[269] The abbey church.
[270] Robert (d.1218?) had lived in a cave near Knaresborough (Yorkshire) and was buried in a nearby chapel: *ODNB*, s.n.
[271] The manor was held by the bishop of Lincoln: *Bk of Fees* 1, pt 1, p. 176; *Valor Ecclesiasticus temp. Henr. VIII Auctoritate Regia Institutus* 4 (Record Commissioners, 1821), p. 6. Richard of Gravesend, bishop 1258–79, was a prominent Montfortian: *ODNB*, s.n.
[272] He occurs in the 1270s (*The Registrum Antiquissimum of the Cathedral Church of Lincoln* 5, ed. K. Major (Lincoln Record Soc. 34, 1940 for 1937), pp. 199–200) and in 1298 (*A Lincolnshire Assize Roll for 1298*, ed. W. S. Thomson (Lincoln Record Soc. 36, 1944 for 1938–39), p. 131).
[273] 6 September.

Dicti autem Robertus et uxor sua quesierunt infantem et inuenerunt eum in puteo et extraxerunt mortuum de puteo et fecerunt planctum magnum et mensurauerunt eum ad comitem Simonem. Et uenit quidem senex inter eos qui dixit eis, 'Ponite puerum inter uos ut recipiat naturalem colorem' et hiis dictis disparuit senex. Et ita factum est et reuixit inter illos.

wife searched for the infant and they found him in the well. They pulled his body out of the well and made great lamentations and they measured him to Earl Simon. An old man came and stood between them and said, 'Place the boy between you so that he can receive your natural warmth,' and the old man disappeared. And so it was done and the boy came back to life between them.

Miracles from the Melrose chronicle
London, British Library, Cotton MS Faustina B IX

198 [fol. 67v] Factum est ergo ut mox perempto Simone et exuto ab armis in quibus iacebat mortuus, quidam ex filiis Belial accederent ad corpus eius abscidentes ei manus et pedes, de quarum altera manu sic se habet uera relatio. Erat quidam marchius in comitatu Cestrie. Hic erat cum Edwardo in bello Eusamie qui post bellum arripiens interfecti Simonis manum de qua ante dictum est, misit illam per clientem inpietatis sue ad uxorem suam ut gauderet de interfectione inimici, cuius interfectionis certissimum signum erat manus amputata. Cum qua ueniens ad predium domini sui cliens et non inueniens predii dominam domi, properat ad ecclesiam parochialem ubi erat non longe a predio uiri sui sitam. Quo cum uenisset cum manu quam portabat in gremio panniculo inuolutam accessit ad dominam loquens ei in aure de interemptione Simonis. Ac inquit, 'Istud est signum occisionis eius,' uolens ostendere ei manum amputatam. Set mulier, ne uerecundaretur uel forte metuens Deum, [fol. 68r] tunc cum persisteret in oratione sua noluit manum uidere set neque attrectare, licet cliens instanter persuaderet ei ut allatam acciperet et penes se retineret. Cui perperam suadenti ait domina, 'Opperire donec diuina fuerint percelebrata.' Ad iussum igitur domine secedens stabat in multitudine populi ut asculteret missam. Et factum est dum eleuaretur sacrosancta hostia et populus eleuaret manus suas pariter et cliens ad Dominum a sacerdote eleuatum adorandum, ecce manus sancti uiri quam baiularat satelles diaboli satellitis supra capud eius absque omni sensibilitate eius diuinitus est eleuata ita ut preeminencia altitudinis melius cerni potuisset quam manus preeminentioris hominis de omni multitudine hominum qui ibi tunc aderant. Que dum adoraret Dominum maiestatis in eleuatione eius de qua dictum est, ut inclinauerat se uersus altare ad adorandum eum, omni dicto citius iterum reclinata est in id ipsum unde exierat non sine uirtute diuinitatis, panniculo quo inuoluebatur inuento integre

Miracles from the Melrose chronicle

London, British Library, Cotton MS Faustina B IX, fols 67v–68v, 71v–72r

198 And so it was that, as soon as Simon was killed and stripped of the armour in which he lay dead, some of the sons of Belial approached his body and cut off his hands and feet, of which one hand is the subject of a true story, as follows. There was a marcher[1] in Cheshire. He was with Edward in the battle of Evesham and it was he who, after the battle, seized the forementioned hand of the slain Simon and, by a male retainer of his unholy self, sent it to his wife so that she should rejoice in the killing of an enemy, of whose killing the hand was a very certain token. On coming with it to the manor house of his lord and not finding the lady of the house at home, he proceeded to the parish church where she was, which stood not far from her husband's house. When he got there with the hand, which he carried in his embrace wrapped in a piece of cloth, he approached the lady and spoke in her ear about Simon's killing. And wishing to show her the severed hand he said, 'This is the token of his killing.' But the woman, not to be embarrassed, or perhaps fearing God, declined to see the hand or even to feel it while she was still at her prayers, although the retainer insistently urged her to take the present and keep it with her. In response to this unseemly pressure the lady told him to keep it covered up until the celebration of divine service was completed. He therefore withdrew at the lady's command and stood with the general congregation to hear the mass. And so it was that when the sacred host was elevated and the people, including the retainer, raised their hands in adoration of the Lord whom the priest had lifted up, lo and behold, the holy man's hand, which the minion of the Devil's minion was carrying, was raised above the man's head by divine power without him being aware of it, so that its exalted height could be seen above the hands of the tallest man in the whole crowd of men that were there at the time. While the priest was adoring the lord of majesty in his elevation as has been said, and as he was bowing towards the altar in reverence to him, the hand returned by divine power, in less time than one could say it, to rest in the same place from which it

---
[1] A landholder in the marches of Wales.

consuto ut prius erat penitus absque omni animaduertibilitate baiulantis. Cuius nouitatis miraculum perpendens mulier quam predixi Deum metuentem, ait clienti post misse celebrationem, 'Manum illam quam dominus meus per te misit ad me, reporta ad illum, quoniam non intrabit in domum meam.' Perculsa enim erat miro stupore ex inuisa et inaudita uisione noui miraculi, propter quod ait clienti, 'Dignus est ultione magna quicumque est ille qui manum illam abscidit.' Narrauitque uisionem secreto clienti, quam non omnes set plures ex fidelibus Christi qui ibi tunc aderant uidere meruerunt, precipiens ei ut uisionem quam audierat, ueniens ad dominum suum fideliter ei enarraret. Pergit igitur seruus propere cum manu quam baiularat ad dominum qui eum miserat. Non enim intrauit in domum domine sue sicut illa promiserat propter manum allatam. Vnde uidetur quod erat una ex fatuis mulieribus que tam sanctam manum tam fatue recusarat, quod non fuit factum sine consilio diuinitatis omnia bene disponentis. Non enim erat dignus uir eius, filius Belial, possidere in domo sua manum tante sanctitatis et ideo creditur transisse ad possessorem Deo prouidente multo meliorem. Set quomodo uel ubi deuenerit prorsus ignoro.

199 [fol. 68r] Iuxta quoddam oppidum in Northumbria est domus preclara in qua degunt canonici Premonstratensis [fol. 68v] ordinis Deo seruientes. Ad hanc domum delatus est pes Simonis per uirum felicis memorie, dominum Iohannem de Wescy dominum burgi de Alnewike, fundatorem et patronum domus canonicorum quos predixi. Quo cum permansisset per aliquot menses omnino incorruptus inuentus est. Vnde propter durationem tante incorruptionis in pede sancti hominis merito inuente, canonici eiusdem abbatie, que uocatur abbatia de Alnewyke quoniam iuxta opidum de Alnewyke posita est, propter reuerenciam summi conditoris fecerunt pedi incorrupto calciamentum de argento purissimo. In quo quidem pede uisa est plaga inter minimum articulum eiusdem pedis et inter conuicinatum sibi inmediate articulum, uel ex cultello nescio an uel ex gladio facta. Non enim sufficiebat amputanti pedem sancti uiri quod multipliciter <detrunccatus>[a] erat in corpore nisi ipse per maiorem maliciam adderet ei uulnus in pede. Accidit autem in diebus illis ut quidam burgensis prediues Noui Castri super Tynam grauissime infirmaretur ita ut fere omnis motus auferretur ab eo. Non enim potuit mouere pedem de lecto, non manum ad os deducere, non aliquod officium sui corporis

---

[a] detrunctatus MS.

had emerged, and the cloth in which it had been wrapped was found to be all sewn up as it was before, without the bearer being aware that anything had happened. The woman of whom I have spoken, contemplating a miracle of such strangeness and fearing God, said to the retainer after the celebration of the mass, 'That hand which my lord has sent to me by you, take it back to him because it shall not enter my house.' Indeed she was so overcome by extraordinary astonishment at the sight of the unprecedented and unheard-of new miracle that she said to the retainer, 'Whoever it was who cut off that hand deserves to be severely punished.' She told the retainer privately about the apparition, which many of Christ's faithful who were present, but not all of them, were worthy to see, and commanded him that when he got back to his lord he should tell him truthfully of the vision that he had heard about. The servant therefore went quickly to the lord who had sent him, carrying the hand with him. But, just as she had stipulated, he did not enter the lady's house, because of the hand he was carrying. Thus it might appear that, by so foolishly rejecting a hand so holy, she was a foolish kind of woman; but it was not done without guidance from the divinity who directs all good things, for her husband, a son of Belial, was not worthy to keep a hand of such holiness in his house. It is therefore believed to have passed, by God's providence, to a much better possessor, but I have no idea by what means or where to.[2]

199   Near a town in Northumberland is a notable house in which canons of the order of Prémontré dwell, serving God. One of Simon's feet was taken to that house by Sir John de Vescy, a man of happy memory, lord of the borough of Alnwick, the founder and patron of the house of canons of whom I have just spoken.[3] When it had remained there for some months it was found to be totally incorrupt. So, because of the permanence of the incorruption found in the foot through the merit of the saintly man, the canons of the same abbey, which is called Alnwick abbey because it is situated near the town of Alnwick, made a shoe of the purest silver for the uncorrupted foot, out of reverence for the supreme creator. On the foot was seen a cut between the little toe and the toe immediately next to it; I do not know whether it was from a knife or from a sword. Certainly, it was not enough for the man who cut off the saint's foot that he had been mutilated many times about the body, unless he himself should, with added spite, give him a wound to the foot. It happened in those days that a very rich burgess of Newcastle upon Tyne became gravely ill, so that he was deprived of almost all movement. For he could not move his foot from the bed or put his hand to his mouth or perform

---

[2] This is a version of **14**.
[3] He had died in 1289: *ODNB*, s.n. He was a 'founder' of the abbey in the sense of 'benefactor'; the original founder was his ancestor Eustace fitz John.

exercere, set nec attrectari ab aliquo uoluit. Tanta enim calamitate ingentissime inualitudinis per totum corpus erat obsessus ut mallet quasi mori quam de lecto ammoueri propter incredibile pondus sue infirmitatis. Cui quadam nocte apparuit uox in sompnis ei dicens, 'Surge cras mane et aliquantulum alleuiaberis ex hac infirmitate, pergensque apud Alnewycum inuenies ibi in abbatia canonicorum Premonstratensium pedem Simonis de Monte Forti. Apud illum', inquit uox, 'pedem recipies sanitatem optimam'. Qui crastina die summo mane consurgens aliquantulum, prout uox diuina ei predixerat, alleuiatus, non tamen absque penalitate graui ascendit equum. Deinde quam citius potuit uenit Alnewycum. Cumque introisset domum religiosorum prefatorum, prout potuit descendens de equo mox properauit ad pedem sancti uiri uisendum. Quod cum compertum fuisset canonicis Deo deuotis, duo ex illis, ut per uiam compendii accederet burgensis adhuc supra modum egrotans ad pedem, ne forte nimis laboraret in eundo uersus pedem tulerunt pedem contra illum de loco requietionis sue cum reuerencia in calciamento quo erat indutus. Ad cuius calciamenti deosculandi tactum antequam eger potuisset appropinquare, ex solo uisu calciamenti integram meruit a Deo recipere propter merita Simonis sospitatem.

200 [fol. 71v] Huic sancto uiro nonnulli qui detraxerunt post mortem eius ignominiosam mortem subire meruerunt. Quorum unus erat canonicus quidam de Alnewic qui postquam nimis superflue uno die derogauerat Simoni, nondum enim uenerat pes eius ad domum illam, in crastino illius diei cum debuisset surgere de lecto suo nullum oculum inuenit in maledicto capite suo. Peierarat enim pridie per oculos Dei quod Simon fuit proditor regis Anglie et procerum suorum, et ideo nec mirum ceciderunt oculi eius per se de capite eius, diuina ultione plectente eum propter Simonem. In loco uero utriusque oculi inueniebatur suf[fol. 72r]fossio profunda et horribilis, qui eodem die subito obiit.

201 [fol. 72r] Quidam alius uere anathema diaboli qui absciderat uirilia sancti uiri Simonis, post duos annos tanti sceleris perpetrati, morte turpissima mortuus est in Scotia, submersus in magno profundo flumine Thayensi fluente ad mare iuxta nobile oppidum de Perht. De quo cum debuisset extrahi inuenti sunt super uentrem eius duo scrabones mire turpitudinis pedes suos adeo fortiter in ipso uentre fixos habentes ut uix euelli potuissent.

any function of his body, but nor did he wish to be touched by anyone. Indeed, throughout his body he was overwhelmed by such a weight of massive disability that he would almost have preferred to die than be moved from his bed, on account of the unbelievable burden of his infirmity. One night a voice came to him in his sleep saying, 'Rise tomorrow morning and you shall be to some extent relieved of this infirmity; and go to Alnwick where, in the abbey of the Premonstratensian canons, you will find the foot of Simon de Montfort, and in its presence', said the voice, 'you shall receive complete good health.' The next day, he got up very early in the morning and, somewhat relieved just as the divine voice had foretold, he mounted his horse, though not without severe pain. He then went as quickly as he could to Alnwick, and when he had entered the foresaid religious house he dismounted as best he could from his horse and hastened straight away to see the saint's foot. When this became known to the canons devoted to God, two of them brought the foot reverently from its resting-place to meet him, in the shoe within which it was enclosed, so that the burgess, who was still extremely ill, might approach the foot in the shortest way lest he should perhaps struggle too much in making towards the foot. Before the patient could get near enough to touch the shoe and kiss it, from the mere sight of the shoe he was allowed by God to have a complete recovery through the merits of Simon.

200 The few who disparaged this saint after his death deserved to suffer an ignoble death. One of them was a canon of Alnwick who had quite excessively denigrated Simon one day, before his foot had yet arrived at that house. On starting to rise from his bed the next day, he found that he had no eyes in his accursed head. In fact he had sworn falsely by God's eyes the previous day that Simon was a traitor to the king of England and his magnates; therefore it was no wonder that his eyes fell from his head of their own accord as a punishment to him for Simon's sake. Indeed, at the site of each eye was to be found a deep and horrible cavity, and he died suddenly the same day.

201 Another man, truly a cursed minion of the Devil, who cut off the genitals of St Simon, died a very nasty death in Scotland two years after that crime was committed, drowned in the great and deep river Tay, which flows into the sea near the noble town of Perth. When they went to pull him out they found two appallingly ugly crabs on his belly with their claws so firmly fastened to the belly that they could scarcely be pulled off.[4]

---

[4] This is a version of **202**, which clearly dates the event to 1273.

A miracle from the Lanercost chronicle (202)
London, British Library, Cotton MS Claudius D VII

[fol. 192v] Regina Scotie Margareta inter hec et alia sua grauamina, precipue de morte patris et dubio reditu fratris, profunde desolata, una uesperarum apud Chinclevin, aere serenato post cenam sumptam, solacii causa super ripam fluminis de Tay perrexit spaciari, comitantibus se armigeris et ancillis, sed specialiter confessore suo, qui mihi gesta intimauit. ¶ Affuit inter ceteros armiger pomposus cum suo garcione qui, attestantibus superioribus, sibi a fratre fuerat commendatus. Et cum sederent in quodam supercilio litoris, descendit ille ad manus abluendas quas luto infecerat ludendo. Isto sic stante semiinclinato, una ancillarum a regina incitata clam accessit et eum intra \oram/ aluei impulit. Qui alludens facto et gratum habens, 'Quid', inquit, 'curo? Natare scio et si ulterius fuero.' Spacians sic in alueo et aliis applaudens, ex inopinato sensit sibi uoraginem corpus absorbere, et clamans ac eiulans nullum habuit qui ad eum accideret nisi seruulum suum, qui prope ludens clamore assistentium impetuose cucurrit in profundum, et ambo absorti sunt in momento coram oculis omnium. Sic inimicus Symonis ac Sathane satelles, qui perditionis se dixit fuisse causam strenui militis, coram omnibus periit.

A miracle from the Lanercost chronicle (202)

London, British Library, Cotton MS Claudius D VII, fol. 192v

Amidst her various tribulations Queen Margaret of Scotland was feeling deeply distressed, especially over her father's death and with anxiety about her brother's return. By way of relief one evening after supper she went out from Kinclaven[1] for a stroll on the bank of the river Tay while the weather was fine, accompanied by squires and maids, and in particular by her confessor,[2] who told me what happened. ¶ With the rest of them was a certain boastful squire with his groom; according to his superiors the squire had been recommended to her by her brother. And while they were seated overlooking the water's edge, this squire went down to wash his hands, which he had soiled with mud while playing. While he was standing thus, half bent over, one of the maids, prompted by the queen, crept up and pushed him over the edge into the river. Treating the matter as a joke and taking it kindly, he said, 'What do I care? Even if I were farther out, I know how to swim.' Wading about like that in the water and congratulating the others, he was disconcerted to feel his body being swallowed up by a deep hole. He shouted and wailed but nobody would go to him except his young servant who was playing nearby. He rushed recklessly into the deep water to the shouts of the bystanders, and both of them were instantly swallowed up in view of everybody. Thus perished, in front of everyone, Simon's enemy and Satan's minion, who claimed to have been the cause of that bold knight's downfall.[3]

---

[1] The remains of Kinclaven castle stand above the right bank of the Tay about ten miles north of Perth. The chronicle records this event under 1273. Margaret's father King Henry III of England had died in the previous November and her brother Edward I, then abroad, would not return to England until August 1274.
[2] A Franciscan friar: *Chron. Lanercost* (1839), p. 97.
[3] This is a version of **201**.

Anno milleno (203)

Cambridge, Gonville and Caius College, MS 349/542

[fol. 10v]
Anno milleno bis centenoque uiceno
Ter iam quintoque denique luce quoque,
Heu milleno bis centeno terque uiceno
Anno quintoque denique luce quoque,
5 Augusti quarta uera de Virgine parta
Luce Symon querit prelia sicque perit
Corpore non anima nam celsa petens fugit ima
Et postrema dies fit sibi prima quies.
Martis luce cadit cum uim ui pellere[a] uadit.
10 Lux festo uacua congruit esse sua.
O pugil anglorum, tu fidus[b] amator eorum
Pro quis castrorum non fugis ipse chorum.
O capud illorum, manus et pes atque cor horum
Pro causa quorum tis facis ipse forum
15 Singula membrorum uendens pro pace tuorum.
O pie mercator, inclite large dator
Dans corpus morti periure membra chohorti.
O magne fidei uir, bone serue Dei,
Iniuste pateris quia ius uir iuste tueris.
20 Sed quia ius queris in nece uictor eris.
Ha Deus in celis merito manet iste fidelis
Passus pro patria uulnera seua pia
Causa nam sponte populo pro paupere monte
De forti dictus nec uulnere nec nece uictus.
25 Iam bene de monte forti dictus quia sponte,
Fortiter ut fortis, fert horrida uulnera mortis.

[a] pellere] *In margin (in the same hand)* †melius† defendere.
[b] fidus] *In margin (in the same hand)* uel decus.

Anno milleno (203)

Cambridge, Gonville and Caius College, MS 349/542, fol. 10v

In the year one thousand, two hundred, three score and five, and at dawn (alas, at dawn in the year one thousand, two hundred, three score and five) on the fourth of August, in a true dawn born of the Virgin, Simon sought battle and thus perished in the body but not in the soul. In seeking the highest he escaped the lowest, and the next day became his first respite. On a Tuesday he fell; with force he went forth to banish[1] force. [10] The day, being void of any calendar feast, was proper to be his. O defender of the English, their faithful[2] friend, for whom you do not flee even from a 'company of hosts'.[3] O their head, their hand, foot and heart: of yours you even hold a market on behalf of their cause, selling each of your limbs for the peace of your people. [16] O holy merchant, renowned and generous giver, giving your body to death and your limbs to a perjured gang.[4] O man of great faithfulness and good servant of God, you suffer unjustly, O just man, for you protect the law. [20] Since you seek the law, however, in death you shall be the victor. Ah, God! This faithful man who suffered cruel wounds for his country in a pious cause deservedly dwells in heaven, for he is called a 'strong mountain' (*monte de forte*) for poor people. [24] Defeated by neither wounds nor death he is well called the 'strong mountain' (*de monte forti*) at present, for as a strong man he willingly bears the horrid wounds of death with strength. But the 'high

---

[1] banish] *In the margin in the same hand* †better† deny.
[2] faithful] *In the margin in the same hand* or glorious.
[3] The Vulgate (Cant. 7: 1) has 'choros castrorum', for which the Douay–Rheims translation has 'companies of camps'; but in the present context the Wyclif translation is more apt: 'cumpenyes of oostis' (S. of S. 6: 12).
[4] A reference to those who had sworn in 1258 to support each other in the reform movement and had since defected.

Immo de monte celso potius quia fonte
Alto celorum nutritur ciuis eorum.
Hic periurorum domitor terrorque malorum,
30 Spes oppressorum, uox uulgi, corque piorum,
Examplar morum, multorum laus populorum,
Religiosorum tutor pro posse uirorum,
Hic auersorum sociorum fraude suorum
Ensibus addictus atroces pertulit ictus
35 Atque truces rictus comes et martir benedictus.
Hic numquam fictus a fictis sepe relictus
Attamine inuictus iam lumine splendet amictus.
O facinus triste, bisacutis ceditur iste,
Ferro truncatur, hastis gladiisque foratur.
40 Lingua, capud, manus atque pedes, pectenque pudenda
Singula sunt abscisa uiro feritate stupenda.
O mors plangenda, mors cum gemitu referenda,
Mors anglis flenda, mors, mors sine fine dolenda,
Mors ulciscenda, mors dira morte luenda.
45 O mors terrenda, mors[a] militibus metuenda
Per quos horrenda tam turpia tamque pudenda
Et tam miranda tam uilia tamque nefanda
Militie flori Symoni fiunt et honori
Omnis militie, fonti riuoque sophie.
50 Res detestanda, res pessima, res miseranda.
Res fit ei uilis ori cum uirga uirilis
Imprimitur propria proprio. Pia Virgo Maria
Que peperit Christum cito palma uindicet istum.
Ve facienti, ueque fauenti, ueque iubenti,
55 Ve praue genti mala tot fieri patienti.
¶ Cum patre ui capitur, moritur, sepelitur
Filius Henricus martir milesque pudicus.
Signa probant mille quod et hic sit sanctus et ille,
Milleque languentes illis laudes referentes.
60 Vos Alienore coniux et filia, more
Vestro deflere nolite uirum quia uere
Martir honoratus est nunc et glorificatus.
Ipsum quippe bonum meruistis habere patronum
Intercedentem pro uobis uosque fouentem.

[a] mors] *At the end of the line (in the same hand) and marked for insertion.*

mountain' would be better, for he drinks at the well in the height of heaven as one of its citizens. [29] This conqueror of perjurers and terror of the wicked, the hope of the oppressed, the voice of the common people and the heart of the faithful, the model of conduct, praised by many of the people, the guardian of the religious to the best of his power, being deceitfully subjected to the swords of his opposing comrades,[5] the blessed earl and martyr endured savage blows and fierce grimaces. [36] He who was never false while often abandoned by false people, undefeated by corruption now shines clothed in light. O woeful crime! He was cut down by double-edged axes, he is mutilated with an iron blade, he is pierced with spears and swords. [40] Tongue, head, hands, feet and genitals were all cut off from the man with astonishing savagery. O deplorable death! O death to be related with a shudder! O death to be wept over by the English! O death, death, to be endlessly mourned! O death to be avenged! O death to be paid for by a dreadful death. [45] O death to cause terror, a death to be feared by the soldiers who inflicted such horrific, disgraceful, shameful, astounding, vile and wicked things on Simon, the flower of knighthood, the source of all knightly honour and the fount and stream of wisdom. [50] A detestable thing, the worst thing, a pitiable thing, a vile thing was done to him when his own male organ was thrust into his own mouth. O holy Virgin Mary who bore Christ, may you quickly vindicate this man with the palm of glory. Woe to him who did that, woe to him who approved of it, and woe to him who ordered it. Woe to the wicked people who allowed such evil things to be done.[6]

[56] ¶ With the father, the son Henry was taken, died and was buried, a martyr and a virtuous knight.[7] A thousand signs show that both of them were saints, with a thousand sick people telling their praises. [60] O you, the Eleanors, wife and daughter,[8] do not weep as you do for this man, for truly he is now honoured and glorified as a martyr. Indeed, you have earnt this advantage: that of having a patron interceding for you and cherishing you.

---

[5] His erstwhile supporters, principally Gilbert of Clare earl of Gloucester.
[6] i.e. the king and Edward.
[7] Henry de Montfort.
[8] Eleanor countess of Leicester, Simon de Montfort's wife, and Eleanor their daughter.

| 65 | ¶ O comes egregie, lucis nunc incola die,
| | Regula iusticie, sancte pie serue Marie,
| | Martiribus Christi sociari iam meruisti
| | Et Domino sisti pro quo tot dira tulisti.
| | Nunc tormentorum memorum memor esto tuorum.
| 70 | Sancte tuis natis ostendas uim pietatis,
| | Militibus teneris quibus de iure teneris,
| | Binos maiores binosque tuere minores.
| | Assiduus Symonis sis custos atque Guydonis
| | Almaricoque precibus succurre citoque.
| 75 | Tu presto mesto Ricardo tutor adesto.
| | Nate predicte[a] fer opem dicteque relicte.
| | Exheredatis et rebus ui spoliatis
| | Et desolatis tibi quondam consociatis,
| | Vita priuatis pro te, tecumque necatis
| 80 | Et iam defunctis olim tibi federe iunctis,
| | Ac modo captiuis tentis in carcere uiuis,
| | Per te solamen det eis Deus omnibus. Amen.

---

[a] predicte] *In margin (in the same hand)* uel proprie.

[65] ¶ O excellent earl, dweller now in a place of light, model of justice, holy and faithful servant of Mary, you have now deserved to be in the company of Christ's martyrs and to be set before the Lord for whom you bore so many evils. Think now of the anguish of your worried family. [70] O saint, extend the power of your holiness to your sons, the young knights, the two elder and the two younger, whom you are rightfully bound to protect. Be the constant guardian of Simon and Guy[9] and support Amaury with prayers, and come soon to the mournful Richard as a ready protector.[10] [76] Bring help to the foresaid[11] daughter and widow. To the disinherited[12] and those despoiled of their possessions by force, those ruined people once your companions, and to those deprived of life, killed with you and for you and now dead, who were once united in partnership with you, and to those captives kept alive in prison, may God give comfort to them all through you. Amen.

---

[9] Simon de Montfort the younger and Guy de Montfort, second and fourth sons of Earl Simon.
[10] Amaury de Montfort the third son, a young clerk, and Richard de Montfort the fifth, an esquire. Richard was alive in 1266 (C. Bémont, *Simon de Montfort Earl of Leicester 1208–1265*, ed. and transl. E. F. Jacob (Oxford, 1930), pp. 259–60) but no later mention of him has been found.
[11] the foresaid] *In the margin in the same hand* or your own.
[12] In September 1265 after a period of unregulated spoliation the Crown began formally to confiscate the estates of all former Montfortians; it was not until October 1266 that the disinherited were offered an opportunity to buy them back: Jobson, *First English Revolution*, pp. 150–2, 157.

Chaunter mestoit (204)

London, British Library, Harley MS 2253

[fol. 59r]
Chaunter mestoit / mon cuer le voit / en un dure langage.
Tut enploraunt / fust fet le chaunt / de nostre duz baronage
Qe pur la pees / si loynz apres / se lesserent detrere,
Lur cors trencher / e demenbrer / pur salver Engletere.

5   Ore est ocys / la flur de pris / qe taunt savoit de guere,
Ly quens Mountfort. / Sa dure mort / molt enplorra la terre.

Sicom je qui / par un mardi / firent la bataile.
Tot a cheval / fust le mal / sauntz nulle pedaile
Tresmalement / y ferirent / de le espie forbie
10   Qe la part / Sire Edward / conquist la mestrie.

Ore est ocis, etc.

Mes par sa mort / le cuens Mountfort / conquist la victorie.
Come ly martyr / de Caunterbyr / finist sa vie.
Ne voleit pas / li bon Thomas / qe perist seinte eglise.
15   Ly cuens auxi / se combati / e morust sauntz feyntise.

Ore est ocys, etc.

Sire Hue le fer / ly Despencer, / tresnoble justice,
Ore est atort / lyvre a mort / a trop male guise,
Sire Henri / pur veir le dy, / fitz le cuens de Leycestre,
20   Autres assez, / come vus orrez, / par le cuens de Gloucestre.

Ore est ocis, etc.

Qe voleint moryr / e mentenir / la pees e la dreyture
Le seint martir / lur fra joyr, / sa conscience pure,

Chaunter mestoit (204)

London, British Library, Harley MS 2253, fols 59r–59v

With harsh words must I sing; my heart is aware of that. All made tearfully was the song about our gentle barons, who let themselves be destroyed for the sake of a peace so far off[1] and allowed their bodies to be slashed and dismembered to protect England.

Now is slain that precious flower, Montfort the earl, who knew so much about war. England will lament his cruel death.

[7]   It was on a Tuesday, so I believe, that they fought the battle. The calamity was that they were all on horseback. Without any infantry,[2] they fought there so forlornly with their burnished swords that Sir Edward's side won the day.

Now is slain, etc.

[12]   But by his death Montfort the earl won the victory. He ended his life like the martyr of Canterbury.[3] The good Thomas did not wish holy church to perish; the earl, too, fought and died without relenting.

Now is slain, etc.

[17] Bold Sir Hugh le Despenser the most noble justiciar and, in truth, the earl of Leicester's son Sir Henry and many others, are now wrongfully delivered up to death by the earl of Gloucester[4] in a manner too wicked, as you shall hear.

Now is slain, etc.

[22] In his natural fairness the holy martyr will bring joy to those willing to die to maintain peace and right, as well as to anyone who would die to help the

---

[1] No peace agreement would be reached until 1 July 1267: Jobson, *First English Revolution*, pp. 159–60.
[2] The infantry had fled the field before battle was joined: Cox, *Battle of Evesham*, pp. 23–4.
[3] Thomas Becket archbishop of Canterbury, murdered in 1170.
[4] Gilbert of Clare, a former ally of Simon de Montfort, was one of the commanders of the army that defeated him at Evesham.

Qe velt moryr / e sustenir / les houmes de la terre
25 Son bon desir / acomplir, / quar bien le quidom fere.

Ore est, etc.

Pres de son cors, / le bon tresors, / une heyre troverent.
Les faus ribaus / tant furent maus / e ceux qe le tuerent.
Molt fust pyr / qe demenbryr / firent le prodhoume
30 Qe de guerrer / e fei tener / si bien savoit la soume.

Ore est, etc.

Priez touz, / mes amis douz / le fitz seinte Marie
Qe lenfant / her puissant / meigne en bone vie.
Ne vueil nomer / li escoler / ne vueil qe lem die
35 Mes pur lamour / le salveour / priez pur la clergie.

Ore est ocys / la flur de pris / qe tant savoit de guere,
Ly quens Montfort. / Sa dure mort / molt enplurra la terre.

[fol. 59v]
Ne say trover rien / quil firent bien, / ne baroun ne counte.
Les chivalers / e esquiers / touz sunt mys a hounte.
40 Pur lur lealte / e verite / que tut est anentie
Le losenger / purra reigner / le fol pur sa folie.

Ore est ocis, etc.

Sire Simoun / ly prodhom / e sa compagnie
En joie vont / en ciel amount / en pardurable vie.
45 Mes Jesu Crist / qe en croyz se mist, / Dieu, enprenge cure
Qe sunt remis / e detenuz / en prisone dure.

Ore est ocys, etc.

men of this land towards achieving his worthy aim, for we believe he was doing something good.

Now is, etc.

[27] Next to his body, that fine treasure, they found a hair shirt. The false scoundrels were so wicked, and they that slew him. What was much worse, they caused the worthy man to be dismembered, who knew so well all about fighting and keeping faith.

Now is, etc.

[32] My dear friends, pray all of you to St Mary's son that he lead the young one in a good life as the mighty heir.[5] I do not want to name the scholar.[6] I do not want anyone to mention him but, for love of the Saviour, pray for the clergy.

Now is slain that precious flower, Montfort the earl, who knew so much about war. The land will deeply lament his cruel death.

[38] I cannot think of anything to say about what they did right, either barons or earls. The knights and esquires were all brought low.[7] Despite their loyalty and honesty, which has come to nothing, the sycophant will be able to rule, and the fool too, despite his foolishness.[8]

Now is slain, etc.

[43] The worthy Sir Simon and his companions[9] are going joyfully to heaven above in eternal life. But may Jesus Christ who, as God, put himself on the cross, take into his care those who are kept behind and held in harsh imprisonment.

Now is slain, etc.

---

[5] Simon de Montfort the younger, Earl Simon's second and eldest surviving son until 1271.
[6] The earl's second surviving son Amaury, a cleric and learned writer, some of whose works survive: *ODNB*, s.n.
[7] Earl Simon's chief supporters had been mostly below the rank of earl or baron: Maddicott, *Simon de Montfort*, pp. 248–50, 255–6.
[8] Possibly a direct reference to King Henry, whose personal weaknesses and consequent lapses of judgement were well known: D. Carpenter, *Henry III: The Rise to Power and Personal Rule 1207–1258* (New Haven and London, 2020), pp. 55–6, 712, 716.
[9] Chiefly Henry de Montfort and Hugh le Despenser: see **186**.

Chaunter mestut (205)

Dublin, Trinity College, MS 347

[fol. 2v]
<Chaunter> mestut <mun quer> *** <dure langage>[a]
Tut enplurant fu fet le chant de nostre barnage

Qui pur la pes si loins apres se lessa detrere
Sun cors trencher pur ben saver la gent de Engletere.

5   Ore est occis la flur de pris ke tant saveit de guere
Li quens Munfort sa dure mort enplura Engletere.

Si cum qui par un mardi fini la bataylle
Tut a cheval firent le mal san ren de petaylle.

Ore est apert cum sire Edeward cunquit la mestrie
10   Mes pur sa mort li quens Munfort cunquit victorie.

Atort est tue e demembre ore ad Deu la vie aye
Cum li martyr de Canterberi se finist sa vie.

Ne voleit pas seint Thomas ke perist seinte eglise
Li quens ausi cumbaty e murut sen fayntise.

15   Pur nus saver e deliverer de males leys enterre
Se cumbatist e mort suffrit. Tut arme sur la †bere†

Pres de sun cors li bon tresors une here truverent
Li faus ribaus \tant/ firent maus ke si li tuerent.

Mult fu pite quant demembre remistrent li prudume
20   Ke de gerrer pur nus sauver si ben saveit la sume.

Huge Despenser li noble ber la dreiturel justise
Ore est atort livre a mort ne sey en quele guyse.

---

[a] *Some characters in line 1 have been lost by trimming at the top edge of the leaf.*

Chaunter mestut (205)

Dublin, Trinity College, MS 347, fols 2v–3r

*** harsh words must I sing, my heart *** All made tearfully was the song about our barons,

who let themselves be destroyed for the sake of a peace so far off[1] and let their bodies be slashed to protect well the people of England.

[5] Now is slain that precious flower, Montfort the earl, who knew so much about war. The land will deeply lament his cruel death.

[7] It was on a Tuesday, so I believe, that the battle ended. The calamity was that it was all on horseback, without any infantry.[2]

[9] Now is it clear how Sir Edward's side won the day. But in spite of his death Montfort the earl won the victory.

[11] He was wrongly killed and dismembered. Now God has protected his life. He ended his life like the martyr of Canterbury.[3]

[13] Saint Thomas did not wish holy church to perish. The earl, too, fought and died without relenting.

[15] To save us and deliver us completely from bad laws, he fought and suffered death. All armed on the †bier†,

[17] next to his body, that fine treasure, they found a hair shirt. The false scoundrels were so wicked, who thus slew him.

[19] It was a great misfortune when they caused the worthy man to be dismembered, who knew so well all about fighting to save us.

[21] Hugh le Despenser the noble baron, the righteous justiciar, is now wrongly delivered up to death, I know not in what manner,

---

[1] No peace agreement would be reached until 1 July 1267: Jobson, *First English Revolution*, pp. 159–60.
[2] Cox, *Battle of Evesham*, pp. 23–4.
[3] Thomas Becket archbishop of Canterbury, murdered in 1170.

E sire Henri pur veirs vus di fiz li quens de Leycestre
E autres ases cum oy avet par li quens de Gloucestre.

25 Li quens Symon par sun dreit nun od sa compaignie
En joye sunt a cel lamunt en pardurable vie.

Mes Jesu Crist ke nus tuz fist de ceus enprenge cure
Ke sunt remis e pris e mis en prisun si dure.

[fol. 3r]
<Je> ne puis truver en ky fier en sei barun ne cunte[a]
30 <Li> chivaler e li esquier tus sunt mys a hunte.

Pur lur leaute pur verite ke tut est enentye
<Li> losenger pura regner li fol pur sa folie.

<Ore> est mort li bon cunte. Deu li faz verai pardun
<Occis> esteit en la bataile a Evisham par treisun.

35 <Deus> vus envei un leun ke enprenge venganse.[b]
<Si> en frai bon chansun.

---

[a] *Some characters in line 29 have been lost by trimming at the top edge of the leaf. Some characters at the beginnings of lines 29–36 have become obscured in the binding.*
[b] ke enprenge venganse] *added by the same hand at the end of line 35, after lines 35–6 had been bracketed as a couplet.*

[23] and in truth so are the earl of Leicester's son Sir Henry and many others, as you have heard, by the earl of Gloucester.[4]

[25] Earl Simon, by his rightful name, and his companions[5] are going joyfully to heaven above in eternal life.

[27] But may Jesus Christ, who made us all, take into his care those who are kept behind, and taken and put in such harsh imprisonment.[6]

[29] I can think of no-one whom I can trust, be they barons or earls. The knights and esquires are all brought low.[7]

[31] Despite their loyalty and despite their honesty, which has come to nothing, the sycophant will be able to reign, and the fool too, despite his foolishness.[8]

[33] Now the good earl is dead. May God give him true mercy. He was killed in the battle of Evesham through treachery.

[35] May God send you a lion[9] who will exact vengeance. Then will I make a fine song of it.

---

[4] Gilbert of Clare, a former ally of Simon de Montfort, was one of the commanders of the army that defeated him at Evesham.
[5] Chiefly Henry de Montfort and Hugh le Despenser: see **186**.
[6] Cf. 203 line 81 (apparently written c.1266).
[7] Earl Simon's chief supporters had been mostly below the rank of earl or baron: Maddicott, *Simon de Montfort*, pp. 248–50, 255–6.
[8] Possibly a direct reference to King Henry, whose personal weaknesses and consequent lapses of judgement were well known: Carpenter, *Henry III 1207–58*, pp. 55–6, 712, 716.
[9] The Montfort shield of arms displayed a white lion on a red field.

Illos saluauit (206)

London, British Library, Cotton MS Otho D VIII

[fol. 261r]
    Illos saluauit Mons Fortis quos superauit.
Carceribus dati sunt multi, non cruciati.
Militie flores anglorum nobiliores
Anglos rexere, qui mortem post subiere,
5   Vt sum daturus \<nece\> qua sit Mons periturus.
Ecclesie festa Leus hec dant tempora mesta
Quo bellum primum multis fecit capud imum.
Annus et Henrici regis quo sunt inimici
Grecus si detur eheu longa mihi semper habetur.
10   Ecclesie festa Leus hec dant tempora mesta
Quo bellum primum multis fecit capud imum.
Bella dabat que lis Leus est uocitata fidelis,
In qua distortum fuerat nil primitus ortum.
Excipitur sanguis quem fuderat impius anguis.
15   Anglia plaudebat dum Mons hanc sorte regebat.
Morti Monte dato diro ruit Anglia fato.
Simonis huic \nomen/ magnum sibi contulit omen.
Miles preclarus, armis super omnia gnarus,
Quem gens gallorum produxit, dux fit eorum.
20   Quam desponsauit germanam regis amauit,
Anglorum gentis regem per cuncta uerentis.
Hic fuit anglorum dux et protector eorum.
Namque duos reges cupientes uertere leges
Anglorum uicit, prius ut gens singula dicit,
25   Hiis nimium parcens quorum mala non \<fuit arcens\>.
Eius et adiutor comes et fuit undique \<tutor\>
De Clare Gilebertus, stabilis non inde repertus.

Illos saluauit (206)

London, British Library, Cotton MS Otho D VIII, fols 261r–262r

Montfort spared those whom he defeated; many were given imprisonment and not put to death;[1] and they would come to have dominion over the flowers of English knighthood, the most noble of Englishmen, who met their death, as I shall tell, in the violent manner by which Montfort was to die. [6] These times render mournful the festal date of Lewes,[2] where for many men the first battle[3] made the greatest into the least; if King Henry's regnal year, in which they were at enmity, were to be stated in Greek, alas I would certainly feel that it was rather long-winded. [10] These times render mournful the festal date of Lewes, where for many men this first battle made the greatest into the least.[4] The which fine (*bella*) conflict (*lis*) is called 'Lewes the trusty', in which nothing hitherto established had been changed. The blood was taken that a wicked snake had shed. [15] England rejoiced while Montfort by good fortune ruled her. When death came to Montfort England fell headlong to dire misfortune. Simon's reputation conferred great power upon himself. A brilliant soldier, supremely skilled in arms, whom the French people brought forth, he became one of their noblemen. [20] He loved the sister of the king,[5] who gave her to him in marriage, in preference to any of the king's English subjects. He was a nobleman of the English and their defender. Indeed, he defeated the two kings[6] who wanted to overturn the laws of England, and was excessively lenient towards them, as all the people are already saying, and not preventing their evil-doing. [26] And his assistant, comrade, and defender everywhere was Gilbert of Clare,[7] who was found to be inconsistent

---

[1] Under the settlement reached after Montfort's victory at Lewes, most of his opponents who had not fled were allowed to return home; a few were held to ransom and some were kept as hostages; no-one was executed: Maddicott, *Simon de Montfort*, pp. 272–3.
[2] 14 May 1264.
[3] The second battle was at Evesham.
[4] It is not clear whether this repetition is intentional.
[5] Eleanor widow of William Marshal earl of Pembroke.
[6] Henry III king of England and his brother, Richard earl of Cornwall and king of the Romans. Both were defeated at Lewes.
[7] Earl of Gloucester.

Inter quos mira cito postea ferbuit ira.
Mittitur ut flamen quo uiret tempore gramen
30 Rege coronato deademate quo decorato.
Inter eos creuit furor et discordia seuit.
Nam bello captum diadem***
Fautor dum cressit hominum concordia ***
Quod mox expressit Gilebertus, ab <inde> ***
35 Edwardo mandat ut ei per singula <pandat>
Velle suum certe socius sibi fiet ***
Vt confundantur barones seu <perimantur>
Per quos tentus erat ad quod nil <se> ***
Custodes uicet ut eosdem pactio <dicet>
40 Consilioque pari sibi possint <consiliari>.
Fugerat Edwardus custodes ut <leopardus>
Vt placuit propere comitis mandata ***
Qui fuerant uiui, uiui Leus a <be>***
Hii demandantur et eis cito <consolidantur>.
[fol. 261v]
45 Simonis ad uillam ueniunt, predantur et illam.
Mannos dum rapiunt audaces robore fiunt.
Armis nudati barones sunt superati,
Quique remansere uitas uix optinuere.
Iure canum uilla Keynworth uocatur, et illa
50 Sunt bona nulla data quia gens ibi fit spoliata.
Ensem uibrauit Gilebertus ulnere strauit
Set Holwellensem qui contra non tulit ensem.
Consiliis aptus est hinc sine crimine captus.
Forsan si queris quantum uixit tria teris,
55 Sexta fit et nona qua sumpsit celica bona.
Spiritus in celis eius prece sit Michelis.
Sic sic traduntur qui non in pace reguntur,
Nam pax nulla datur ubi concio sic separatur.
Secum duxerunt homines ibi quos rapuerunt.
60 Ad Warewiche ueniunt proceres, post inde recedunt.
Armis ditati properant ad bella parati

in that regard. Soon afterwards remarkable anger erupted between them. [29] It arose like a flame at the time when the grass was growing,[8] when Earl Simon was adorned with a diadem like a crowned king. Hatred grew between them and discord raged. For the crown captured in battle *** As the benefactor grew in status, harmony between the men *** as Gilbert made clear a little later, from there *** [35] He sends word to Edward that each of them should individually announce his definite wish *** to become the other's comrade, so that they would defeat or kill the barons by whom Edward was held, to which nothing himself *** Edward should overcome the guards so that an agreement would declare that they would be able to consult one another about a plan. [41] Edward had fled from his captors like a leopard,[9] as he wished to *** quickly to the earl's message.[10] Those who had survived, and are alive from *** Lewes, are summoned to unite with them quickly. [45] They come to Simon's town[11] and pillage it. When they seize the horses, the bold acquire strength. Stripped of their arms, the barons were overcome and those who were left barely saved their lives.[12] [49] Kenilworth (*Keynworth*) is rightly called the 'town of dogs' (*canum uilla*); there is nothing of value there because the inhabitants were plundered. Earl Gilbert brandished his sword and struck down and wounded Holwell, who did not, however, carry a sword against him. A skilled counsellor, he was taken thence without having committed any crime. [54] If you happen to enquire how long he survived, three hours would be too little; the sixth hour came, and the ninth, at which he received heaven's bounty. Michael's prayer is that his spirit be in heaven.[13] Those who are not ruled peacefully are thus treated, for no peace is given where society is divided thus. [59] They took with them the men whom they had seized there. The noblemen come to Warwick.[14] Afterwards they withdraw from there. Furnished with arms they

---

[8] In the spring of 1265.

[9] Edward had earlier been likened to a leopard on the ground that he was both fierce and untrustworthy: *Song of Lewes*, p. 14, lines 417–34. See ibid. pp. 86, 89; Ambler, *Bishops in the Political Community*, pp. 174–5.

[10] On 28 May 1265, under a pre-arranged plan, Edward escaped from custody at Hereford on a speeding horse: Maddicott, *Simon de Montfort*, pp. 333–4.

[11] Kenilworth.

[12] Edward and his allies raided the camp of Simon de Montfort the younger at Kenilworth at dawn on 2 August 1265: Cox, *Battle of Evesham*, pp. 11–13.

[13] At Kenilworth Master Stephen of Holwell, one of Earl Simon's clerks, had been removed from a church and beheaded on the orders of Earl Gilbert: 'Annales Londonienses', *Chronicles of the Reigns of Edward I and Edward II* 1, ed. W. Stubbs (Rolls Series, 1882), pp. 1–251 (at p. 68). Earl Gilbert had then seized the estate at Little Holwell (Bedfordshire) that Stephen had settled on his mother Maud for her life (*Cal. Inq. Misc.* 1, p. 187) and which in 1255 had been held under Ramsey abbey by William of Holwell (*Cartularium Monasterii de Rameseia* 1, ed. W. H. Hart and P. A. Lyons (Rolls Series, 1884), p. 458). Michael, the author of these verses, may have been a monk of Ramsey (A. G. Rigg, *A History of Anglo-Latin Literature, 1066–1422* (Cambridge, 1992), pp. 202–3, 370) and therefore particularly interested in Stephen's fate.

[14] *Recte* Worcester: Cox, *Battle of Evesham*, p. 14.

Vt sic Mons Fortis subeat discrimina mortis.
Mars donat mortem, necat hunc dum forte cohortem.
Fortes prostrati <nece>[a] sunt heu sic superati.
65 Militie flores uitas capiunt meliores.
Martirio freti florent super ethera leti.
O mors quam dira quod nulli parcit in ira,
Nam ruit ense pater natus nati quoque frater.
Ex ipsis funus tamen haud tunc pertulit unus.
70 Multi sunt dempti qui sunt pro pace perempti
Nec pax ulla datur melior pars dum superatur.
Anglia terra teres, dic cur gemis et modo meres
*** mortem quem uix cono dicere fortem
<Nam> capud anglorum fuit et conquestor eorum
75 <In> pugna prima, cui manent nimis ima
***ius et Henricus anglorum natus amicus
***m ruit ense graui, mors illum depulit a ui.
*** <Dispensator> ruit illic pacis amator
***bus anglorum dabitur pax sanguine quorum
80 *** <sanguinea> nece <concorruit> ampla chorea
***<que multorum fusum fuit> ema uirorum.
***<bis> etiam uere d<uo bi>s sibi lustra fuere
***us uixit mihi gens ut plurima dixit.
*** hiis propere iungas tibi si placuere.
85 *** <nunquam> rore proprio maduere <cruore>
***<ore patrie> pro pacis amore.
***<eges> multos faciunt sibi reges.
*** <fatur> quod sit raptum rapiatur
***<letu> quid in hoc contingere cetu
90 ***<iebant>, qui meriorem capiebant.
*** <conflictu> Simon ruit ensis in ictu.
*** <abscisum>, summo petiit paradisum.
*** Domini dum singula uestis
Ex ipso rapitur qui nudus ibi reperitur.
95 Trunccat et inde manus quidam miser atque <prophanus>
Atque pedes. Christo duce mundo fertur ab isto.
Vt multi referunt comitis putibunda <tulerunt>
Membraque sperserunt agris, post hoc abicerunt.
Sic sic trunccatus sit omnino spoliatus,

[a] necc *MS*.

go forth prepared for battle so that Montfort might thus undergo death. Mars is the giver of death as he boldly kills that army. [64] The strong are laid low by death and are defeated thus, alas. The flowers of knighthood receive better lives. Confident in their martyrdom they flourish happily above the ether. O, how dire is the death that in its anger spares no-one, for a father is cut down by the sword of his own son, and so is a brother. [69] Funeral rites were accorded to scarcely one of them at that time. Nor was any peace granted when the better side was overcome. You will say, 'Tell me, O land of England, why do you now groan and grieve?' *** hardly call death strong, like an army. [74] For he was the leader of the English and their conqueror in the first battle. Of whom there remain in the lowest place *** and Henry the son,[15] friend of the English. *** fell by a cruel sword. Death drove away his strength. *** Despenser[16] fell there, a lover of peace. [79] To the *** of the English shall be given peace by the blood of those of whom a large company fell together *** in a bloody killing *** the *haima*[17] of many men was poured out. *** also truly they have been together twice two lustres[18] *** lived, as many people told me. [84] *** hasten to unite them with you if you wish to. *** have never shed a drop of their own blood *** of the country for the love of peace. Kings make many *** for themselves. *** says that what may be stolen should be stolen. [89] *** what to happen with the company in this *** who received sorrow. *** conflict Simon fell to the blow of a sword. *** cut off, he attained the supreme paradise. *** of the Lord when every garment was taken from him, who was there found naked. [95] And some wretched and wicked man cuts off his hands and feet. Led by Christ he is carried from this world. As many relate, they took away his genitals and scattered his limbs over the land and after that got rid of them. [99] Cut up like that, he would be completely stripped and, castrated thus, he undergoes

---

[15] Henry de Montfort.
[16] Hugh le Despenser, justiciar of England, Simon de Montfort's chief minister.
[17] Ancient Greek for 'blood'.
[18] A lustre is a period of five years.

100 Et sic castratus summos patitur cruciatus.
Framea lictoris fuit anglis causa doloris.
Cur? Quia pellexit comitem rex quem male rexit.
Celum signa <dabat>[a] quoniam sol non<radiabat>
Et motum terre dedit hora ferissima <guerre>.
105 Dum sic bellatur, Domini gens dum cruciatur,
Tunc pluit et tonuit, imbres dedit <etheris ira>
Ingens grando fuit quo possis dicere <mira>.
Rumphea cum lite tulit illi gaudia <uite>.
Nam nece condignis parcens fuit ille <malignis>.
110 Anglis prodesset licet hic silicernius esset,
Cuius et in morte misera ruit Anglia forte.
Iusticiis plena fuit anglica terra serena.
Non tibi sint frustra totum bis .l. et duo lustra
Ac unum restat quo se Christus manifestat,
115 Carnis habens spolia de uirgine sumpta Maria.
Si grece loqueris, si tempora bellica queris,
Tu pi bis pone, sima xi, set et epsilon uenietur,
Annum compone belli qui sic <tibi detur>;
Imera si ponas augusti pridie nonas
120 Quo bello fortes Hevesham cecidere <cohortes>
Qui sic prostrati superant dum sunt superati.
Hec domus est Eue. Contra gens ruit inclita seue
Nam male traduntur misera nece dum feriuntur.
  Post Euesham bellum scelus excercere <nouellum>
125 Quidam ceperunt, qui ceci mente fuerunt.
Mandat Clarensis Gilebertus, acutus ut ensis,
Seruis ut propere faciant fera tempora guerre
Terras ut lustrent, dominos quibus hii cito frustrent.
Semper abutuntur qui pessima iussa sequuntur.
130 Diuino more proprio Deus hoc tulit ore
Ne quis mendicum nec quisquam fallat amicum,
Tractet per uicum male quisquam non inimicum,
Ne sit et incestus quo quis sit iure scelestus.
Christi mandata postponit gens scelerata,
135 Nam spoliat uillas [blank] spoliabitur illas.
Vnde Berengarius Ramesenses exspoliauit
Quique fide uarius manes sibi iure parauit.

[a] dabant MS.

the utmost abuse. The assassin's sword was the cause of sorrow to the English. Why? Because the king invited the earl in but governed him badly. The sky gave signs inasmuch as the sun did not shine and the fiercest hour of warfare produced an earthquake. [105] While the battle went on thus, while the Lord's people were thus being killed, it then rained and thundered, the wrath of the ether produced storm clouds, and there was a huge hailstorm that you might say was unnatural. With the strife, the sword brought him the joys of life. [109] For in death he was merciful to those malignants who deserved the same. He had done well by the English although he had been an old man, and by his death a wretched England fell by mischance into ruin. Full of justices was the peaceful English land. [113] The whole of twice fifty-two lustres would not be futile for you if there remained one of them in which Christ were to show himself, having received the spoils of the flesh from the Virgin Mary. If you speak Greek and are seeking the date of the battle, put two times *phi*, plus *sigma*, plus *xi*, and then add *epsilon* to make the year of the battle, which would thus be given to you;[19] [119] and the day if you put the day[20] preceding the nones of August, on which strong forces were cut down at Evesham who, thus laid low, conquered while being conquered. This was the home of Eve.[21] An illustrious people fell cruelly in opposition, for they were mistreated by a wretched death when slain.

[124] After the battle of Evesham some who were mentally blind began to commit a fresh crime. Gilbert of Clare, sharp as a sword, orders his servants quickly to make the wartime cruel in such a way that they would seek out lands of which they would promptly deprive the lords. [129] Those who obey the truly bad commands continue to commit abuses. As is God's way, God has said this himself, that one should not cheat a beggar or a friend, nor wickedly drag through the street someone not an enemy, nor commit sexual acts in circumstances where one would be guilty under the law. [134] Those wicked people put aside Christ's commands, for they plunder townships [*blank*] *** those, they shall be plundered. Thus did Berengar[22] plunder anyone of any sort among Ramsey's people who had supplied goods for him lawfully and in faith. This man did not keep fealty; he was a knight

---

[19] In Ancient Greek the letters *phi*, *sigma*, *xi*, and *epsilon* represented respectively 500, 200, 60, and 5.
[20] 4 August.
[21] A fanciful derivation of 'Evesham'.
[22] Berengar le Moyne. After the battle of Evesham he seized Montfortian estates arbitrarily (*Cal. Inq. Misc.* 1, pp. 254–5) and was granted others by the king (*Rot. Selecti*, p. 251). Royalist keeper of the peace in Huntingdonshire (the county of Ramsey abbey), he was empowered early in 1267 to raise money locally to fight the Montfortian rebels holding out in the Isle of Ely: *Cal. Pat.* 1266–72, p. 132.

Non tenet ille fidem, dominos spolians eques idem.
Hic eques <extiterat> quem nutriuit Rameseya.
140 Qui mala multa ferat det Christus et alma Maria.
Vt pascat toruos donet Deus in cruce coruos
Et similes eius subeant per <tempora> peius.
[fol. 262r]
Vt nequeant cerni, flammis urantur Auerni,
Ni reddant rapta ni restituant male capta.
145 Agnus, ouis, uitulus, gallus, gallina, uel auca,
Bos, equus, ac aries, porcorum copia pauca,
Queque remanserunt miseris cibus ipsa fuerunt.
Hiis tanquam dignis sit potus sulphur[a] et ignis.
Nulla referta bonis est uillula religionis
150 Quam non predentur miseri, qua non dominentur.
Multas iacturas subeunt pro tempore duras
Hos per predones sacrate religiones.
Pauca relatiua fuerant animalia uiua.
Sunt ablatiua quia non sunt ulla datiua.
155 Actio passiua meroris erat genitiua.
Heccine gens atra uillis abduxit aratra.
Inculte terre iacuerunt tempore guerre,
Orrea triturant, mala tempora dummodo durant.
Pacem firmare uolunt rex quam reprobare.
160 Gens ea presumpsit, gens effera, gens mala cum sit.
Regia mandata postponit gens scelerata
Nam contra iura rapit omnia gens peritura.
Dilecti parum sunt ciues Londoniarum.
Exheredantur multi uillaque fugantur;
165 Nam contra morem domine fecere pudorem
Exulat unde cito nato ductore petito,
Semper et exosi regine suntque dolosi.
Oderat hos peius Edwardus filius eius.
Vrbi pax detur a Christo ne superetur.
170 Si tamen hoc mores ueteres faciat meliores,
<Anglica terra> ferax in qua gens plurima uerax
Nunc fremit atque gemit ut singula gaudia demit
Nescia uenturi cuius sit subdita iuri,
Sub quo custode, sub Christo uel sub Herode,

---

[a] potus sulphur] \b/ sulphur \a/ potus MS.

plundering lords. [140] He had emerged as a knight whom Ramsey nurtured. May Christ and gentle Mary grant that he may endure many evils. May God grant that in torment he may feed the savage ravens[23] and that those like him may suffer worse in due course; may they be consumed by the flames of hell so that they disappear from sight, unless they return what they have seized and restore what they have wickedly taken. [145] Whatever were left – a lamb, a sheep, a calf, a cock, a hen, a goose, an ox, a horse, a ram, many pigs or a few – were food for those scoundrels just as, for those who deserve it, may the drink be fire and brimstone.[24] [149] There is no small religious settlement that the scoundrels would not despoil and would not dominate. For a time the holy religious suffer many severe losses at the hands of those robbers. Few livestock had been returned (*relatiua*). [154] They are taken (*ablatiua*), for they are none of them given (*datiua*). Passive (*passiua*) action is productive (*genitiua*) of sorrow. These menacing people took away the ploughs from townships; the lands lay untilled during the war. They thresh the barns while the bad times last. [159] They wish to secure a peace, which the king wishes to reject. Those people have taken those things, a savage people, for they are an evil people. Those wicked people set aside the king's commands, for contrary to the law those people seize everything perishable.[25] The citizens of London are too little respected. [164] Many of them are disinherited and driven from the city. For he who dishonours a lady contrary to accepted conduct is soon banished thence, the son having been put in command, and those who are deceitful remain hateful to the queen too. Edward her son hated them even more.[26] [169] May peace be granted to the city by Christ, lest it be overcome. Even if this should make the old ways better, the fertile English land, in which is a truth-loving people, now moans and groans and thus abandons every joy, not knowing what is to come, to whose jurisdiction it should be subject, under what authority, under Christ's or under

---

[23] feed the savage ravens] A metaphor for 'lie dead on the battlefield'.
[24] fire and brimstone] Cf. Ps. 10: 7.
[25] Ramsey abbey and its neighbourhood were troubled by both royalists and rebels during the Ely campaign: *Cal. Pat.* 1266–72, pp. 33, 220; *Flores Historiarum* 3, p. 13; 'Chronicon vulgo dictum Thomae Wykes', *Ann. Monastici* 4, pp. 6–319 (at pp. 207–8).
[26] On 13 July 1263 a mob of Londoners had hurled missiles and insults at the queen as her boat approached London bridge. On this and on the penalties inflicted on disloyal Londoners after the battle of Evesham see Williams, *Medieval London*, pp. 219, 232–9.

175 Sub custode bono sub solo siue patrono,
An plures reges plures facient sibi leges
Vt sit destructa lex anglica uel male ducta.
Absit ut hoc detur lex anglica quod reprobetur.
O pie seruorum Iesu miserere tuorum.
180 Vt pax ecclesie prece detur firma Marie.
Christe regens terram, nostram cito destrue guerram,
Nam sunt exosi cuntis fere relligiosi
Hos affligendo uel eorum iura tenendo
Tu cito da pacem, tu destrue quemque rapacem,
185 Comprime uersutos, nos fac hoc tempore <tutos>,
Et malefactores humiles fac et <meliores>.
Sis memor illorum, qui scandis ad astra polorum,
Pro quibus e celis ueniens uerbo Gabrielis.
Nobis sis egis qui semper in ethere degis
190 Ne male fallatur tua gens seu <destituatur>
Donis sanctorum qui possidet ordo <uirorum>.
Pro dolor eu, equites discindunt sanguine lites
Qui querunt pacem per terram sepe feracem.
Non est inuentus presul qui crimine tentus
195 Non sit, uel funus capiens ex patribus unus
Post Thomam uere qui pacem querat habere
Qui domet immites effuso sanguine lites.
Tempore decliuo populo Deus obsecro uiuo
Succurras uere quia multi iam periere.
200 Exheredati proceres sunt rege iubente
Et male tractati, Waleran <Roberto> dicta ferente.
Exheredati si fiant connumerati,
Millia cum binis deca bis sunt acta ruinis.
Tunc extorqueri gazas gens nescia ueri
205 Iussit et ut terra nusquam maneat sine <guerra>.
Religio certe, que non deliquit aperte,
Gente feroce satis mala pertulit improbitatis
Vasta sit ut terra mox oritur altera guerra.
Incendunt uillas iterato pir uolat illas
210 Ac inimicorum male tractant tecta suorum.
Exheredati, qui sint per secla beati,
Hoc mala fecerunt iacturas nam subierunt.
Dum gens ieiunat socios sibi quisquis adunat

Herod's, whether under a good authority and under a single ruler, or whether a multiplicity of kings should make a multiplicity of laws in such a way that the law of England should be destroyed or badly administered. Far be it that it should come to this, that the law of England be discredited. [179] O merciful Jesus, have pity on your servants. O Christ, ruler of the land, quickly put an end to our warfare so that a settled peace may be given to the church in accordance with Mary's prayer.[27] [182] Since religious men are hated by nearly everyone in striking them or taking hold of their rights, do give peace quickly, subdue anyone who is rapacious, repress the cunning deceivers, make us safe at this time, and make the evildoers humble and better people. [187] Just as you ascended to heaven, remember those for whom you came from above in accordance with Gabriel's message.[28] Be a shield to us, you who dwell for ever in the ether, lest your people be badly cheated or deprived by mere men of the gifts that they possess from saints.[29] [192] Alas and alack, knights escalate disputes with bloodshed while, in many instances, seeking peace throughout the fertile land. There is no bishop to be found who is not in the grip of sin, or a single one of the prelates after Thomas who truly seeks to have peace by choosing death and who subdues harsh quarrels by the shedding of his own blood.[30] [198] I beg you, O God, to help the downcast surviving people in good time, for truly many are now perishing. Eminent persons are being disinherited at the king's behest and badly treated, with Robert Walerand conveying the orders.[31] [202] If the disinherited should be numbered, twice *deka*[32] thousand, doubled, have been driven to ruin. At that time a body of people ignorant of truth ordered treasure to be seized by force, and that the land should nowhere be left without warfare. The religious, who have certainly not offended openly, have endured enough evil from the unjust behaviour of a savage set of people in such a way that the land should be laid waste as soon as further fighting breaks out. [209] They burn townships repeatedly and rob them too, and they wickedly pull down the roofs of their enemies. The disinherited, who should have been forever blessed, behaved badly in this way, for they carried out acts of destruction. [213] While people are fasting[33] they associate whomsoever to themselves so that the royalist

---

[27] See Luke 1: 51–2.
[28] See Luke 1: 31–3.
[29] Many religious houses of Anglo-Saxon origin had been founded or endowed by saints.
[30] About half of the English bishops had been Montfortian supporters or sympathizers but all of them quietly submitted to royal and papal authority after the battle of Evesham: S. T. Ambler, 'The Montfortian bishops', in Jobson (ed.), *Baronial Reform and Revolution*, pp. 139–51 (at pp. 139–40).
[31] It was alleged that Walerand, one of Henry III's chief ministers, was behind the king's decision to formally disinherit any who had supported Montfort: *ODNB*, s.n. It was certainly he who announced the policy to Parliament in September 1265: 'Annales prioratus de Wigornia', *Ann. Monastici* 2, pp. 355–564 (at p. 455).
[32] Ancient Greek for 'ten'.
[33] In Lent.

Vt confundatur pars regia seu perimatur.
215 Non parcunt uite dum quis fert, 'Ite, redite,
Nulli parcatis, inimicos quin perimatis.'
Est populus certus nimis est quod fiscus apertus
Regis nam uelle dedit anglos sepe procelle.
Ecclesiam nescit de qua rex sponte recessit
220 Consilio nati semper bellare parati.
Cetibus hiis claris, o rex, cur sic operaris?
Cur tantas gentes non excipiendo parentes
Exheredasti, mala quo tibi sponte parasti?
Ni tibi sit cura pereas post Pascha futura.
225 Mauult namque mori gens ut subdatur <honori>
Quam se merori dare uel uiuendo <dolori>.
Heu dolor est fari. Cur debet rex <reprobari>?
Nam spoliatorum <bona post> destructa ***

side should be confounded or destroyed. They do not spare lives when someone says, 'Come and go, spare no-one, let us destroy the enemy.' The people are certain that the king's purse is open too much, for wanting that, often, gave the English over to civil commotion. [219] The king does not know the church from which he has willingly withdrawn at the instigation of his son, who is always ready to make war. Why, O king, do you behave thus towards these illustrious communities? Why have you disinherited so many people, not excepting their families, whereby you have willingly prepared troubles for yourself? [224] Unless this becomes of concern to you, may you perish after the coming Easter.[34] For people would prefer to die, and thus sacrifice themselves to honour, than to surrender themselves to mourning or to living in sorrow. Alas, to speak is sorrow. Why must the king be reproved? [228] Because the possessions of his plunderers afterwards destroyed ***

---

[34] 28 March 1266.

Vbi fuit mons (207)

Cambridge, Gonville and Caius College, MS 85/167

[fol. ii r]
¶ Vbi fuit mons est uallis
Et de colle fit iam callis
Heus et strata publica.

Propter casum dire sortis
5 Debilis est factus fortis
Non per sua merita.

Bellicosus infirmatur,
Alter <Sampson> trucidatur,
<Lamentatur> Anglia.

10 Symon pro simplicitate
Marchionum feritate
Cadit cesus framea.

Die martis bellum creuit,
Cadit \H/ector, Rachel fleuit
15 Pro cesis in area.

Comparatur hic Vluxi
Nam pro fide crucifixi
Non timebat milia.

Rexit uigor in Achille
20 Set et Symon talis ille
Qui pungnat pro patria.

Primus natus <rexit> frenum,
Non permisit alienum
Dare patri uulnera.

Vbi fuit mons (207)

Cambridge, Gonville and Caius College, MS 85/167, fol. ii r

¶ Where there was a mountain is now a valley, and from a hill is now made a path, alas, and a common highway.[1]

[4]   A strong man is now made weak because a cruel fate has befallen him and not because of his deserts.

[7]   A fighting man is made a casualty. Like another Samson, he is slain. England laments him.

[10]   Simon is fallen for the sake of honesty, pierced by a spear, through the savagery of the marchers.[2]

[13] On a Tuesday (the day of Mars) the battle took place. Hector fell,[3] and Rachel wept for those cut down in the field.[4]

[16] He is like Ulysses;[5] indeed because of faith in the Crucified he did not 'fear thousands'.[6]

[19] In Achilles strength predominated, and Simon is such as he, fighting for his country.[7]

[22] His eldest son[8] held on to the reins and did not allow anyone to wound his father.

---

[1] Cf. Luke 3: 5 (alluding to Is. 40: 4).
[2] The army that defeated Earl Simon was led by holders of lordships in the marches of Wales.
[3] In the *Iliad* Hector is the foremost Trojan hero.
[4] See Jer. 31: 15, cited in Matt. 2: 18 with reference to the Slaughter of the Innocents.
[5] Ulysses (Odysseus in Greek) is a Greek hero in the *Iliad* and the central figure of the *Odyssey*.
[6] Cf. Ps. 3: 7.
[7] In the *Iliad* Achilles is a Greek hero.
[8] Henry de Montfort.

25　Dum durauit non expauit
　　Pater enses set certauit
　　Propter pacis[a] federa.

　　Pater prole confortatur,
　　Proles patrem consolatur
30　Dum durarent prelia.

　　Non fuerunt duo tales
　　In amore speciales
　　Infra mundi climata.

　　Abel Ade sociatur,
35　Abel prius inmolatur,
　　<Cadit> Adam postea.

　　In Henrico rosa uernat
　　Et in rosa si quis cernat
　　Sat †apereri†† <lilia>.

40　Martir fertur per ruborem
　　Et per album fertur florem
　　Virgo sine macula.

　　Dixit quidam, ut Pilatus,
　　Qui in bello principatus
45　Tenuit dominia,

　　'Redde, redde, comes fortis.
　　Eris aut pro certo mortis
　　Datus ad suplicia.'

　　'Hunc', fert alter, 'occidatis
50　Vlli uiuo non parcatis
　　De sua familia.'

　　Omnes clamant 'Moriatur!'
　　Comes instans meditatur
　　De superna patria.

55　'Reddo me omnipotenti.

---

[a] *Altered from* patris *by the same hand.*

[25] As long as he endured, the father feared nothing but fought for the peace agreement.[9]

[28] While the fighting lasts, the father is encouraged by the son and the son gives reassurance to the father.

[31] There were no two such close friends in any corner of the world.

[34] Abel is united to Adam. Abel is killed first and Adam falls afterwards.

[37] In Henry a rose blooms, and inside the rose, if anyone should perceive it well enough, a lily †opens†.

[40] A martyr is signified by a red flower, and by a white flower is signified a spotless virgin.

[43] Someone who had a leading role in the battle said, like Pilate,

[47] 'Yield, yield, mighty earl, or you will certainly be given the penalty of death.'

[50] Another said, 'You should kill him! You should not spare the life of any of his followers.'

[53] They all cry, 'May he die!' while the fervent earl contemplates the world above.

---

[9] Possibly a reference to the settlement agreed at the Hilary parliament of 1265: Maddicott, *Simon de Montfort*, pp. 318–20.

Vitam meam do uiuenti
Deo pro uictoria.'

Tunc uenerunt loricati
Nimis graues et irati
60 Cum magna superbia

Cupientes preualere
Non potentes amouere
Pedibus scansilia.

Firmiter incedit equo.
65 Cadit equus non ab equo
Perforatus lancea.

Hunc occidunt conspirantes,
Introducunt ignorantes
In celi palacia.

70 Quando martir exspirauit,
'Montem Fortem', exclamauit,
'Summe pater adiuua!'

Caput eius mutulatur
Et os eius perforatur
75 Certans pro iusticia.

Manus, pedes detrunccantur
Et de morte cuncti fantur
Vili sibi tradita.

Omnes illi confundantur
80 Per quos eius uiolantur
Nature uirilia.

Thomas martir nuncupatur,
Sic Christus, sicut datur
Symon pro iusticia.

85 Passi sunt in ista terra
Pari pena pari guerra
Ambo cruciamina.

[56] 'I yield myself to the Almighty. I give my life to the living God for the sake of victory.'

[59] Then came men in hauberks with great arrogance who were extremely strong and angry.[10]

[61] They wanted to defeat him but could not shift the stirrups from his feet.

[64] Firmly he advanced on his horse but the horse falls, not because it is unequal to its role but because it is pierced by a lance.

[67] The conspirators killed him and unwittingly conducted him into the heavenly palace.

[70] When the martyr died, he cried out, 'Highest father, come to Montfort's aid!'

[73] In fighting for justice, his head was cut off and his face was pierced.

[76] His hands and feet are cut off and everyone bears witness to the foul death inflicted on him.

[79] May all those be put to shame by whom his male organs of generation are violated.

[82] Thomas the martyr,[11] like Christ and like Simon, is sacrificed for the sake of justice.

[85] They have suffered on this earth by equal punishment and equal struggle, and each under torment.

---

[10] Possibly the twelve assassins appointed to kill Earl Simon at Evesham: see Laborderie, Maddicott and Carpenter, 'Last hours of Simon de Montfort', p. 408; *Chron. Lanercost* (1839), p. 76.
[11] Thomas Becket archbishop of Canterbury, murdered in 1170.

Symon gratis passus fuit
Et pro terra cesus ruit,
90 Thomas pro ecclesia.

Comes regi sociatur
Qui Oswaldus nuncupatur
Equa per certamina.

Nabuzardan subner[u]auit
95 Et hunc uita superauit
Continens ieiunia.

¶ Hic Robertum sequebatur
Cuius uita comendatur
Certa per miracula.

100 Dictis eius uir obedit.
Fert Robertus, Symon credit
De statutis talia:

'Si uerum confitearis
Et pro dictis moriaris
105 Magna feres premia.'

'Quod uir iustus patiatur
Satis liquet et probatur
Per magna tonitrua.'

Est lorica duplex ei
110 Et examen huius rei
Fit per eius spolia.

Extra bene uir armatur,
Quisquis uidens hoc testatur
Per signa bellifica.

115 ¶ Loricatur subtus stricte.
Hanc non tulit miles ficte
Tendens ad celestia.

Nec contentus est hac ueste.
Inuocato Deo teste
120 Induit cilicia.

[88] Simon suffered willingly and was cut down for the sake of this land, as was Thomas for the church.

[91] The earl is united with the king called Oswald by their similar ordeals.[12]

[94] He disempowered Nabuzardan and overcame him by a life of keeping fasts.[13]

[97] ¶ He was a follower of Robert,[14] whose life is commended by undoubted miracles.

[100] The man obeys his teachings. Robert pronounces such maxims as these and Simon believes them:

[103] 'If you are to declare the truth and to die for the sake of these sayings you will receive a great reward.'

[106] 'It will be evident enough by great thunderclaps that a just man is suffering and is approved.'[15]

[109] He has a twofold hauberk, and the evidence of that comes when the armour is taken off him.

[112] On the outside the man has a good hauberk[16] and that, as anyone can see, is confirmed by its martial appearance.

[115] ¶ Underneath, he has a tight hauberk such as no knight wore falsely when reaching for heavenly things.

[118] In fact he was not satisfied with the former garment but, calling on God as his witness, put on a hair shirt.

---

[12] In 642 Oswald, the Christian king of Northumbria, had been killed in battle against the pagan Penda of Mercia; his body was dismembered by the victors and miracles were afterwards attributed to him; Earl Simon's feast day, 4 August, immediately preceded Oswald's: *ODNB*, s.n.

[13] Nabuzardan was a military commander under Nebuchadnezzar II king of Babylon and pillaged Jerusalem in 597 BC. In the Septuagint Nabuzardan's title is inaccurately rendered as 'chief cook' (LXX 4 Reigns 25: 8–12), whence he was taken in the Middle Ages to exemplify gluttony (e.g. *Gesta Romanorum: or, Entertaining Moral Stories*, transl. C. Swan, ed. W. Hooper (London, 1894), p. 346).

[14] Robert Grosseteste.

[15] The battle of Evesham had been immediately preceded by a thunderstorm: Cox, *Battle of Evesham*, pp. 21–2.

[16] A coat of mail.

¶ Symon, Symon, modo dormis.
Quam mors tua sit enormis
Clamat uox ad sydera.

Ante tuum Christe uultum
125 Non relinquas hunc inultum
Pro tua clemencia.

Hii coniuncti sunt uictores
Et sunt uiuis altiores
Nam uiuunt in gloria.

130 Firmiter sunt \hii/ ligati
Qui nec morte separati
Nec sunt in militia.

¶ Et Radulfus Basset dictus
Miles eius est conflictus
135 Patiens pericula.

¶ Et de Baylol dictus Guydo
Signa feris corde fido
Cuntis aparencia.

Vires eius probitatis
140 Vir in fide constans satis
Ostendebat dextera.

Quando Symon fuit cesus
Guydo sicut nondum lesus
Signum fert in lancea.

145 Signum iusti nunquam ruit.
Semper exaltatum fuit
Inter tua brachia.

Euasisse potuisti
Tamen magis elegisti
150 Symonis consortia.

Interfectis in agone
Spe mercedis et corone
Christe dona grandia.

[121] ¶ O Simon, Simon, you are only sleeping. Our voice cries to high heaven that your death is a crime.

[124] O Christ, in your mercy, may you not leave this thing unpunished before your very eyes.

[127] These men are united together in victory and are higher than the living, for they live in glory;

[130] these are firmly bound together, who are separated neither in death nor in arms:

[133] ¶ Ralph Basset, his knight, has also fought and undergone the dangers.[17]

[136] ¶ And Guy de Balliol,[18] may you with a faithful heart give signs[19] that are visible to all.

[139] A man utterly steadfast in faithfulness, he showed the strength of his valour with his right hand.

[142] When Simon was cut down, Guy, as yet unharmed, is bearing the standard on a lance.

[145] The just man's standard never fell and was always lifted high in your arms.

[148] You could have escaped, but you chose rather to be with Simon.

[151] O Christ, to those killed in anguish give hope of a great reward and a crown.

---

[17] Ralph Basset of Drayton, a rich Midlands knight and an active supporter of Earl Simon: *ODNB*, s.n.
[18] Guy de Balliol had been Earl Simon's standard bearer at Evesham: *Chron. Melrose* (1835), p. 200; Laborderie, Maddicott and Carpenter, 'Last hours of Simon de Montfort', p. 408. He was the eldest son of Henry de Balliol chamberlain of Scotland: *ODNB*, s.n. 'Balliol [Baliol], Henry de'.
[19] i.e. miracles.

Symon, Symon, si uixisses
155 Currere non permisisses
Raptores in patria.

Quis nos potest defensare?
Venietne ultra mare
Exspectata uenia?

160 ¶ Custos pacis heu necatur
Et ad litus applicatur
Nauis cum discordia.

Incessanter angli flere,
Modo possunt redolere.
165 Non habent remedia

Nisi Deus mittat eis
Vindictam de dictis reis
Qui fecerunt scelera.

Ne subuertant alieni
170 Istam terram dolo pleni,
Super hanc considera.

Amen.

[154] O Simon, Simon, if you had lived you would not have allowed robbers to roam the country.[20]

[157] Who can defend us? Will hoped-for help be coming from across the sea?[21]

[160] ¶ The guardian of the peace is dead, alas, and a ship bringing discord is brought ashore.[22]

[163] The English can only weep and mourn incessantly and have no relief

[166] unless God send vengeance for the said matters upon those who have done wicked deeds.

[169] Lest aliens should utterly destroy this land with guile, give thought to her.[23]

Amen.

---

[20] Widespread depredations were made by royalists and by Montfortian rebels during the unrest that followed the battle of Evesham and which lasted until 1267: Jobson, *First English Revolution*, pp. 150–60.

[21] In May 1266 Simon de Montfort the younger was rumoured to be gathering forces in France for an invasion of England, and in September that was still considered a possibility: *Cal. Pat. 1258–66*, pp. 664–5; L. J. Wilkinson, *Eleanor de Montfort: A Rebel Countess in Medieval England* (London and New York, 2012), pp. 127–9.

[22] Possibly a reference to the landing at Dover on 31 May 1267 of a force of knights under the counts of Saint-Pol, Boulogne and Guines to assist the king against the rebel occupiers of London: *Chron. Canterbury–Dover*, p. 246; *Flores Historiarum* 3, p. 16; Oxnead, p. 243.

[23] Soon after the battle of Evesham there were rumours of numerous royal grants of land to 'aliens': Jobson, *First English Revolution*, p. 154. In 1267 an alleged influx of foreigners to the lands, church and government of England remained among the rebels' grievances: Rishanger, *De Bellis*, pp. 561, 563–4.

Vulneratur karitas (208)

London, British Library, Harley MS 746

[fol. 103v]
Vulneratur karitas, amor egrotatur,
Regnat et perfidia, liuor generatur.
Fraus primatum optinet, pax subpeditatur.
Fides uincta carcere nimis desolatur.

5 ¶ Amur gist en maladie, charite est nafre,
Ore regne tricherie, hayne est engendre.
Boidie ad seignurie, pes est mise suz pe.
Fei nad ki lui guie, en prisun est lie.

¶ In presenti tempore non ualet scriptura
10 Sed sopita ueluti latent legis iura.
Et nephandi generis excecata cura
Nullo sensu preuio formidat futura.

¶ Ne lerray ke ne vus die, ne vaut ore escripture
Mes cum fust endormie e tapist dreiture.
15 De la gent haye avugle est la cure
Ke el ne dute mie venjance a venir dure.

[fol. 104r]
¶ Resistentes subruunt iniquitatis nati.
Perit pax ecclesie, regnant et elati.
Hoc silendo sustinent improbi prelati
20 Mortem pro iusticia recusantes pati.

¶ Les contre estanz abatent li fiz de felonie.
Lors perit seinte eglise quant orgoil la mestrie.
Ceo sustenent li prelaz ki se ne peinent mie.
Pur dreiture sustenir nolent perdre vie.

Vulneratur karitas (208)

London, British Library, Harley MS 746, fols 103v–104r

[*Latin*] Kindness is wounded and love sickens, while treachery rules and hatred is bred. Deceit has gained the upper hand and peace is trodden down, while faithfulness lies bound and utterly helpless in prison.

[*French*] [5] ¶ Love lies sick, kindness is wounded. Now treachery rules and hatred is bred. Deceit has the upper hand and peace is trodden underfoot. Faithfulness has no-one to lead it and is bound in prison.

[*Latin*] [9] ¶ At the present day the written word is not valued and the rule of law seems to be hidden away and asleep. And the blind preoccupation of a wicked people has no apprehension of things to come.

[*French*] [13] ¶ I shall not omit to tell you that the written word is not valued now and justice is hidden away. Blind hatred is the people's preoccupation, for they have no apprehension at all of harsh vengeance to come.

[*Latin*] [17] ¶ The sons of iniquity strike down those who resist. The peace of the church perishes while the proud hold power. The unprincipled prelates are supporting this by being silent, unwilling to suffer death for the sake of justice.[1]

[*French*] [21] ¶ The sons of iniquity strike down those who resist. Thus does holy church perish while pride rules it. The prelates, who do not exert themselves at all, are supporting this. They are not willing to lose their lives for the sake of supporting justice.

---

[1] About half of the English bishops had been Montfortian supporters or sympathizers but all of them quietly submitted to royal and papal authority after the battle of Evesham: Ambler, 'Montfortian bishops', pp. 139–40, 149–51.

25　¶ Strata pace penitus, amor refrigescit.
　　Tota tellus Anglie merore madescit.
　　Omnisque dilectio dulcis euanescit.
　　Cuncti consolatium querunt quo quiescit.

　　¶ Pes est acravante e amur refreidie.
30　La terre est desconforte e de plur enmoistie.
　　Amur e amiste tut est anentie.
　　Ni ad nul ki ne quert confort e aye.

　　¶ Patre carent paruuli pupilli plangentes
　　Atque matre orphani fame iam deflentes.
35　Qui in primis penitus fuerunt potentes
　　Nunc subcumbunt gladio, plorant et parentes.

　　¶ Asez i ad des orphanins grant doel demenanz,
　　Ke lur parenz sunt mis a fins, dunt il en sunt dolenz.
　　Cil ki en comencent furent mult pussanz
40　Sunt suzmis a le espeye, e plorent li parenz.

　　¶ Ecce praui pueri pauperes predantur.
　　Ecce donis diuites dolose ditantur.
　　Omnes pene proceres mala machinantur.
　　Insani satellites liuore letantur.

45　¶ Li enfanz felons sen vunt la povere gent preer.
　　Li riches a tort enrichiz sunt de autri aver.
　　A peyne i ad haute home ki cesse mal penser.
　　De hayne sunt haitez li felons esquier.

　　¶ Ecce uiri confluunt undique raptores.
50　Ecce pacis pereunt legisque latores.
　　Dogmata despiciunt truces hii tortores
　　Et prodesse nequeunt sancti confessores.

　　¶ De tote parz venent li bers ravisanz.
　　Ore perissent de pes e de la ley li sustenanz.
55　Enseignement refusent ces cruels tormentanz.
　　Espleyt ne poent fere cil ki vunt prechanz.

　　¶ Hii conuerti respuunt uirtute sermonum,
　　Neque curam capiunt de uita uirronum.
　　Omnes simul rapiunt ut mos est predonum.
60　Hiis uindictam ingere Deus ultionum.

[*Latin*] [25] ¶ Peace is wholly cast down and love grows cold. All the land of England grows wet with tears, and all gentle affection is vanishing. Everyone is trying to find where comfort lies.

[*French*] [29] ¶ Peace is cast down and love is grown cold. The land is without solace and wet with tears. All love and friendship are brought to nothing. Nor is there anyone who is not looking for comfort and help.

[*Latin*] [33] ¶ Little waifs weep without a father and hungry orphans now mourn without their mother. Those who had full strength to begin with are now fallen under the sword and their families weep.

[*French*] [37] ¶ There are many orphans displaying much grief that their parents have been put to death, on account of which they mourn them. Those who were very strong to begin with have been put to the sword and their families weep.

[*Latin*] [41] ¶ See how wicked young men plunder the poor while the rich are artfully enriched with gifts. Nearly all the great are involved in plotting evil things while their senseless adherents delight in hatred.

[*French*] [45] ¶ The wicked young men set out to plunder the poor people. The rich are wrongfully enriched with other people's property.[2] There is hardly any great man who ceases to contemplate wickedness. The lawless esquires delight in hatred.

[*Latin*] [49] ¶ See how men come together everywhere to rob, while those who uphold peace and the law perish.[3] These cruel tormentors despise religious teaching, and holy confessors are unable to achieve anything.

[*French*] [53] ¶ The men who rob come from everywhere. Those who uphold peace and the law now perish. These cruel tormentors reject any teaching. Those who set out to preach are unable to achieve anything.

[*Latin*] [57] ¶ They refuse to reform in response to sermons, nor do they care about the lives of property holders. They all rob in gangs as is the way of thieves. Heap vengeance upon them, O 'God of revenge'![4]

---

[2] Royal policy from September 1265 to October 1266 was to confiscate the estates of Montfort's alleged supporters and grant them to loyalists: Jobson, *First English Revolution*, pp. 151–2, 157.
[3] Widespread depredations were made by royalists and by Montfortian rebels during the unrest that followed the battle of Evesham and which lasted until 1267: ibid. pp. 150–60.
[4] Cf. Ps. 93 (AV 94): 1.

VULNERATUR KARITAS

¶ Si il se ne volent amender pur dit ne pur fesance
Mes pur tuer quant ont poer ben ont la voillance.
Trestuz en funt ravine, de Deu nen ont dotance.
Cels metez a declin, sire Deu de venjance.

[*French*] [61] ¶ Thus they do not want to reform themselves in response to words or deeds, but have the keen desire to kill whenever they have the power to. They all commit robbery and have no fear of God. Destroy them, Lord 'God of revenge'!

Calendar entries

209 Barking abbey calendar
London, British Library, Cotton MS Otho A V

[fol 2v, under 4 August] Simonis de Monte Forti

210 Barking abbey calendar
Oxford, University College, MS 169

[fol. 4v, under 4 August] Simonis de Monte Forti

211 Beaulieu abbey calendar?
London, British Library, Harley MS 2951

[fol. 129v, under 4 August] Anno Domini MCClxv occisus est Symon de Monteforti

212 Tavistock abbey calendar
Cambridge, Corpus Christi College, MS 210

[p. 30b] 1265. Sancti Simonis de Monte Forti die .4. augusti

213 Evesham abbey calendar
London, British Library, Lansdowne MS 427

[fol. 13r, under 4 August] Occisio Symonis Montis Fortis sociorumque eius

214 Evesham abbey calendar
London, British Library, Cotton MS Vespasian A VI

[fol. 183r] Anno Domini M°CC^{mo}lx°v^{to} <Occisio>[a] Symonis Montis Fortis sociorumque eius pridie nonas augusti

---

[a] Octauo *MS*.

Calendar entries

209   Barking abbey calendar
London, British Library, Cotton MS Otho A V, fol. 2v

[4 August] Of Simon de Montfort

210   Barking abbey calendar
Oxford, University College, MS 169, fol. 4v

[4 August] Of Simon de Montfort

211   Beaulieu abbey calendar?
London, British Library, Harley MS 2951, fol. 129v

[4 August] In the year of our Lord 1265 was killed Simon de Montfort

212   Tavistock abbey calendar
Cambridge, Corpus Christi College, MS 210, p. 30b

1265. Of Saint Simon de Montfort on the 4th day of August

213   Evesham abbey calendar
London, British Library, Lansdowne MS 427, fol. 13r

[4 August] The killing of Simon de Montfort and his companions[1]

214   Evesham abbey calendar
London, British Library, Cotton MS Vespasian A VI, fol. 183r

In the year of our Lord 1265. The killing of Simon de Montfort and his companions on 4 August

---

[1] Chiefly Henry de Montfort and Hugh le Despenser: see **186**.

Salue Symon: antiphon, versicle and response (215)
London, British Library, Cotton MS Vespasian A VI

[fol. 183r]
[Antiphona]
Salue Symon Montis Fortis
Totius flos militie
Duras penas passus <mortis>
<Pro statu>[a] gentis Anglie.
5   Sunt de sanctis inaudita
Cunctis passis in hac uita
Quemquam passum talia,
Manus, pedes, amputari
Caput, corpus, uulnerari
10   Abscidi uirilia.
Sis pro nobis intercessor
Apud Deum qui defensor
In terris <extiteris>.[b]

[Versus] Ora pro nobis beate Symon
[Responsio] Vt digni efficiamur promissionibus Christi.

[a] Pro statu] Prost'tor MS.
[b] exterritas MS.

Salue Symon: antiphon, versicle and response (215)

London, British Library, Cotton MS Vespasian A VI, fol. 183r

[Antiphon]
Hail, Simon de Montfort, flower of all knighthood, who suffered the harsh pains of death for the sake of the English people. [5] None of the saints who suffered in this life knew any such suffering: to have hands and feet severed, head and body wounded and genitals cut off. [11] May you, who lived as our defender on earth, be an intercessor for us with God.

[Versicle] Pray for us, O blessed Simon
[Response] That we may be made worthy of the promises of Christ.

Salue Symon: motet (216)

Cambridge, Jesus College, Old Library Manuscripts, Old Library, QB5

[fol. 139r]
***
***
***

Pro <statu>[a] gentis Anglie.
5 Sunt de sanctis inaudita
Cunctis <passis>[b] in hac uita
Quemquem passum talia,
Manus, pedes, amputari
Capud, corpus, uulnerari
10 Abscidi uirilia.
Sis pro nobis intercessor
Apud Deum qui defensor
In terris extiteris.

[a] stratu *MS.*
[b] passus *MS.*

Salue Symon: motet (**216**)

Cambridge, Jesus College, Old Library Manuscripts, Old Library, QB5, fol. 139r

*** for the sake of the English people. [5] None of the saints who suffered in this life knew any such suffering: to have hands and feet severed, head and body wounded and genitals cut off. [11] May you, who lived as our defender on earth, be an intercessor for us with God.

Rumpe celos (217)

Cambridge, Cambridge University Library, MS Kk.4.20

[fol. 77v]
¶ Rumpe celos et descende capud Iesu martirum,
Signis sacris et ostende comitis martyrium.
Arma, scutum, comprehende contra uires hostium.

Heu dolorum nos multorum torquet infor[tu]nium.
5   Simon cesus cadit Iesus Anglie presidium,
Comes fidus regni sidus, decus et flos militum.

Est iactura nimis dura regno et ecclesie.
Simon fortis casum mortis causa rei pupplice
Sumit; cadit dum inuadit prelium perfidie.

10   Iuris sator exstirpator fuit iniusticie,
Effugator et dampnator <fraudis>[a] et iniurie,
Pacis dator et seruator plebis et ecclesie.

Quis anglorum nunc regnorum tuetur prudencia?
Militaris expers paris pre[ter]mitur prestancia.
15   Plebi cleri forma ueri cedit sapiencia.

Tu qui pro salute mundi crucis pressus pertica
Da post casum putibundi fati sit in gloria.
Simon celi letabundi per eterna secula. Amen.

[a] fraudes MS.

Rumpe celos (**217**)

Cambridge, Cambridge University Library, MS Kk.4.20, fol. 77v

¶ Rend the heavens and come down,[1] Jesus chief of martyrs, and show forth the earl's martyrdom with sacred signs.[2] Take up weapons and a shield against hostile forces.

[4]   Alas, misfortune torments us with many sufferings. Cut down, Simon falls injured, the protector of England, the faithful earl, the kingdom's guiding light, the glory and flower of knighthood.

[7]   The damage to kingdom and church is exceedingly severe. Simon the strong takes on the penalty of death in the cause of the public good; he falls when he attacks the army of faithlessness.

[10]   Cultivator of the law, he was an eradicator of injustice, a banisher and condemner of falsity and wrong, a giver of peace and a preserver of the common people and the church.

[13]   Who now watches over the good sense of the English realms? Deprived of such a knight, leadership is abandoned. The sound wisdom of the true clergy withdraws from the common people.[3]

[16]   O thou, who for the salvation of the world was subdued by the rod of the cross, grant that Simon, after succumbing to a humiliating fate, should be in the glory of a joyful heaven for all eternity. Amen.

---

[1] Cf. Isa. 64: 1.
[2] i.e. miracles.
[3] About half of the English bishops had been Montfortian supporters or sympathizers but all of them quietly submitted to royal and papal authority after the battle of Evesham: Ambler, 'Montfortian bishops', pp. 139–40, 149–51.

Mater Syon (**218**)

Cambridge, Cambridge University Library, MS Kk.4.20

[fol. 77v]
Mater Syon[a]

¶ Mater Syon iocundare
Tantum decus dilatare.
Tibi uenit nouus dare
Noua martyr gaudia.

5   Comes Symon Thomam querit,
Causam Thome Simon gerit,
Et cum Thoma falsas terit
Leges per martyrium.

Thomas tytan orientis,
10   Simon sydus occidentis,
Vir uterque pie mentis
Pungnat pro iusticia.

Presul Thomas ueritatem
Se[r]uans dampnat prauitatem.
15   Pungnans dedit libertatem
Qua floret ecclesia.

Israelis Symon murus
Plebi clero profuturus
Pro utroque pungnaturus
20   Dura passus prelia.

Nunc uterque pugil fortis
Post occasum dire mortis
In agone sacre sortis
Migrat ad celestia. Amen.

[a] Added in red between first two stanzas.

Mater Syon (218)

Cambridge, Cambridge University Library, MS Kk.4.20, fol. 77v

Mother Zion

¶ Be joyful, mother Zion, that your glory should increase so greatly. A new martyr comes to you to give new joy.

[5] Earl Simon seeks after Thomas, Simon conducts Thomas's cause, and with Thomas he crushes wrongful laws through martyrdom.

[9] Thomas the sun of the east, Simon the star of the west,[1] each man with holy intent fights for justice.

[13] Archbishop Thomas, serving the truth, condemns wickedness. By fighting he bestows that liberty on which the church thrives.

[17] Simon was destined to be a defensive wall[2] for the common people and clergy of Israel[3] and to fight for both, enduring a hard battle.

[21] May each of those mighty warriors, after an end by cruel death in a martyrdom with holy result, now pass over into heaven. Amen.

---

[1] The appearance of the Western Star, also called Hesperus or the Evening Star, signified the end of the day.
[2] After the battle of Lewes the Montfortians were advised to 'make themselves into a wall': *Song of Lewes*, p. 14, line 408.
[3] The plight of the English people before the battle of Lewes had been likened to that of the Israelites under Pharaoh: ibid. p. 3, line 73.

Nequit stare (**219**)

Cambridge, Cambridge University Library, MS Kk.4.20

[fol. 77v]
¶ Nequit stare set rotare fortuna mutabilis
Per quam scita mors uel uita uenit admirabilis.

En iam primus set nunc ymus flos florum militie
Regnat modo ruit modo, pacem zelans Anglie.

5 Heu uir fortis Montis Fortis, corpus tuum moritur,
Denudatur, mutilatur, per partes diuiditur.

Amputatur capud, datur, mulieri mittitur.
Non uilescit nec sordescit, Baptiste coniungitur.

Set mens fortis hora mortis [non] morte percutitur.
10 Sullimatur, coronatur, in celis recipitur.

Hoc monstrauit, hoc probauit sol priuatus lumine,
Terre motus, orbis totus tunc percussus fulmine.

Die martis marce Martis transit in uigilia
<Par>[a] amici dominici cum sua militia.

15 Deridebat et pedebat scutifer ignobilis,
Male sonans quasi plorans necem plangens comitis.

Laus sit Deo nil ab eo post exisse dicitur.
Tumens uentre gemens mente derisor confunditur.

Symon ergo mortis ergo fac ne nos concuciat,
20 Te tutore te ductore Christus nos suscipiat.

[a] Per *MS*.

Nequit stare (**219**)

Cambridge, Cambridge University Library, MS Kk.4.20, fol. 77v

¶ The changeable wheel of Fortune, by which is made the awesome decree of death or life, will not stay still but revolves.

[3] Lo, the greatest now and not the least, the flower of the flowers of knighthood, at one moment rules and at another is cast down, ardent for the peace of England.

[5] Alas, Montfort, you strong man, your body dies, is stripped, mutilated and split into parts.

[7] Your head is cut off and given away, and is sent to a woman.[1] It has become neither debased nor sullied; it is associated with the Baptist.[2]

[9] But at the hour of death a strong conviction is not struck down by death. It is exalted, crowned, received in heaven.

[11] This was shown, this was proved, by a sun deprived of light, by an earthquake, by the whole world then hit by lightning.[3]

[13] On a Tuesday (*die martis*) he passes from the field of Mars with his army in the evening like a friend of the Lord.

[15] A lowly squire mocked and farted, making a foul sound like weeping to lament the earl's violent death.

[17] Praise be to God, nothing afterwards is said to have come out of him. With swollen belly and groaning mind, the one who mocked is confounded.

[19] Therefore, Simon, make it so that death may not shake us so that, with you as our guardian and leader, Christ may receive us.

---

[1] Maud wife of Roger Mortimer: *Cron. Maiorum*, p. 76; Rob. Gloucester 2, p. 765; *Chron. et Annales*, p. 37; Rishanger, *De Bellis*, p. 543.
[2] John the Baptist's severed head had been presented to the stepdaughter of Herod Antipas: Matt. 14: 6–11; Mark 6: 21–8.
[3] The battle of Evesham had been immediately preceded by a thunderstorm: Cox, *Battle of Evesham*, pp. 21–2.

Adhuc rota precor tota prosterne maliuolos
Quos leuasti que prostrasti quam plures beniuolos.

Nonne uides non est fides in tota prouincia.
Iura iacent, leges tacent, mutescit ecclesia.

25 Violatur, spoliatur, nec ligat sentencia.
Quis quid fari quot in mari nunc fiunt facinora.

Quot dampnantur quot necantur spiritus et corpora.
Capiuntur, rapiuntur naues mercimonia.

Confundantur, prosternantur perpetrantes talia
30 Nisi cessent et emendent tot commissa crimina.

Vt hoc fiat et sic fiat 'Amen' dicant omnia.

[21] I pray to you again, O wheel, wholly to cast down the malevolent ones whom you raised up when you cast down so many people of good will.

[23] Do you not see? There is no faith in all the land. Rights lie idle, the laws are silent, the church is struck dumb.[4]

[25] Any pronouncement is violated, is despoiled, and is not binding. Who can say how many offences are now committed on the sea?

[27] How many souls are damned and bodies killed? How many ships are captured, robbed of their cargoes?[5]

[29] May the perpetrators of such things be confounded and cast down if they do not cease and do not make amends for so many crimes committed.

[31] That this should be, and should be so, may all things say 'Amen'.

---

[4] About half of the English bishops had been Montfortian supporters or sympathizers but all of them quietly submitted to royal and papal authority after the battle of Evesham: Ambler, 'Montfortian bishops', pp. 139–40, 149–51.

[5] Until March 1266 the Cinque Ports, still in Montfortian hands, were conducting a campaign of piracy against commercial shipping in the Channel: A. Jobson, 'The maritime theatre, 1258–1267', in Jobson (ed.), *Baronial Reform and Revolution*, pp. 218–36 (at pp. 233–5).

O decus militie (Cambridge MS) (220)

Cambridge, Cambridge University Library
O decus militie (Cambridge MS), MS Kk.4.20

[fol. 77v]
[Antiphona]
    O decus militie gentium anglorum,
    Comes Leicestrie, dextra oppre[s]sorum,
    Sanguine commercio ius tenes celorum;
    Posce nobis miseris uitam beatorum.

[Versus] Magna est gloria eius in salutari tuo.

[Collecta] Deus qui beatum Symonem martyrem tuum uirtute constancie in agone suo communisti, quique illi ad renouandum Britannie regnum milites inclitos associasti, tribue nos eius precibus adiuuari qui celebri martyrio meruit consummari. Per [Dominum nostrum Iesum Christum].

O decus militie (Cambridge MS) *(220)*

Cambridge, Cambridge University Library, MS Kk.4.20, fol. 77v

[Antiphon]
O earl of Leicester, glory of the knighthood of the English people, right hand of the oppressed, by purchase with your blood you have attained the justice of heaven. Implore the life of the blessed for our miserable selves.

[Versicle] His glory is great in thy salvation.[1]

[Collect] O God, thou who fortified the blessed martyr Simon with the power of endurance in his agony and joined unto him renowned knights for the renewal of Britain, grant that we may be helped by the prayers of him who deservedly accomplished a famous martyrdom. Through [our Lord Jesus Christ].

---

[1] Ps. 20: 6 (AV 21: 5).

O decus militie (Cologne MS) (221)

Cologne, Historisches Archiv der Stadt Köln, Best. 7010 (Wallraf) 28

[fol. 84v]

Symonis comitis ac sociorum martirum 4º augusti[a] antiphona

O decus militie gentium anglorum,
Comes Lecestrie,[b] dextra oppressorum,
Miles regis glorie, apoteca morum,
Posce nobis miseris uitam beatorum.

Versus. Letamin[i] in Domino.

Collecta. Deus pro cuius pace et ueritate gloriosus sanguis beati Symonis martiris effunditur concede propitius ut qui ipsius sociorumque eius beneficia implorant pace perfrui mereantur eterna. P[er] D[ominum nostrum Iesum Christum].

---

[a] 4º augusti] *At the end of the line (probably in the same hand) and marked for insertion.*
[b] Lecestrie] *First five letters written over an erasure.*

O decus militie (Cologne MS) (221)

Cologne, Historisches Archiv der Stadt Köln, Best. 7010 (Wallraf) 28, fol. 84v

Antiphon of Earl Simon and his companions,[1] martyrs, on 4 August
O earl of Leicester, glory of the knighthood of the English people, right hand of the oppressed, knight of the king of glory, storehouse of decency, implore the life of the blessed for our miserable selves.

Versicle. Be glad in the Lord.[2]

Collect. O God, for whose peace and truth was shed the glorious blood of the blessed martyr Simon, graciously grant that they who implore his help and that of his companions[3] may be deemed worthy to enjoy everlasting peace. Through [our Lord Jesus Christ].

---

[1] Chiefly Henry de Montfort and Hugh le Despenser: see **186**.
[2] Ps. 30 (AV 32): 11.
[3] Chiefly Henry de Montfort and Hugh le Despenser: see **186**.

Miles Christi (222)

Cambridge, St John's College, MS F.1 (formerly MS 138),
former fols 127v–128r (now detached)

[Voice I]
Miles Christi gloriose
Symon certans in agone
Pro iusticia
Qui constanter conseruasti
5   A subuersione
Fidem Christi tibi datam
Et a lesione
Vt nos mundet a delictis
Satisfactione
10 Et in ***

[Voice II]
Plorate ciues Anglie
Magnanimum Lecestrie
Qui bellans pro iusticia
Prostratus est in Anglia.
5   O zelus[a] ineffabile
[O] nephas <innarrabile>
Quo fit pius ob emulis
Morti datur et meritis
Dum pungnat pro iusticia.
10 Prauorum ruit framea
Fideles ***

---

[a] Ronald Woodley suggests emendation to scelus *(crime)* in *Music & Letters* 63 (1982), p. 344.

Miles Christi (222)

Cambridge, St John's College, MS F.1 (formerly MS 138),
former fols 127v–128r (now detached)

[Voice I] O Simon, by fighting to the death for justice as a glorious soldier of Christ you staunchly kept [5] from overthrow and harm that faith in Christ which was given to you, so that he might cleanse us of our sins by penance [10] and in ***

[Voice II] O citizens of England, weep for the great-hearted earl of Leicester who was cut down battling for justice in England. [5] O the wonderful zeal, O the unspeakable wickedness, by which he is made blessed. While he fights for justice he is given over to death by his enemies and by those who deserve it themselves. He falls to the evildoers' spear. [10] The faithful ***

Select Bibliography

Ambler, S. T., *Bishops in the Political Community of England, 1213–1272* (Oxford, 2017)

Baker, G., *The History and Antiquities of the County of Northampton*, 2 vols (London, 1822–41)

Bartlett, R., *Why can the Dead do Such Great Things?* (Princeton and Oxford, 2013)

Carpenter, D., *Henry III: Reform, Rebellion, Civil War, Settlement 1258–1272* (New Haven and London, 2023)

—— *Henry III: The Rise to Power and Personal Rule 1207–1258* (New Haven and London, 2020)

Cox, D. C., *The Battle of Evesham: A New Account*, 2nd edn (Evesham, 2019)

—— 'The tomb of Simon de Montfort: an enquiry', *Transactions of the Worcestershire Archaeological Soc.* 3rd ser. 36 (2018), pp. 159–71

Dyer, C., *Standards of Living in the Later Middle Ages: Social Change in England c.1200–1520*, 2nd edn (Cambridge, 1998)

Eyton, R. W., *Antiquities of Shropshire*, 12 vols (London, 1854–60)

Fernandes, M., 'The Northamptonshire assize jurors: The role of the family as a motivating force during the Barons' War', in R. Eales and S. Tyas (eds), *Family and Dynasty in Late Medieval England: Proceedings of the 1997 Harlaxton Symposium* (Donington, 2003), pp. 38–55

Finucane, R. C., *Miracles and Pilgrims: Popular Beliefs in Medieval England* (London, 1977)

Gordon, E. C., 'Accidents among medieval children as seen from the miracles of six English saints and martyrs', *Medical History* 35 (1991), pp. 145–63

Gransden, A., *Historical Writing in England c.550 to c.1307* (London, 1974)

—— 'Some manuscripts in Cambridge from Bury St Edmunds abbey: Exhibition catalogue', in A. Gransden (ed.), *Bury St Edmunds: Medieval Art, Architecture, Archaeology and Economy* (British Archaeological Association Conference Transactions 20, 1998), pp. 228–85

Jacob, E. F., *Studies in the Period of Baronial Reform and Rebellion, 1258–1267* (Oxford, Oxford Studies in Social and Legal History 8, 1925)

James, M. R., *A Descriptive Catalogue of the Manuscripts in the Library of Gonville and Caius College* (Cambridge, 1907)

Jobson, A. (ed.), *Baronial Reform and Revolution in England 1258–1257* (Woodbridge, 2016)

—— *The First English Revolution: Simon de Montfort, Henry III and the Barons' War* (London, 2012)

Knowles, C. H., 'The disinherited, 1265–1280: A political and social study of the supporters of Simon de Montfort and the resettlement after the Barons' War' (Univ. of Wales Ph.D. thesis, 1959)

—— 'The resettlement of England after the barons' war, 1264–67', *Transactions of the Royal Historical Soc.* 5th ser. 32 (1982), pp. 25–41

Laborderie, O. de, J. R. Maddicott and D. A. Carpenter, 'The last hours of Simon de Montfort: A new account', *EHR* 115 (2000), pp. 378–412

Lefferts, P. M., 'Two English motets on Simon de Montfort', *Early Music History* 1 (1981), pp. 203–25

Maddicott, J. R., 'Follower, leader, pilgrim, saint: Robert de Vere, earl of Oxford, at the shrine of Simon de Montfort, 1273', *EHR* 109 (1994), pp. 641–53

—— *Simon de Montfort* (Cambridge, 1994)

Prothero, G. W., *The Life of Simon de Montfort Earl of Leicester with Special Reference to the Parliamentary History of his Time* (London, 1877)

Shields, H., 'The *Lament for Simon de Montfort*: An unnoticed text of the French poem', *Medium Aevum* 41 (1972), pp. 202–7

St Lawrence, J. E., 'The *Liber miraculorum* of Simon de Montfort: Contested sanctity and contesting authority in late thirteenth-century England' (Univ. of Texas Ph.D. thesis, 2005)

Tyson, D., 'Lament for a dead king', *Journal of Medieval History* 30 (2004), pp. 359–75

Valente, C., 'Simon de Montfort, earl of Leicester, and the utility of sanctity in thirteenth-century England', *Journal of Medieval History* 21 (1995), pp. 27–49

—— *The Theory and Practice of Revolt in Medieval England* (Aldershot and Burlington, VT, 2003)

Warton, T., *The History of English Poetry*, ed. R. Taylor, 3 vols (London, 1840)

Williams, G. A., *Medieval London: From Commune to Capital*, 2nd edn (London, 1970)

Wilson, L. E., 'Writing miracle collections', in S. Katajala-Peltomaa, J. Kuuliala and J. McCleery (eds), *A Companion to Medieval Miracle Collections* (Leiden, 2021), pp. 15–35

Index of Persons and Places

Roman numerals refer to the introductory pages, while arabic numerals refer to the numbered texts. Names are spelled as in the translations. Unidentified names are enclosed in quotation marks. Identified places are defined by their ancient (pre-1831) counties.

Ab Lench (Worcs.)   136
Aconbury priory (Herefs.)   124
Adam the chaplain (from Ab Lench), *or* Adam Chaplain   136
Adam the clerk (from 'Odebury'), *or* Adam Clark   134, 135
Adelard
   John   135
   Thomas   135
Agnes
   from 'Blythe'?   167
   from Boston   26
   from Radstone   58
   from Sulgrave   34
Alan (Aleyn)
   John   109 n.155
   Maud   109
   Ralph   110
   Robert   109
'Aldewik', Robert of, prior of Gloucester abbey   123
Alexander
   Agnes   54
   William   54
Aleyn   *see* Alan
Alice
   from Bretforton?   53
   from Burton Overy   7
   from 'Chaddelee'   113
   from Hereford   28
   'mother' of Henry of Studley   10
   sister of William, rector of Warrington   72
   wife of Gilbert (from Derby)   67

Alnwick abbey (Northumb.)   199, 200
Andrew, rector of Chelveston   30
Angevin
   John   191
   Reynold   98
   Stephen   191
Armitt, Richard, *or* Richard the hermit   139
Arnould, count of Guînes   207 n.22
Astley, Thomas of   1
Astwell (Northants.)   59 n.88, 106 n.147
Astwell
   Joan of   106
   Roger of   106
Atch Lench, William of   140
Atteheye, Thomas   177
Aubourn (Lincs.)   175
Aumale, countess of   *see* Reviers, Isabel de
Auvergne, Robert d', count of Boulogne   207 n.22
Avice (from Dunchurch)   174
Avon, river   1
Aylestone (Leics.)   111
'Ayse' (Ayre?), William   172

Badbury (Wilts.)   170 n.230
Badbury
   Simon   170
   Stephen   170
Badger, Richard, *or* Richard the badger   xviii, 3
Bakewell, John of   108
Balliol
   Guy de   1, 207 lines 136–50
   Henry de   207 n.18

INDEX OF PERSONS AND PLACES

Banbury, William of   56
Barate, Ralph   40
Barking abbey (Essex)   xlv
Basset
    Ralph (of Drayton)   1, 207 lines 133–5
    Ralph (of Sapcote)   102 n.142
Baston (Lincs.)   xlv
Beauchamp
    John   1
    William (d.1269)   xviii, xxxiv, 3, 9 n.22
    William (d.1298), earl of Warwick   9 n.22
    family   40 n.68
Beaulieu abbey (Hants.)   xlv
Becket, St Thomas, archbishop of Canterbury   196, 204 lines 13–14, 205 lines 12–13, 206 line 196, 207 lines 82–90, 218 lines 5–21
Bedford (Beds.)   1
Bedfordshire   see Bedford; Bletsoe; Dunstable; Holwell, Little
Bedworth (Warws.)   37 n.64
'Belbeworth', Mabel of   18
Belbroughton (Worcs.)   see Bell, Brians; Hurst Farm
Bell, Brians, in Belbroughton (Worcs.)   115
Belle, 'Gelbreda'   76
Benedict (Benedist)
    John   117, 179
    Simon   117, 179
Bengeworth (Worcs.)   137
Bennet, priest (from Wells)   150
Berkshire   xxiv; see also Coldridge; 'Cordebreg(g)e'; Newbury; Ufton Nervet
Bernard, Gilbert   52
Berrick Prior (Oxon.)   97
Besford (Worcs.)   96 n.131
'Besseborne'   40
'Besseforde'   96
'Bideford', Henry of, abbot of Pershore   130 n.184
Bidford on Avon (Warws.)   33
Birmingham, William of   1
Bletsoe (Beds.)   189
'Blythe', Maud of   168
Bohun
    Humphrey de (d.1265)   1, 33 n.58

Humphrey de (d.1275), earl of Hereford   1 n.8
    Joan de   see Quincy, Joan de
'Bokyngeham', Walter of   166
Bond
    Alexander le   53
    John le   53 n.82
Bossoun, Guarin   93
Boston (Lincs.)   26
Boughton Malherbe (Kent)   112 n.158
Boulogne, count of   see Auvergne, Robert d'
Bounde, Henry   160
Brackley (Northants.)   64
'Braddewell'   121
Brauncewell
    John of   143
    Thomas of   143
Breconshire   see Bronllys; Pipton
Bretforton (Worcs.)   4, 53, 54, 55
Brians Bell, in Belbroughton (Worcs.)   115
Bridgnorth (Salop.)   xxxiii, 79
Brill (Bucks.)   xxiv, 109, 110
Briouze, Maud de, m. Roger Mortimer   219 n.1
Broadwater (Suss.)   xliv
Broadwell (Glos.)   121 n.172
Bronllys (Brec.)   118
Broom, Elizabeth of   33
Brown (Brun)
    Henry   16 n.31
    John   xxii, 16
    William   16 n.31
Bruern abbey (Oxon.)   141
Brun   see Brown
Buchan, countess of   see Quincy, Elizabeth de
Buckinghamshire   see Brill; Studley priory; Winchendon, Over
Buckland (*unspecified*)   12
Buckland (Glos.)   12 n.26
Buckland, Ralph of   5
Burd, Margery de la   41
Burton Overy (Leics.)   7
Burton upon Trent (Staffs.)   196
Bury St Edmunds abbey (Suff.)   xxxiv, xlviii
Butler
    Angaret   193

90

Hugh   20
Robert   20
William (d.1280)   41 n.69
William (d.1283)   193
William (d.1334)   193
Butlers Marston (Warws.)   193

Cambridgeshire   *see* Childerley, Little; Ely, Isle of; Whaddon
Canterbury (Kent)   52, 91, 92, 154, 155, 157, 176, 177
   St Augustine's abbey   xxxviii
Canterbury, archbishop of   *see* Becket, St Thomas
Canterbury
   Alexander of   92
   Richard of   52
   Wilcock of?   92
Cantilupe (Cantlow)
   Joan, m. Henry Hastings   11
   John   11 n.25, 21 n.17
   Margery   *see* Cumin, Margery
   St Thomas, bishop of Hereford   21, 22
   Walter, bishop of Worcester   1 n.4, 99 n.136
   Walter (the same?)   99
   William   11 n.25, 21 n.17
Castlemorton (Worcs.)   20
Causefeylde, Roger   xl
'Chaddelee'   113
Chadley (Warws.)   113 n.159
Chandler (Chanteler; Chaunteler), Henry, *or* Henry the chandler   4, 55
Channel, English   219 lines 26–8
Chanteler, Henry   *see* Chandler
Chaplain
   Adam, *or* Adam the chaplain   136
   Henry, *or* Henry the chaplain   37
   Philip, *or* Philip the chaplain   118
   Richard   4
   Robert *or* Robert the chaplain   140, 141
   Roger, *or* Roger the chaplain   24
   William, *or* William the chaplain, *or* William Margary the younger   127
Châtillon, Guy de, count of Saint-Pol   207 n.22
Chaunteler, Henry   *see* Chandler

Chelveston (Northants.)   30
Cheshire   xxiv, 198
Chichester, bishops of   *see* St Leofard, Gilbert de; Wich, St Richard of
Child, William   79
Childerley, Little (Cambs.)   144 n.205
Childerley
   Henry of   144 n.205
   Margery of   144
   Maud of   144
   Nicholas of   144
   Nicholas of (the same?)   144 n.205
Chilham, Alice of   92
Chipping Norton (Oxon.)   36
Chubb, John, abbot of Tavistock   xlvi
Chyldessonne, Richard   134, 135
Cinque Ports confederation   24 n.41, 38 n.66, 219 n.5; *see also* Dover; Hythe; Rye; Woodchurch
Clare
   Alice of, countess of Gloucester   *see* Lusignan, Alice de
   Gilbert of, earl of Gloucester
      breaks with Montfort   xxxi, 206 lines 26–43
      at Worcester   1
      executes Stephen of Holwell   206 lines 51–5
      at Evesham   1
      blamed for Evesham deaths   203 n.5, 204 line 20, 205 line 24
      orders revenge after Evesham   206 lines 126–8
   Maud of, countess of Gloucester   *see* Lacy, Maud de
Clark
   Adam, *or* Adam the clerk   134, 135
   Ralph, *or* Ralph the clerk   8
   William, *or* William the clerk   48
Clifford, Maud, m. (1) William Longespee, (2) John Giffard   118 n.164
'Cliffton'   xl
Cockerel, Edmund   78
Codnor (Derb.)   192 n.258
Coldridge (Berks.)   80 n.115
Coleville, Walter de   1, 175 n.236
Cologne charterhouse (Germany)   xlviii
Colston, William   194

Comyn, Elizabeth (*or* Isabel), countess of
   Buchan   *see* Quincy, Elizabeth
Corby (Lincs.)   182
Corby, Robert   181
'Cordebreg(g)e' (Berks.)   80
Cornish, Lawrence   145
Cornwall, earl of   *see* Richard
Courtenay, Hawis de, m. (1) John de
   Neville, (2) John of Gaddesden
   xliv, 117, 179
Coventry (Warws.)   86
Crepping, Robert of   1
'Crest', Thomas of   75
Crevequer, Robert de   180 n.240
Croft, William of   122
Croughton
   John   63
   John (the same?)   63 n.94
'Culne', John of   62
Culworth
   Hugh of   34 n.59, 100 n.137
   Richard of   15 n.30, 34 n.59, 100 n.137
   'Robert' (Richard?) of (the same?)   15
Cumberland   *see* Lanercost priory
Cumin, Margery, m. John Cantilupe   11

Dale abbey (Derb.)   108
Darlaston (Staffs.)   46
Darlingscott, Robert of   129
David (from 'Cordebreg(g)e')   80
Deacon
   Henry, *or* Henry the deacon   196
   Robert, *or* Robert the deacon   115
Dene, in Wingham (Kent)   156 n.216
Dene
   Emm of   156
   Richard of   156 n.216
'Deneburne', Agnes of   112
Dennis, abbot of Beaulieu   xlv
Derby (Derb.)   67, 108
Derby, countess of   *see* Quincy, Margaret
   de
Derby, earls of   *see* Ferrers
Derby
   Alan of   66
   Avice of   66
   Ralph of   68
Derbyshire   xxiv, 90; *see also* Codnor;
   Dale abbey; Derby

Deschalers
   Geoffrey (d. by 1267)   71
   Geoffrey (d.1284)   71 n.100
Despenser, Hugh le
   death   xxxi, 1, 204 lines 17–18, 205
      lines 21–2, 206 line 78
   grave   xxxvi, 186
   heavenly reward   204 line 43, 205 line
      25, 213, 214, 221
   miracles   xxxiii, 186
Deverois, William   1
Devon   xxiv, 88, 164?, 165; *see also*
   Tavistock abbey
Devon, countess of   *see* Reviers, Isabel de
Dogsthorpe, in Peterborough (Northants.)
   xliv
Donne, John   xxvii–xxviii
'Donninton'   107
Dover (Kent)   39 n.67, 207 n.22; *see also*
   Cinque Ports confederation
Drayton Bassett (Staffs. and Warws.)   1,
   207 n.17
Droitwich (Worcs.)   94
Dunchurch (Warws.)   174
Dunnington (Warws.)   107 n.150
Dunstable (Beds.)   191
   priory   191 n.257
Durham cathedral priory (co. Dur.)   xlvii
Durham, bishop of   *see* Stichill, Robert of
Durham, Richard of   xli

Edmund, earl of Lancaster (as earl of
   Leicester)   30 n.53
Edward II, king of England   xxxvii
Edward (Sir Edward), son of Henry III
   title   xxx n.53
   escape   xxxi, 71 n.99, 206 lines 35–44
   Kenilworth raid   206 lines 45–8
   at Evesham   1, 198, 203 line 55, 204
      line 10, 205 line 9
   hostile to Londoners   206 lines 166–8
   instigates neglect of church   206 lines
      219–20
   warlike nature   206 line 220
   as King Edward I   202
Eleanor
   princess, m. Simon de Montfort, earl of
      Leicester   152 n.214, 203 lines
      60–4, 76

INDEX OF PERSONS AND PLACES

    of Provence, m. Henry III   206 n.26
    daughter of Emm (from Aubourn)   175
Ellis
    dean of Warrington   119
    son of William (from Milton)   32
Ellis, George   xliii
Elmley Castle (Worcs.)   xxxiv, xxxvi, 9
Ely, Isle of (Cambs.)   xxxiv, 206 nn.22, 25
Emm (from Aubourn)   175
Essex   95, 197; *see also* Barking abbey; Rickling; Sheering; Waltham Holy Cross abbey
Evesham (Worcs.)   xxiv, xxxix
    abbey   *see* Evesham abbey
    battle   1, 17, 131, 198, 204 lines 7–10, 205 lines 7–9, 206 lines 61–123, 207 lines 13–72
    battlefield (Green hill)   1, 3, 52, 68, 70, 73, 112
    churchyards   1
    Earl's well (Battle well)   xxii, xxxvi, xxxviii, 3, 4, 5, 6, 7, 8, 9, 158, 181, 191, 195
    parochial chapels   1
    'Siveldeston'   1
    vicar of   140, 141
Evesham abbey (Worcs.)   xxi, xxxvi, 1, 28 n.49
    abbots   *see* Whitchurch, William of; Wykewone, John
    abbot-elect   *see* Marlborough, William of
    altar of Holy Cross   xxxvi, 195 n.266
    calendars   xlvi
    choir   xxxi, xxxvi, 29 n.51, 38
    librarian   140
    miracles witnessed at   93, 140, 172, 194, 196
    Montfortian burials   xvii, xxxi, xxxiii, xxxvi, 15, 29 n.51, 52, 125, 132, 136, 186, 191, 192, 195, 196, 203 lines 56–7
    rood   xxxvi, 195 n.266
    offerings received
        arrowhead   77
        bent pennies   xxii, 6, 186
        candles   xxii, 16, 72, 78, 83, 89, 95, 108, 139
        chick   34

        money   xx, xxi, 142, 189
        peacock's tail   114
        wax images   xxii, 49, 50, 95, 101, 154, 155, 176, 187, 190
    prior   84, 93
    St Wulfsige's tomb   xx, xxxi, xxxvi, 29
Falcutt (Northants.)   59 n.88
'Fancote', James of   27, 59
'Farle', William of   *see* 'Sarle'
Farou
    Maud   152
    family   152 n.213
Fawdon, in Newcastle upon Tyne (Northumb.)   151 n.211
Feckenham (Worcs.)   132 n.188, 134, 135; *see also* Hunt End
Feckenham forest (Worcs.)   135 n.192
Ferrers
    Agnes de, m. William de Vescy   25 n.42
    Margaret de, countess of Derby   *see* Quincy, Margaret de
    Robert de, earl of Derby   15 n.29, 25 n.42, 30 n.53
    William de (d.1254), earl of Derby   15 n.29
    William de (d.1287), earl of Derby   7 n.19, 30 n.53
Feypo
    Christian   29
    Richard   29, 31, 87?
    Roger   29
    Simon   31
Filby (Norf.)   xxiv, 76
Filby
    John of   76?, 78
    family   76 n.106
Fillot (Fillote)
    Alice   132
    Christine   132 n.189
    John   132
    Richard   132
Fittleton (Wilts.)   75 n.104
fitz John
    Eustace   199 n.3
    John   1, 160
FitzAlan
    John (d.1267)   36 n.63
    John (d.1272)   36 n.63

INDEX OF PERSONS AND PLACES

Fladbury, Felice of   19
Folville, Eustace de   8 n.21
Forde, Walter le   149
Fors, Isabel de, countess of Devon and of Aumale   *see* Reviers, Isabel de
France   50, 207 n.21
Frettenham, Ralph of   xlvii
Fuller, Roger, *or* Roger the fuller   94
Furber, John, *or* John the furber   86
Furness (Lancs.)   172

Gaddesden
   Hawis of   *see* Courtenay, Hawis de
   John of   117 n.161
Gainsborough (Lincs.)   xxiv, 162
Gamages, Robert de   161
Gatton
   Alice of   112 n.158
   Alice of (the same?)   *see* Malherbe, Alice
Gatwick, Ralph of   xxxviii
Gaunt, Gilbert de   1
'Geddewolde'   37
Germany   *see* Cologne charterhouse
Giffard
   John   118 n.164
   Maud   *see* Clifford, Maud
   Osbert   131
Gilbert
   from Derby   67
   from Warrington   44, 47 n.74
Glendon (Northants.)   35
Gloucester (Glos.)   123, 126
   abbey   123
Gloucester, countesses of   *see* Lacy, Maud de; Lusignan, Alice de
Gloucester, earl of   *see* Clare, Gilbert of
Gloucestershire   xxiv, 169; *see also* Broadwell; Buckland; Gloucester; Hawkesbury; Mickleton; Tewkesbury; Todenham; Tortworth; Washbourne, Great; Winchcombe abbey
Godde, John   118
Grate
   Alice   134
   Nicholas   132, 134
Gravesend, Richard of, bishop of Lincoln   120 n.170, 197 n.271

Great Washbourne (Glos.)   40 n.68
Grendon (Warws.)   105
Grendon
   Gregory of   102, 103, 104, 105
   Robert of   105 n.145
   Scholace of   105 n.145
Grey
   John de (d.1266)   192 n.258
   John de (d.c.1271)   1, 192 n.258
   Richard de   1, 192 n.258
Grimbald
   Gillian, m. William of 'Northburgh'   51
   Robert   51 n.80
Grosseteste, Robert, bishop of Lincoln   xxix, 17, 129 n.182, 207 lines 97–108
Guînes, count of   *see* Arnould
'Gulac' ('Gulak'), Nicholas of   145, 146
Gullafre
   Henry   60
   William   60
Gunnell (from Ketton)   192
Guy
   from Pinley   159
   from Warrington   43

Hales, William of   184, 185
Halliwell, James Orchard   xliv
Hampshire   *see* Beaulieu abbey; Romsey
Hanbury (Worcs.)   133 n.191
Hansard (Hanseoticus), Otes   93
Harcourt
   Saher de   18 n.35, 111 n.157
   William de   18 n.35, 111 n.157
   family   111 n.157
Hardel
   John de   163
   John (the same?)   163 n.222
   Robert, the elder   181
   Robert (fl. 1257) (the same?)   181 n.245
   Robert, the younger   181
   Robert (d.c.1280) (the same?)   181 n.245
Harlow (Northumb.)   151 n.211
Harlow, John of   151
Hartlebury
   John   132
   Sarah   132

94

INDEX OF PERSONS AND PLACES

Hastings
  Henry   1, 11 n.25, 37 n.64, 51 n.80, 111 n.157
  Joan *see* Cantilupe, Joan
Hawis (from Heddon?)   89
Hawkesbury (*unspecified*)   60
Hawkesbury (Glos.)   60 n.90, 130
Haymunde, William   64
Heddon (Northumb.)   89
'Hekynton'   190
Helmsley (Yorks.)   61
Henry III, king of England
  treats Montfort badly   206 line 102
  profligacy causes unrest   206 lines 217–18
  at Lewes   xxx, 206 line 23
  at Kempsey   1
  at Evesham   1, 203 line 55
  rejects peace   206 line 159
  disinheritance policy prolongs crisis   206 lines 222–3
  considered a fool   204 line 41, 205 line 32
  his death imagined   206 line 224
  his death   202
Henry VI, king of England   xxi
Henry, son of Gunnell (from Ketton)   192
Henry the chandler (from Bretforton), *or* Henry Chandler   4, 55
Henry the chaplain (from 'Geddewolde'), *or* Henry Chaplain   37
Henry the deacon (from Burton upon Trent), *or* Henry Deacon   196
Henry the leech (from Canterbury), *or* Henry Leach   176
Hercy, Richard   142
Hereford (Herefs.)   28, 69 n.98, 71 n.99, 118, 206 lines 39–43
  Franciscan friary   128
Hereford, bishop of *see* Cantilupe, St Thomas
Hereford, earl of *see* Bohun, Humphrey de (d.1275)
Hereford, Richard of   69
Herefordshire *see* Aconbury priory; Hereford; Leominster; Mordiford
Hertfordshire *see* 'Shendeworth'
'Hicclebury'
  John of   107
  Rose of   107

Hill
  Nicholas   118
  Stephen   118
Hillborough (Warws.)   107 n.148
Holcombe (Oxon.)   98
Holme family   76 n.106
Holwell, Little (Beds.)   206 n.13
Holwell
  Maud of   206 n.13
  Stephen of   206 lines 51–6
  William of   206 n.13
Holy Land   61 n.92
'Homerton', John of, prior of Malton   25
Horseman, Roger   12
Hoyvill, Hugh de   1
Hugh
  father of Richard (from Berrick Prior)   97 n.133
  father of William   70
Hunt End, in Feckenham (Worcs.)   135 n.194
Hunte
  Hugh   134, 135
  Richard   134, 135
  Richard (the same?)   135 n.192
Huntingdonshire   206 n.22; *see also* Ramsey
Hurst Farm, in Belbroughton (Worcs.)   115 n.160
Hurst. William of the   115, 116
'Hyda', Walter de   xliv
Hyde
  Joan de la *see* Neville, Joan de
  Walter de la   xliv, 117 n.162
'Hyke', John of   83
'Hylamtre', William of   116
Hythe (Kent)   24; *see also* Cinque Ports confederation
Hythe, West (Kent)   24

Inkberrow (Worcs.)   132, 134
Inkberrow, Reynold of   xx
Ireland   xxxviii, xliii, 29, 31, 87
Isabel (from London)   187

James (from Warrington)   45
John
  abbot of Bruern   141
  chaplain of Bretforton   4, 53, 54

INDEX OF PERSONS AND PLACES

John (*cont.*)
   Eustace fitz   199 n.3
   of Filby?   76
   John fitz   1, 160
   vicar of 'Sellinge'   91
John the furber (from Coventry), *or* John Furber   86
Johnson, Samuel   xxxvii
Jordan (from Boston), Thomas son of   26

Kempsey (Worcs.)   1
Kempt, John   xl
Kenilworth (Warws.)   xviii, 1, 3, 175 n.236, 206 lines 45–50
   castle   xviii–xix, xxxiv, 1, 35 n.60, 103
   priory   1
Kent   xxiv, 92, 188; *see also* Boughton Malherbe; Canterbury; Dene; Hythe; Hythe, West; Milton (*unspecified*); Milton next Gravesend; 'Sellinge'; Thanet; Wingham; Woodchurch; Wormshill
Ketton (Rut.)   192
Kibworth Harcourt (Leics.)   18 n.35
Kinclaven castle (Perths.)   202
Knapp, O.G.   xlvi
Knaresborough (Yorks.)   196 n.270
Knaresborough, Robert of   129 n.182, 196

Lacy, Maud de, m. Richard of Clare, earl of Gloucester   6 n.164
Lancashire   *see* Furness; Ribble and Mersey; Warrington
Lancaster, earls of   *see* Edmund; Lancaster, Thomas of
Lancaster, Thomas of, earl of Lancaster   xlviii
Lanercost priory (Cumb.)   xli
Leach
   Alice   176
   Henry, *or* Henry the leech   176
Lece the meadmaker (from London), *or* Lece Meadmaker   195
Leicester (Leics.)   xxiv, xxxix
   abbey   64 n.95
   Dominican friary   180
Leicester, countess of   *see* Eleanor
Leicester, earls of   *see* Edmund; Montfort, Simon de (d.1265)

Leicester
   Piers   35
   Piers of (the same?)   35 n.60
   Piers of (another?)   35 n.60
Leicestershire   *see* Aylestone; Burton Overy; Kibworth Harcourt; Leicester; Sapcote
Lench, Ab (Worcs.)   136 n.195
Leominster (Herefs.)   13
'Lesseberge', Henry of   137
Lettice (from Aylestone)   111
'Lewerk' ('Luwerk')
   Simon   143
   William of   144
Lewes (Suss.)   xxxix
   battle   xxx, xxxvii, xliii, 131 n.185, 206 lines 1–15, 74–5
   Song of Lewes   xxx, 61 n.9, 80 n.2
Lincoln (Lincs.)   17, 143
Lincoln, bishops of   120, 182 n.246; *see also* Gravesend, Richard of; Grosseteste, Robert
Lincoln, Hugh of, abbot of Dale   108
Lincolnshire   xlv, 138; *see also* Aubourn; Baston; Boston; Corby; Gainsborough; Lincoln; Louth
Little Childerley (Cambs.)   144 n.205
Little Holwell (Beds.)   206 n.13
Little Washbourne (Worcs.)   40 n.68
Llywelyn ap Gruffudd, prince of Wales   118 n.164
Lombard, Peter   xlii
London   71, 181, 183, 184, 185, 187, 195, 206 lines 163–9
   Bridge ward   181 n.245
   Fisher Street   149
   Fleet Street   195
   London bridge   187
   St Bride parish   195
   St Magnus the Martyr parish   181 n.245
   St Martin Vintry parish   181
   St Dunstan parish (*unspecified*)   163
   Edward's hostility to   206 lines 166–8
   rebel occupation   15 n.30, 207 n.22
London
   Clement of   79
   William of   190
Longespee, Maud   *see* Clifford, Maud
Louth (Lincs.)   197

Ludlow (Salop.) xlii, 71
Lullingstone, Christian of 157
Lusignan
    Alice de, m. Gilbert of Clare, earl of Gloucester 6
    William de *see* Valence, William de
Luttrell, Alexander 61
'Luwerk' *see* 'Lewerk'
'Lydeham' (Oxon.) 158

Mabel, nun of Studley 82
Malherbe, Alice, m. Robert of Gatton? 112
Malton, New (Yorks.) 25 n.42
Malton, Old (Yorks.) 25 n.42
    priory 25
Mandeville, William de 1
Maniword
    Agnes 69
    Reynold 69
Mare
    Henry de la 117 n.162
    Joan de la *see* Neville, Joan de
Margaret, m. King Alexander III of Scotland 202
Margary
    Richard 127 n.181
    William, the elder 127
    William, the younger, *or* William the chaplain, *or* William Chaplain 127
Marlborough, William of, abbot-elect of Evesham xxxvi
Marsh, Adam 146 n.208
Marshal, Roger 181
Marston, Butlers (Warws.) 193
Mary (from Chipping Norton) 36
Maud
    from Radstone 57
    wife of William son of Hugh 70
Maule
    Christian de *see* Valognes, Christian de
    Piers de 49 n.78
    William de 49?, 95
Mauncelle (Maunsel)
    Margaret 169
    Margaret (the same?) 169 n.229
    William 169
    William (the same?) 169 n.229

Meadmaker, Lece, *or* Lece the meadmaker 195
Melrose abbey (Roxb.) xli
Mersey, river 45
    land between Ribble and (Lancs.) 119
Michael
    monk of Ramsey? xliii, 206 line 56
    vicar of Over Winchendon 171
Mickleton (Glos.) 4
Milton (*unspecified*) (Kent) 32
Milton next Gravesend (Kent) 32 n.57
Monmouthshire *see* Netherwent
Montfort
    Amaury de xlii, 203 line 74, 204 line 34
    Eleanor de (d.1275), countess of Leicester *see* Eleanor, princess
    Eleanor de (d.1282) 203 lines 60–4, 76
    Guy de xlii, 1, 203 line 73
    Henry de 174 n.235
        death 1, xxxi, xxxiii, 186, 203 lines 56–7, 204 lines 19, 43, 205 line 23, 206 lines 76–7, 207 lines 22–42, 213, 214, 221
        burial xxxi, xxxvi, 186
        miracles and sainthood xxxiii, 186, 203 lines 58–9
    Piers de (d.1265) 1, 113 n.159, 159 n.218
    Piers de (d.c.1287) 113 n.159, 159 n.218
    Richard de xlii, 203 line 75
    Simon de (d.1265), earl of Leicester
        badly treated by Henry III 206 line 102
        and the common people 203 line 30, 217 lines 12, 15, 218 line 18
        and the poor 84, 203 line 23
        likened to Becket xxvii, 204 line 13, 205 line 12, 207 lines 83–90, 218 lines 5–21
        considered old 23, 117, 197, 206 line 110
        hair shirt xxix, xxxi, 204 line 27, 205 line 17, 207 lines 115–20
        armour 131, 207 line 109
        burial xvii, xxxvi, 15, 29 n.51, 52, 125, 132, 136, 186 n.248, 191, 192, 195, 196

Montfort, Simon de (d.1265) (*cont.*)
    Opusculum de nobili Simone   xli
    Vita   74 n.103
  Simon de (d.1271)   xlii, 1, 160 n.220,
    203 line 73, 204 line 33, 206 n.12,
    207 n.31
  family heraldry   205 line 35?
Mordiford (Herefs.)   15 n.29
Mortimer, Maud   *see* Briouze, Maud de
Morton, Castle (Worcs.)   20
Moulton, Thomas of   26 n.45
Moyne, Berenger le   206 lines 136–41
Munchensi, William de   1, 32 n.57, 132 n.188
Murray, Gilbert   xlvi
Muscegros, John de   20 n.36
Myton
  Henry of   11
  William of   11

Neirun (Neyrnut)
  Richard   99
  Richer (the same?)   99 n.135
Netherwent (Mon.)   161
Neville
  Hawis de   *see* Courtenay, Hawis de
  Hugh de   1, 117 n.161
  Joan de, m. (1) Henry de la Mare, (2) Walter de la Hyde   117, 179
  John de (d.1246)   xliv, 117 nn.162, 163
  John de (d.1282)   117 n.161
Newbold on Stour, in Tredington (Worcs.)   16 n.11
Newbury (Berks.)   152
Newcastle upon Tyne (Northumb.)   199; *see also* Fawdon
Newmarket, Adam of   1
Newminster abbey (Northumb.)   77
Neyrnut   *see* Neirun
Nicholas
  steward of Thomas Cantilupe   22
  priest (the same?)   22 n.38
Norfolk   *see* Filby; Norwich cathedral priory; St Benet of Holme abbey; Thurne
Northampton (Northants.)   35 n.60, 120, 153
  Dominican friary   56

Northamptonshire   xxiv, 106, 147; *see also* Astwell; Brackley; Chelveston; Dogsthorpe; Falcutt; Glendon; Northampton; Peterborough; Radstone; Sulgrave; Syresham; Weston Favell; Whistley park; Whitfield
'Northburgh'
  Gillian of   *see* Grimbald, Gillian
  William of   51 n.80
Northumberland   xxiv, 151; *see also* Alnwick abbey; Fawdon; Harlow; Heddon; Newcastle upon Tyne; Newminster abbey
Northumberland, 'Cutting' of   77
Northumbria, king of   *see* Oswald, St
Northumbria, earl of   *see* Waltheof
Norton, Chipping (Oxon.)   36
Norwich cathedral priory (Norf.)   xlvii
Noveray
  Alexander, prior of Leicester Dominicans   180
  Robert   180

Obthorpe, Hugh of   xlv
'Odebury'   135
'Odebury', Richard of   135
Offenham (Worcs.)   127
Olive (from Leominster)   13
Olney, Robert of, prior of St Frideswide's, Oxford   122
'oogredeford'   15
Oswald, St, king of Northumbria   207 lines 91–3
Over Winchendon (Bucks.)   171
Oxford (Oxon.)   23, 101, 122
  Franciscan friary   146
  St Frideswide's priory   122
Oxford, earl of   *see* Vere, Robert de
Oxfordshire   xxiv; *see also* Berrick Prior; Bruern abbey; Holcombe; 'Lydeham', Norton, Chipping; Oxford

Palmer
  Lettice   101
  Simon   101 n.140
Pattishall, Simon of   189

Pecche
  Gilbert   182 n.246
  Hugh   182 n.246
  Philip   182
  Robert   182 n.246
Pembroke, earl of   *see* Valence, William de
Pepre
  Richard   100
  Robert   100
Pershore abbey (Worcs.)   130
Perthshire   *see* Kinclaven castle
Peterborough (Northants.)
  abbey   xxxviii, xliv, 74
  see also Dogsthorpe
Peverel
  Hugh   88
  Joan   88
  Margery   88
'Peytun', Roger of   138
Philip (from Bretforton)   53
Philip the chaplain (from Bronllys), *or* Philip Chaplain   118
Pickering, William of   154, 155
Pinley (Warws.), partly extra-parochial, partly in Rowington   159
  priory   159 n.218
Pipton (Brec.)   118 n.164
Pomeroy
  Henry de la (d.1281)   65, 165
  Henry de la (d.1305)   165
'Pytyltone'   75

Quincy
  Ela de, m. Alan la Zouche   7 n.19
  Elizabeth (*or* Isabel) de, m. Alexander Comyn, earl of Buchan   7 n.19
  Hawis de, m. Baldwin Wake   33 n.58
  Joan de, m. Humphrey de Bohun (d.1265)   33 n.58
  Margaret de, m. William de Ferrers, earl of Derby   7 n.19
  Robert de   33 n.58
  Roger de, earl of Winchester   7 n.19

Radstone (Northants.)   57, 58, 59 n.88
Ralph
  from Woodchurch   39
  son of Gilbert (from Derby)   67

Ralph the clerk (from 'Sepham Burland'), *or* Ralph Clark   8
Ramsey (Hunts.)   206 lines 136–7
  abbey   xliii, 206 nn.13, 22, 25
Reims, Jean de   50
Reviers, Isabel de, countess of Devon, m. William de Fors, count of Aumale   57 n.87, 160
Reynold
  from 'Besseforde'   96
  from Gainsborough   162
Ribble and Mersey, land between (Lancs.)   119
Richard, earl of Cornwall and king of the Romans   206 line 23
Richard
  from Berrick Prior   97
  vicar of Wingham   156
Richard the badger (from Evesham), *or* Richard Badger   xviii, 3
Richard the hermit (from Warrington) *or* Richard Armitt   139
Rickling (Essex)   83 n.119
Ridware, Adam of   1
Rigon, Reynold   122
Ritson, Joseph   xliii nn.8, 9
Robert
  canon of Malton   25
  chaplain of Ab Lench   136 n.195
  St (*unspecified*)   129
  St, abbot of Newminster   77 n.111
  squire of Alexander Luttrell   61
Robert the chaplain, vicar of Evesham, *or* Robert Chaplain   140, 141
Robert the deacon, *or* Robert Deacon   115
Roger, dean of Warrington   139
Roger the chaplain, vicar of West Hythe, *or* Roger Chaplain   24
Roger the fuller (from Droitwich), *or* Roger Fuller   94
Romans, king of the   *see* Richard, earl of Cornwall
'Romesey', Cecily of   125
Romsey (Hants.)   125 n.178
Ros
  Alexander de   61
  Robert de   61 n.91
  William de   61
Rowington (Warws.)   159; *see also* Pinley

Roxburghshire *see* Melrose abbey
Rutland *see* Ketton; Teigh
Rye (Suss.) 38; *see also* Cinque Ports confederaton
Rye, William of 147, 153

St Benet of Holme abbey (Norf.) 78
St Leofard, Gilbert de, bishop of Chichester 186
St Mary Cray
   John of 188
   Philip of 188
St Philibert, Hugh de 30 n.53
Saint-Pol, count of *see* Châtillon, Guy de
Saltmarsh, Piers 3
Sambourne (Warws.) 10
Samlesbury, Aline of 42
Sapcote (Leics.) 102, 103, 104, 105
'Sarle' ('Farle'?), William of 23
Saxi, William 54
Say, Geoffrey de 83
Scotland 142, 207 n.18; *see also* Kinclaven castle; Melrose abbey; Tay, river
Scotland, queen of *see* Margaret
Scott, Walter xxxviii, xlii
Scrayingham
   Margaret (*or* Margery) of 89
   Nicholas of 89
Seagrave, Nicholas of 1
Secher, Simon 38
'Sellinge' (Kent) 91
'Sepham Burland' 8
Sheering (Essex) 49
'Shendeworth' (Herts.) 144
Sherlonde, Maud 148
Shrewsbury (Salop.) 79
Shropshire *see* Bridgnorth; Ludlow; Shrewsbury
Smyth, Robert xl
Snitterfield (Warws.) 11
Somerset *see* Wells
Song of Lewes xxx, 61 n.9, 80 n.2
Staffordshire *see* Burton upon Trent; Darlaston; Drayton Bassett
Stichill, Robert of, bishop of Durham xlvii
Stratford, Robert of 122
Stratford upon Avon (Warws.) xviii, 3, 25

Studley
   Henry of 10
   Isabel of 10
Studley priory (Bucks.) 82
Sturmy
   Custance 197
   Nicholas 197
   Robert 197
Suffolk *see* Bury St Edmunds abbey
Suffolk, Alexander of 181
Sulgrave (Northants.) 34, 100
Sulgrave, Hugh of, abbot of Ramsey xlii
Surrey, earl of *see* Warenne, John de
Sussex xxiv; *see also* Broadwater; Lewes; Rye; Tortington
Sutton
   Agnes of 178
   Dowse of 178
   Robert of, abbot of Peterborough 74 n.103
Syresham (Northants.) 59 n.88; *see also* Whistley park
Syward, Walter 118

Tadcaster (Yorks.) 194
Tavistock abbey (Devon) xlv–xlvi
Tay, river (Scotland) 201, 202
Taylor, John 56
Teigh (Rut.) 8 n.21
Tewkesbury (Glos.) 6
   abbey 40 n.68
Thanet (Kent) 5, 39
Tholus *see* Tolas
Thomas
   friar (from Leicester?) 180
   son of Jordan (from Boston) 26
Thurne (Norf.) 78
Todenham (Glos.) 173 n.234
Tolas (Tholus)
   Godfrey 133 n.191
   Rose 133
Tortington (Suss.) 117, 179
Tortworth (Glos.) 169 n.229
Tovey, Michael 181
Tredington (Worcs.) 16; *see also* Newbold on Stour
Trent, river 196
Troye, Hugh de 1
Troyes, Guillaume de 50

INDEX OF PERSONS AND PLACES

Trussel, Richard   1
'Tuddenham'   173

Ufton Nervet (Berks.)   99 n.135
Umfraville, Gilbert de   151 n.211

Valence, William de, *or* William de
    Lusignan, earl of Pembroke   xxiv,
    76 n.106, 162 n.221
Valognes
    Christian de, m. Piers de Maule   49
    William de   49 n.78
Verdun, Henry de   46 n.73
Vere, Robert de, earl of Oxford   1
Vescy
    Agnes de   *see* Ferrers, Agnes de
    John de   1, 25 n.42, 199

Wake
    Baldwin   1, 33 n.58
    Hawis   *see* Quincy, Hawis de
Walding, Thomas   173
Walerand, Robert   206 line 201
Wales   xxiv, 1; *see also* Bronllys;
    Netherwent; Pipton
    marches of   xxxi, 198, 207 line 11
Wales, prince of   *see* Llywelyn ap
    Gruffudd
Walter (from 'Lydeham')   158
Waltham Holy Cross abbey (Essex)   84, 85
Waltheof, earl of Northumbria   xxi
Ware, John de la   46
Warenne, John de, earl of Surrey   76 n.106
Warrington (Lancs.)   41, 42, 43, 44, 45,
    47, 139
    dean of   119, 139
    rector of   72, 73
Warwick, earl of   *see* Beauchamp, William
    (d.1298)
Warwickshire   xviii; *see also* Bedworth;
    Bidford on Avon; Chadley; Coventry;
    Drayton Bassett; Dunchurch;
    Dunnington; Grendon; Hillborough;
    Kenilworth; Marston, Butlers;
    Pinley; Rowington; Sambourne;
    Snitterfield; Stratford upon Avon;
    Wellesbourne Mountford
Washbourne, Great (Glos.)   40 n.68
Washbourne, Little (Worcs.)   40 n.68

Washbourne family   137 n.197
Wauncy, Robert de   59 n.88
Wellesbourne Mountford (Warws.)   113
    n.159
Wells (*unspecified*)   150
Wells (Som.)   150 n.210
'Weredech', Alice of   46
West Hythe (Kent)   24
Weston Favell (Northants.)   180
Whaddon (Cambs.)   71
Whistley park, in Syresham (Northants.)
    59 n.88
Whistones (Worcs.)   48 n.76
Whitchurch, William of, abbot of Evesham
    13, 140
Whitfield (Northants.)   59 n.88
Wich
    John of   87
    St Richard of, bishop of Chichester   87
    n.123
William
    from 'Braddewell'   121
    from Milton   32
    from Weston Favell   180
    brother of David (from 'Cordebreg(g)e')
        81
    rector of Warrington   72, 73
    son of Hugh   70
    son of William (from Weston Favell)   180
William the chaplain (from Offenham),
    or William Chaplain, *or* William
    Margary the younger   127
William the clerk (from 'Wistan'), *or*
    William Clark   48
Wiltshire   *see* Badbury; Fittleton
Winchcombe abbey (Glos.)   23
Winchendon, Over (Bucks.)   171
Winchester, earl of   *see* Quincy, Roger de
Wingham (Kent)   156; *see also* Dene
Wirral
    Gilbert of   47
    Robert of   47
'Wistan'   48
Woodchurch (Kent)   39; *see also* Cinque
    Ports confederation
Worcester (Worcs.)   xxiv, 1, 206 line 60
Worcester, bishop of   *see* Cantilupe,
    Walter
Worcester, William   xlv–xlvi

INDEX OF PERSONS AND PLACES

Worcestershire xxxiv; *see also* Bell, Brians; Bengeworth; Besford; Bretforton; Droitwich; Elmley Castle; Evesham; Evesham abbey; Feckenham; Feckenham forest; Hanbury; Hunt End; Hurst Farm; Inkberrow; Kempsey; Lench, Ab; Morton, Castle; Newbold on Stour; Offenham; Pershore abbey; Tredington; Washbourne, Little; Whistones; Worcester
Wormshill (Kent) 112 n.158
Wulfsige, St (of Evesham), tomb of xx, xxxi, xxxvi, 29
Wycombe, Richard of 183

Wykewone, John, abbot of Evesham xxxviii

Yanworth, John of, abbot of Winchcombe 23
Yorkshire *see* Helmsley; Knaresborough; Malton, New; Malton, Old; Tadcaster
Yve
   Robert 91
   Thomas 91

Zouche
   Alan la 59 n.88, 64 n.95
   Zouche, Ela la *see* Quincy, Ela de